ISLAM, HINDUTVA AND CONGRESS QUEST

(A STUDY IN CONFLICTING IDEOLOGIES)

ISLAM, HINDUTVA AND CONGRESS QUEST

(A STUDY IN CONFLICTING IDEOLOGIES)

Ram Gopal

Reliance Publishing House

New Delhi

ISBN : 81-7510-072-9

Published by
Dr. S.K. Bhatia (Life Member ILA & INSA) *for*
RELIANCE PUBLISHING HOUSE
3026/7H, Ranjit Nagar,
New Delhi-110 008 Ph.: 5737377/5722605

Composed by
Geeta Graphics
3026/7H, Ranjit Nagar,
New Delhi- 110008. Ph.: 5786889

Printed by : -
S.S.S. Printers
New Delhi-110002.

PREFACE

For centuries together, the Indian sub-continent, called Hindustan, had been a battlefield of Islamic imperialism, represented by the Crescent, and defensive Hindutva, represented by the saffron colour. The two had almost come to terms by the close of the 18th century when the imperial power of England, represented by the Union Jack, intervened and eclipsed both.

In 1885, the Indian National Congress, comprising the Indian elite of all hues, professing to represent the Indian sentiments as a whole, came into existence and started contending for a gradual transfer of power to it. Its tricolour sought to represent Islam, the Hindutva, and the whiteman at large.

In the 20th century, the British power itself gave way to the emerging new super powers of the USA and the USSR. In their own different styles, both the new super powers helped and supported the freedom movements of the Asian and African countries who had been reeling under the British or other colonial rule of Europe. Consequently, the British and other imperialist powers(like France, Portugal, Germany, Denmark, Holland), withdrew not only from India but also from all their colonies spread over the length and breadth of Asia and Africa. The only imperialist power of Asia was Japan. It also had to withdraw from Korea and China after World War II.

The British recognised the Congress as representing only the upper caste Hindus. So, they carved out Pakistan for the Muslims, following the demand of the Muslim League. The truncated India came to be ruled by the Congress, the most powerful contender of the time. The Congress, however, kept on harping as the Messiah of the Muslims and other minorities, even to the extent of antagonising the Hindu majority.

Now that the Congress is on its last legs, the ancient conflict of the Crescent and the Saffron has come to the fore. The policy followed by Congress for over 75 years has also become a creed which may be termed as "Congressism". It is the epicentre of all the splinter groups formed by ex-Congressmen. The present book is a brief narration of the political games being played around Islam, Congressism, and Hindu revivalism.

The tragedy is that the Hindus and the Muslims who together constitute about 97 per cent of the Indian population have so far refused to realise their true identity and have thus failed to solve any of their problems. Even after getting independence, they have continued to play the foreign tunes. While Muslims have had an overdose of their religion(much of which is politics) Hindus have largely gone irreligious or become victims of false gods, goddesses, and godmen. Partition of India has solved no problem. On the contrary, it has created new problems. Larger part of the energy and resources of India, Pakistan and Bangladesh, are spent on protecting their artificial borders which keep them in a state of perpetual war. The result is that they are always in the international weapons market, buying huge quantities of war material from the developed countries at heavy costs even when they don't have enough to feed and educate their own people. For their public utility services, education, sanitation and development, they look around for foreign aid and loans.

One who knows himself but does not know his enemy is very likely to lose the battle: One who knows neither himself nor his enemy will perish. Only one who knows himself and knows his enemy can hope to survive and win. As things stand today, people of the third world, especially the Hindus, fall in the second category, knowing neither themselves nor their enemies.

Hundreds of books have appeared to tell the story of India's partition and its political turmoil. Most of them are from the actual participating politicians and bureaucrats or by sponsored research scholars. There is hardly one from an unattached person, like the present one. It attempts to explain the actual causes and effects of major political developments, compulsions of the leaders of the freedom movement, and portends of the future. I believe that nothing happens all of a sudden. Our own deeds and misdeeds or of our own forefathers in the past are responsible for our rise and fall. Similarly, our own doings and undoings today will shape the future of our country.

It is often said, "What is the use of talking of past events? Let us concentrate on the present and work for building a new India, brick by brick". Unfortunately, I don't share this view. Such a sermon may be relevant for the advanced countries, like the USA and even China, whose structure is complete and who are making rapid advancement on their adopted methodology. India is different. It is still coming up and taking shape from the debris of the past. In this situation, it will be suicidal to ignore the past events and historical experiences. A person who does not know his assets and liabilities of yesterday, knows only what he has earned today, cannot correctly plan his tomorrow. History provides us our yesterday's balance sheet. Past events of our rise and fall provide us the key to our strength and weaknesses of thought and action. Wrong or concocted history, like a wrong balance sheet, is sure to lead us to wrong directions. I have tried to set the records straight. Some of my findings may not be pleasing to those who are moulded in one or the other school of thought or schism. Considering vastness of the subject, this book is small. So, I had to leave a number of facts which, I think, are already well known.

I express my gratitude to all those authors and publishers from whom I have quoted and my friends Dr. E.C. Chakravorty, (former Director, Historical Division, Ministry of Defence), Shri A.S. Kanwa, (former Principal, Dewan Chand Arya Higher Secondary School, Lodi Road, New Delhi), Shri M. Surya Rao, (Electronic Engineer, MBA, and a voracious reader), Shri R.K. Sharma, Media-writer, a noted Hindi novelist and playwright, and Shri G.N.S. Raghavan, a reputed journalist and author, who all helped me in my endeavour even though some of them hold their own different views and to that extent we agree to disagree, among ourselves Over and above, I am thankful to Dr. S.K. Bhatia, Prop. Reliance Publishing House for bringing out this book.

Factual errors or important ommissions, if any, brought to the notice of the author will be gratefully acknowledged.

Ram Gopal
A-2B/94-A, Ekta Apartment,
Paschim Vihar, New Delhi-63

[illegible] it is still cropping up [illegible] from the depths of my [illegible] in this situation, it will be [illegible] to ignore the past events [illegible] experiences [illegible] you will not [illegible] of yesterday [illegible] what [illegible] today [illegible] History provides us [illegible] strength and weaknesses [illegible] thought and action [illegible] history [illegible] I have tried to set the [illegible] may not be pleasing to those who [illegible] school of thought or scheme. [illegible] this book small [illegible]

I express my gratitude to all those authors and publishers from whom I have quoted and my friends Dr. [illegible] (Former [illegible]) [illegible] Dr. [illegible] who helped me [illegible] Publishing House for bringing out this book.

[illegible] or suggestions, if any, brought to the notice of the author will be gratefully acknowledged.

[illegible]

4-28-94 [illegible] Apartments

[illegible] Vihar, New Delhi-[illegible]

ERRATA

Islam Hindutva and Congress Quest

Ram Gopal

Title Cover		Line 7, for "portends" read "portents".
Back Page		Line 9, for "disasterous" read " disastrous".
		Line 10, for "Khalifat" read "Khilafat".
		Line 23,, after "India's defence" insert (,)
		Line 28, for "reacer" read "reader".
		Line 31, for "the" read "and".
Preface	:	2nd page, line 11 from bottom, For "portends" read "portents"
		3rd page, line 4, from bottom, After "ourselves" add (.)
Text Page no.		
3	:	Line 9 from bottom, for "Mullans" read "Mullahs".
9	:	Line 15, for (d) read (c)
10	:	Line 9 from bottom, after "lawyers" add comma (,)
14		Line 21 from bottom, for the word and figure "In 1883" read "In 1893"
23	:	Line 7 from bottom, for "Present" read "present".
30		Lines 6 and 12, for references "27" and "28" read "26" and "27" respectively.
48		Line 13 from bottom, after "There can" insert "be"
70	:	Line 18, delete "now Rashtra pati Bhawan" and insert "then near Kingsway Camp".
71		Under the heading "MOPLAH REBELLION", in line 3, after "God" close the bracket.
93		Line 16, for "23", in small print, read "Twenty three"
102	:	Line 11 from bottom, for "their" read "there".
121	:	Para 3, line 4, for "Woorld War I" read "World War I".

141	:	Line 16, for "1945" <u>read</u> "1946"
157	:	Para. 4, line 4, for "23rd March <u>read</u> "22nd March"; for "the next day" <u>read</u> "on the 24th".
162	:	In the foot-note, remove line 16 <u>and</u> in line 27, after the words "to become a woman." <u>insert</u> "His final sexual experiment with Manu (grand-niece of Gandhi)".
164	:	Line 8, for "centurary" <u>read</u> "century".
165	:	Line 4 from bottom, for "in" <u>read</u> "is"
171	:	Line 4 from bottom, for "Parayag" <u>read</u> "Prayag".
194	:	Line 8 from bottom, for "bloody war" <u>read</u> "bloody civil war".
214	:	Line 6, for 'Dr. M.S. Golwalkar" <u>read</u> "Shri M.S. Golwalkar".
216	:	Line 10 from bottom, for "they <u>read</u> "the".
223	:	First Line, after "writer", close bracket.
240	:	Line 11 for "bewil derment" <u>read</u> one word "bewilderment".
243	:	Line 5 from bottom, for "United Nationals" <u>read</u> "United Nations"
252	:	Line 10, for "discrimination" <u>read</u> "discrimination".
257	:	In para 3, last line, for "ISA" <u>read</u> "ISI"
264	:	Line 14, for "extravagnt: <u>read</u> "extravagant".

CONTENTS

Chapter I

GROWTH OF ISLAM IN INDIA

As a religion, Islam had entered India during the life-time of Hazrat Mohammed himself in the first half of the seventh century AD. India had trade relations with the Arabs for centuries prior to the advent of Islam. Many Arab traders had, therefore, settled in the coastal areas of the Western Ghats and Kerala, namely Daibal, Broach, Cambay, Sindh, Kutch, Malabar and Kathiawar. They also had their settlements in Kannauj and Varanasi. When Islam became the ruling religion of Arabia, the Arab settlers in India also became Muslims and continued with their trading activities. The Hindu kings of the time provided them all facilities to practise their new found religion and to erect mosques."Sulaiman, Masudi, Ibn Haukal, and Abu Zaid, all agree in praising Balhara (the Vallabhi ruler of Gujarat) for the friendliness which he exhibited towards the Musalmans...Masudi saw his co-religionists practicing their religion openly everywhere."[1]

As a political force, Islam entered India a century later, when Muhammad-Ibn-Kasim, the nephew and son-in-law of al-Hajjaz, governor of Iraq led an Arab invasion on Sindh through the sea route in 712 AD. There had been 15 such invasions earlier but all of them had been repulsed by the brave Hindu (Brahmin) King Dahir. Kasim's success lay in "the treachery of certain Buddhist priests and renegade chiefs who deserted their sovereign and joined the invader."[2] The Arab rule was removed later by the neighbouring Hindu rulers—Chalukyas in the south, Pratihars in the east, and the Karkotas in the north. Arab conquest of Sindh has been described by Mr. Stanley Lane-Poole as "an episode in the history of India and Islam, a triumph without results."[3] But, in 1001, the defeat of the Hindu Raja Jaipal of the Shahiya dynasty of Waihind (Udabhandapur), the ruler of present NWFP of

Pakistan and parts of present Afghanistan, at the hands of the Turkish Sultan of Ghazni, Mahmud, cleared this land route of safe entry to the Indian peninsula.

The Sultan of Ghazni made 17 raids on India from 1001 to 1026, draining the wealth of the country and much of its military resources. He did not establish his kingdom in India, but his occupation of Afghanistan, the North West Frontier areas, and the Punjab served as the key to unlock the Indian interior for subsequent invaders*. Yet, for about next 200 years, no invader stepped in because of the factional and ethnic wars for supremacy among various Muslim chieftains in Western and Central Asia in which the Arabs and the Ghaznavid (Yamini) Turks gave way to the princes of Ghur in the mountainous regions of Afghanistan to the south-east of Herat. Thus, Mohammad of Ghur, known as Mohammad Ghori, marched towards Indian interior and, after removing the Ghaznavid ruler of Lahore, set up his empire in Delhi in 1192. During the intervening period of 200 years, the Hindu rulers of India had been fighting among themselves. They did not ever think of recovering the North West Frontier areas, once lost to Muslim invaders. They kept their eyes closed to the dangers of the fast expanding military power of Islam. Hindu kings for their petty selfish ends, had no qualms in helping a Muslim invader even against their own kith and kins. Although the Muslim rulers had great differences of ethnicity, culture, language, region, which kept them always warring among themselves, their common religion, Islam, forbade them from helping any non-Muslim ruler against a Muslim invader. A classic example is provided by the Mughal king Babur's son Humayun in 1534. His own enemy, Bahadur Shah of Gujarat, had attacked Mewar (Rajasthan). Mewar's Rani Karnavati sent a *Rakhi* to Humayun and solicited his help to thwart the evil designs of Bahadur Shah. Humayun, then at Malwa, received the *Rakhi* with due deference. His ministers advised him to help the Rani so that he should have the Rani's gratitude as well as easy riddance from an arch enemy. Contrary

---

* The strategic importance of NWFP and Afghanistan was well understood by the British. They, therefore, took special care to ensure that these areas remain under the British or with the British friends. Unfortunately, the Indian leaders have not paid due attention to it. Pakistan has been trying hard for many years to have its own or a puppet government in Afghanistan. The Taliban which has, in a civil war, occupied about 2/3rd of Afghanistan, was raised and funded by Pakistan.

to generally held belief, based on a Hindi play by Harikrishna Premi, Humayun declined the suggestion on the ground that his faith did not permit him to attack a Muslim king engaged in a war against an infidel. Thus, Humayun served his faith' though, in the words of the noted historian A. L. Srivastava, he "lost a golden opportunity of winning for his own cause their (Rajput) Sympathy and support, the inestimable worth of which was realised by his son Akbar".[4]

The Islamic rule having been established at Delhi in 1192 went on expanding, though the ruling dynasties changed from time to time upto the Mughal emperor, Aurangzeb (1659-1707). Even then, it is erroneous to call it the Muslim period because, except for the brief periods of Allauddin Khilji and Aurangzeb, the larger parts of India remained under the Hindu rulers. After Aurangzeb, the Mughal empire started crumbling, giving way to Hindu power arising from Maharashtra under Shivaji followed by the Peshwas and from the Punjab in the form of the Sikhs. Although the warriors of Maharashtra and the Punjab were products of the same Islamic tyranny and bore essentially the same Hindu faith, they could not make a common cause. Similarly, in course of time, the religious schism of Shia and Sunni, ethnic prejudices of the Turks, the Mughals, the Pathans, and the native Muslim converts, and regional biases, divided the Muslim forces. In this anarchy of parochial and feudal interests, the British became masters of the vast Indian sub-continent, defeating all the Hindu and the Muslim monarchs during a hundred year war from 1757 to 1857. A number of attempts were made to put up a united front of the Hindu and the Muslim nobilities against the foreign powers, but all of them failed mainly because of the aggressiveness of the Mullahs for whom all Hindus were' kafirs'. The attitude of the Mullahs can be gauged from the fact that when the Hindu (Maratha) rule extended upto the Punjab and the Mughal emperor of Delhi accepted Hindu protection, the Mullahs, led by Shah Walliullah, and Najibullah, the Afghan chief of Ruhelkhand, invited Ahmed Shah Abdali of Afghanistan, to destroy the Hindu power, disregarding the eventuality of doom of the Mughal dynasty and dishonour of the motherland. And, when in 1760 the Maratha army marched from Poona towards Delhi to save the Mughal emperor from Abdali, the Mullahs issued fatwas that no one in the plains of Delhi and Panipat should render any help or make even food supply to the Maratha army.

The defeat of the Maratha army at Panipat (1761) was a severe jolt to the rising Hindu power, but the Maratha forces regrouped soon (though not in their pristine glory) and, after defeating the British forces, brought back in 1772 the exiled Mughal emperor, Shah Alam II, to Delhi. Shah Alam remained a protectorate of the Marathas, the real power of the empire vested in Mahadaji Scindia who was bestowed with the title of Wakil-i-mutlaq, while Mahadaji was a deputy (Naib) of the Peshwa at Poona. By 1792, Mahadaji Scindia had established his ascendancy over the Rajputs and the Jats and his power in Northern India reached its meridian splendour. After Scindia's death in 1795, the Marathas got entangled in a kind of family war in which each one fought for supremacy. This led the Peshwa to enter into a treaty of Subsidiary Alliance with the British and he signed the Treaty of Bassein on 31st Dec. 1802. That was an important landmark in the history of British supremacy in India. By the year 1857, all Indian rulers, Hindu or Muslim, had been subjugated by the British power. The Mughal emperor at Delhi had for a long time remained a puppet first of the Maratha power and then of the British upto 1857 after which he was deposed and moved to Rangoon on a pension. For sentimental reasons alone, neither the Marathas nor the British had thought of removing the Mughal emperor earlier.

Among the Muslim rulers, Aurangzeb had the largest empire. He aimed at bringing the whole of Hindustan under the strict Islamic rule (Nizam-e-Mustafa) of the Sunni school. That was an impossibiltiy. Hindus took up arms against him under the leadership of Shivaji of Maharashtra and Guru Gobind Singh of the Punjab. Within thirty years of Aurangzeb's death, the Mughal empire ceased to be an all India political unit. It was split into numerous independent or semi-independent States. The Deccan, Oudh and Bengal (including Bihar and Orissa) became independent. The Maratha power became supreme. The Jats, near Agra, became independent; the Ruhela Afghans founded their State of Ruhelkhand in the North Gangetic Plains; the Sikhs became independent in the Punjab. The dream of Shivaji of establishing Hindu padpadshahi (rule according to Hindu traditions) could not come true because of his early death. His successors proved unequal to the task. They extended their political power and areas of influence far and wide, but lost sight of the main goal. The

Maratha power split into four houses. One by one all the Muslim as well as Hindu rulers were subjugated by the British in a period of one hundred years.

The mutiny of 1857, the first war of independence to overthrow the British yoke is known to all. There are hundreds of books on the topic. The unique feature of the 1857 revolt was that it originated from the ground level in which the common man, the peasant and the low rank sepoy took active part without any distinction whatever of caste or religion. The failure of the mutiny was mainly because of weak leadership and utter lack of planning and coordination. Nana Saheb Peshwa of Bithur (Kanpur), the main leader and the foremost motivating force in the Central India, disappeared from the scene, very soon. The other leader of the Northern India, Bahadur Shah Zafar, the emperor of Delhi, was very old, almost bankrupt, and an unwilling partner. His own Begum and many of his courtiers are alleged to have been hobnobbing with the British. Above all, well-trained Sikhs of the Punjab and the Gurkhas of Nepal fought on the British side. Contemporary British generals and writers had confessed that, without the support of the Sikhs and the Gurkhas, they could not have survived the uprising of 1857.

The 18th century was a period of great political turmoil, uncertainties and constant wars among various sections of the Indian nobilitis along with a number of European trading companies, who had also joined the fray. The re-deeming feature of the time, however, was the process of Hindu-Muslim rapproachment. A noted historian states:

> "Akbar's reign is remarkably important and instructive for the existence of Hindu-Muslim harmony. Illustrations of this are not lacking even in the reign of Aurangzeb. Alawal, a Muhammadan poet who translated in the seventeeth century the Hindi poem 'Padmavat' into Bengali, was the author of several poems onVaishnava subjects. Abdullah Khan, one of the Sayyid brothers,observed the Basant and Holi festivals; and, Siraj-ud-daulah and Mir Jafar enjoyed holi festivals along with their friends and relatives. It is said that on his death-bed Mir Jafar drank a few drops of water poured in libation over the idol of Kiriteswari near Murshidabad. Daulat Rao Scindia and his officers joined Muharram pro-

> cessions wearing a green dress like Muhammadans. It has been noted by a modern Indian writer on the authority of Jam-i-Jahan Numa, a Persian weekly of the early nineteenth century, how the Durga Puja was celebrated at the Delhi court as late as A. D. 1825."[5]

But, that is only one side of the picture. By and large, the Muslims of foreign origin, namely the Turks, the Afghans, and the Mughals, still bore their distinctiveness with an air of ethnic superiority; they looked down upon not only the Hindus, but even the Muslim converts of India, called 'Hindustani'. They largely kept aloof from the uprising of 1857, partly because they were not sure of its success and partly because they thought that in the event of success, the reins of power would go to Hindu hands. Most of the Hindu kings and nobles, especially in Bengal and Northern India, apprehended a revival of the Islamic rule of which they had been recently delivered by the secular looking Britishers.

The Muslim converts of Hindu ancestry formed a class by themselves. Most of them had come from the low castes and were making all out efforts to get equality with the Muslim aristocracy of foreign origin. They displayed greatest zeal in adopting foreign ways, language, style of living and took pride in denouncing their Hindu ancestry. Owing to these reasons, he (the Indian convert) was cut off like an alien in his own motherland.[6] The truth, however, is that the Indian rulers in general, whether Hindu or Muslim, were least bothered about the fate of millions of farmers small traders, and workmen who had been driven to utter poverty due to the new British policies about agriculture, trade and industry, all meant to fill the coffers of the East India Company, its officers and the Government of Britain. Thus, there was a tremendous public resentment against the British rule, but there was no one to channelise it properly.

REFERENCES

1. Dr. Tara Chand, Influence of Islam on Indian Culture.
2. Advanced History of India, R.C. Majumdars and others, MacMillan & Co, Ltd. 1946, St. Martin's Street, London, p. 182.
3. Ibid, p. 275.
4. Advanced History of India, p. 434.
5. —do— p. 560.
6. A.L. Srivastra, The Sultanate of Delhi. p. 482.

Chapter II

BIRTH AND EARLY YEARS OF CONGRESS

"I thank the Almighty for emancipating this country from the centuries old bondage and placing it under the British rule".[1]

These are the words of Raja Rammohun Roy (1772-1833) about the East India Company's victory in the Plassey war (1757) and consequent removal of the Muslim rule from Bengal.

The British rule in India had a mixed reaction. It was hailed by those who had seen the tyranny of Islamic rule under the Muslim emperors and nawabs. It was cursed by those who had enjoyed patronage of the extravagant and lustful nawabs and kings. The farmers, the tradesmen and craftsmen, especially the weavers, were all hard hit, because of the new agrarian and trade policies of the East India Company. As a result, there were frequent local uprisings in various parts of the country, especially in Bihar, Bengal and South India, even before the armed revolt of 1857.

The failure of the 1857 revolt brought home to Indians their basic weaknesses. The leaders of the majority Hindu community realised that they must first get rid of their age-old shackles of casteism, regional prejudices, illiteracy, superstitions, and defeatism, before they could succeed in any attempt against the British might. Consequently, a number of social and religious reformist organizations, like the Arya Samaj, Brahmo Samaj, Prarthana Samaj, came into being. The British intelligentsia also realised that they could not take the Indian population for granted and must pay heed to Indian sentiments and tone up their administration. On their part, the British started taking certain measures to appease the Indian sentiment.

In the meantime, a new crop of Indian intellectuals, consisting of lawyers, editors, doctors, enterpreneurs and civil servants had been produced by the East India Company and the British Crown. Their only grievance was that they were denied equality of status and remuneration with their white counterparts.

There were many Britishers who studied the Indian problem in great detail and brought before the British parliament the failings of the British government in India which needed redressal.[2] A British ex-ICS officer, Mr. A. O. Hume, took up the Indian grievances. In a letter to Sir Auckland Colvin, he complained about (a) the costly and unsuitable civil courts, (b) the corrupt and oppressive police, (c) the rigid revenue system, and (d) the galling administration of the Arms Act and the Forest Act. He sought (a) justice cheap, sure and speedy, (b) a land revenue system more elastic and sympathetic, and (d) a less harsh administration of the Arms and Forest laws.[3] Hume had also "unimpeachable evidence" of political discontent and "seething revolt" incubating in various districts, based upon the communications of the disciples of various *gurus* to their religious heads. He, therefore, thought of evolving a safety valve for this unrest and the Congress was the outlet. In a letter addressed to the graduates of the Calcutta University, on 1st March, 1883, he asked for just fifty men, good and true, men of unselfishness, moral courage, self-control and active spirit of benevolence. He stated "If only fifty men good and true, can be found to join as founders, the thing can be established and the further development will be comparatively easy." Hume added... "if they cannot renounce personal ease and pleasure, then at present at any rate all hopes of progress are at an end and India truly neither desires nor deserves any better Government than she enjoys."[4]

Hume also consulted the then Viceroy, Lord Dufferin, about forming the Indian National Union (later named as Congress) and was blessed by the latter. Mr. W. C. Bonnerjee, the first president of the Congress, wrote in his 'Introduction to Indian Politics', published in 1898:

> "It will probably be news to many that the Indian National Congress, as it was originally started and as it has since been carried on, is in reality the work of the Marquis of Dufferin and Ava when that nobleman was the Governor-General of India. Mr. A. C. Hume, C.B., had in 1884, conceived the

idea... saw the noble Marquis when he went to Simla early in 1885... Dufferin took great interest in the matter and after considering over it for some time he sent for Mr. Hume... He said there was no body of persons in this country who performed the functions which Her Majesty's Opposition did in England...it would be very desirable in their interest as well as the interest of the ruled that Indian politicians should meet yearly and point out to the Government in what respects the administration was defective and how it could be improved, and he added that an assembly such as he proposed should not be presided over by the local Governor, for in his presence the people might not like to speak out their minds...Lord Dufferin had made it a condition with Mr. Hume that his name in connection with the scheme of the Congress should not be divulged so long as he remained in the country, and his condition was faithfully maintained and none but the men consulted by Hume knew anything about the matter."[5]

In March 1885, it was decided to hold a meeting of representatives from all parts of India at the ensuing Christmas. A circular was issued stating inter-alia that the Conference would be composed of delegates -leading politicians well-acquainted with the English language- from all parts of the Bengal, Bombay and Madras Presidencies. The venue first proposed was Poona but later it was changed to Bombay.

The first two day session of the Indian National Congress was accordingly held at Bombay on 27 and 28 Dec. 1885 under the presidentship of a retired ICS officer, Mr. W.C. Bonnerjee. It was attended by 72 delegates including prominent men like Dadabhai Nauroji, K.T.Telang, Ferozeshah Mehta, a number of professors, lawyers editors, writers and scholars. Reporting about the convention, the Times of India, Bombay, of Feb 5, 1886, sarcastically remarked:

"Only one great race was conspicuous by its absence: the Mohammedans of India were not there. They remained steadfast in their habitual separation."[6]

The report was, however, not wholly correct. Two prominent members of the Muslim community, namely, R.M. Sayani and A.M. Dharamsi, both lawyers at the Bombay High Court, did attend the Congress session. It is noteworthy that a political organisation of middle class Muslims was also formed in 1885 in Calcutta. This Muslim organisation later joined the Congress. The editorial of the Times of India however made a prophetic observation which not only proved correct fifty years later but would seem relevant even today. It stated:

"Political privileges they can obtain in the degree in which they prove themselves deserving of them. But it was by force that India was won, and it is by force that India must be governed, in whatever hands the Government of the country may be vested. If we (the TOI was then owned by the British) were to withdraw, it would be in favour not of the most fluent tongue or of the most ready pen, but the strongest arm and the sharpest sword".[7]

The first session of the Congress expressed loyalty of the Indian people towards the British government in clear and unequivocal terms. It discussed issues relating to administration and taxation and passed a resolution that the British government should appoint a committee to look into the same. Upto 1897, the main aim of the Congress was to secure from the British masters greater rights of recruitment of Indians in higher civil services and certain other concessions, like reform of the legislative council, holding examination for the ICS,both in England and India. Its means were appeals, memorials, memoranda and petitions. The number of Congress delegates increased with each subsequent session. Participation of the Muslims also increased; from 2 in the first session and 33 in the second, it rose to 156 (out of 702) in the sixth session in 1890. Participation of Parsis and Christians was quite appreciable. While the first president of the Congress was a Hindu, thc second one (1886), Dadabhoi Nauroji, was a Parsi, the third (1887), Badruddin Tyabji, was a Muslim, the fourth (1888), David GeorgeYule, was a Christian, the fifth (1889), Sir William Wedderburn, was a European, and the sixth (1890), Sir Pherozshah Mehta, was again a Parsi. In spite of all this, the Congress was termed as a "Hindu" organisation, and rightly so because of the Hindu majortiy. An impression was, however, being created by the British officials that the Muslims were opposed to it. As a reaction to it, one Sheikh Raza Hussein Khan produced in the Congress session of 1888 at Allahabad, a 'fatwa' from the spiritual leader of the Sunni community of Lucknow and declared that "It is not the Muslims but their official masters who were opposed to the Congress".[8] The Sheikh said, "We may differ in religious views, but in our aspirations we are one. We have a common goal, and we are one nation. So in respect of laws all should be treated alike".[9] But the fact remains that quite a large number of Muslim leaders, prominent among them being Sir Syed Ahmed Khan were opposing the Congress and dissuading the Muslims from joining it.

A classic example is one of Badruddin Tayyabji, president of the 1887 session of the Congress. Almost at the same time, Syed Ahmed Khan got his Knighthood. Tayyabji wrote him a letter of congratulation. In reply, the Syed criticised the Congress. Stating that it was against the interests of the Muslim community, he ridiculed Tayyabji for his association with the Congress. The latter first defended his national outlook, but ultimately relented and wrote to A.O. Hume that in view of the increasing hostility of the Muslims, the annual session of the Congress should be prorogued for at least five years. Taking note of the Muslim sentiments, Hume, himself circulated a draft resolution that no subject should be taken up for consideration by the Congress if it was opposed by the Muslim or the Hindu delegates as a body. it was the starting point of Muslim séparation from Hindus and other religious minorities, all together called non-Muslims.

Thus, from the very beginning, the Congress came to regard the Muslims as a separate entity. Not only that. Various acts and gestures of Congress showed that it needed the Muslims more than the Muslims needed the Congress. Taking advantage of this queer situation, the Muslims who joined Congress always bore a domineering posture.

Here is an example. Social reform was made a part of the Congress programme. Alongwith the main session, a National Social Conference used to be held in the same Pandal. In the Social Conference of 1899, a Muslim Mufti from Barreilly was associated. A resolution supporting re-marriage of Hindu child widows came up for consideration. The Mufti sought permission to speak. The presiding officer said, "The resolution concerns Hindus alone; you need not speak."The Mufti said angrily, "Then, why have you tagged the word 'National' with this Conference?" Permission was granted. The Mufti pleaded that the Hindu *Shastras* did not allow re-marriage of widows and, therefore, it was a sin to bring in such a resolution." On another resolution to allow reconversion to

Hindu religion of those who had once gone out and embraced Islam or Christianity, the Mufti again intervened to say, "When a man became an apostate and abandoned Hindu religion, he should not be allowed to come back and contaminate the sacred Hindu society."[10] The Hindu leaders in the Conference, including stalwarts like Ranade, were simply non-plussed. The incident brings out the tragic fact that the Hindus who had brought the two resolutions had not done their home work properly. They had not seen their own scriptures. They had been prompted only by the Western thought-wave. The Mufti had not said anything new. The fact, still mostly unknown and ignored, is that wherever Islamic rule was set up in India, the Qazis and the Muftis interpreted even the Hindu *Shastric* law. And, they did the way it suited them most. The Shariat law does not allow a Muslim to go out of the Muslim fold. Thus, it served the cause of Islam to favour the view that once a Hindu embraces Islam or Christianity, the doors of Hindu religion are closed to him for ever. The Shariat law allows Muslims four wives at a time. Thus, it suited the Muslims to decree that the Hindu widows could not re-marry under the Hindu law. Consequently, thousands of Hindu widows went to Muslim homes. Had the Hindu leaders read their own scriptures, history and known their ancient traditions, they would have found that widow marriage was prevalent among Hindus. The holy Vedas, the original Book of Hindu religion, contain references to widow marriages as well as inter-caste marriages. Emperor Chandra Gupta Maurya's marriage with the daughter of Greek general Seleukos, about 300 BC, is a well known fact of history. Later Hindu *Shastras* do not commend such marriages, but there is no absolute injunction against them. Further, the Vedic edict is 'Krinvanto vishwamaaryam' (let us Aryanise the world). As all the Hindu Dharmashastras were composed much before the advent of Islam or Christianity, they could not lay down anything specific about them or those who, to save their lives or property, adopted either of them, but wanted to come back to their original faith. A ban on such home coming would be violative of the Vedic teaching of converting the world to Aryan fold. Moreover, in the present context, such a ban will be a sin against humanity and freedom of conscience. The very fact that all the people of various hues, like the Shakas, the Huns, the Bactrians, who had come to India before Islam, got converted to

Hindu religion, leaving no trace of their origin, is a glaring testimony of the open door policy of Hindu religion.

ENTRY OF LOKAMANYA TILAK

Even before Bal Gangadhar Tilak attended the Congress session at Bombay in Dec. 1889, he had become a great nationalist leader in his own right. In this session, he proposed that the members of the Imperial Council should be elected by the Provincial Councils instead of being elected by the electoral college. G.K. Gokhale seconded it. It was the first and the last time in Congress proceedings that the two concurred with each other. Tilak's proposal was lost, but his speech made a lasting impact. He got great support from leaders like B.C. Pal, Lajpat Rai, Subramaniam Iyer and Madan Mohan Malaviya. In fact, Tilak gave a wholly new turn to the Congress, in that, he changed its course from loyalty to British government to confrontation, by putting up the demand for self government, 'Swaraj is my birth right'. Tilak laid stress on the service to the people and making Congress an organisation of the masses.

In 1883, Tilak had started Lord Ganesha worship festival as a public function which soon became an annual feature. It was followed by the celebration of Shivaji Jayanti in 1896. The Muslims also participated in these festivals. But, the Anglo-Indian press of the time accused him of communalism, trying to stir up the Hindus against the Muslims. Vehemently refuting this charge, Tilak said:

"Shivaji festival is not celebrated to alienate or even to irritate the Muslims. Times are changed and the Mohammadans and the Hindus are in the same boat so far as political condition of the people is concerned. Can we not both of us derive inspiration from the life of Shivaji under these circumstances?"[11]

No right thinking man can accuse Shivaji of being communal. Indeed, in Maharashtra, Shivaji was held in high esteem both by the Muslims and the Hindus. In the disastrous famine of 1896-97 and during the plague epidemic of March 1897, Tilak did a lot of relief work and, on both the occasions, he served Hindus and Muslims alike. He was, however, critical of Government's pro-Muslim attitude and expressed his anger through the 'Maratha' and the 'Kesari'. Consequently, there was a vilification campaign not only against him but against the whole Brahmin community of

Poona. He was imprisoned on the charge of sedition in July 1897 and released in Sept. 1898. But, the malicious reports of pro-British press of the time against him has formed the source material for a number of Marxist, British and Pakistani historians to denigrate Tilak. For example, a Britisher states:

"The first man to combine Hindu revivalism with active political agitation was Bal Gangadhar Tilak (1856-1920) who inspired an era of religious fanaticism and political violence which lasted until Gandhi introduced other methods in the early 1920s...Tilak can also be regarded as one of the founders of Pakistan, for he and the other revivalist Hindu leaders - and later, Gandhi, who followed in their tradition - used the Hindu religion politically in such a way that Indian Muslim finally became convinced that it would be the Hindus who ruled if Congress ever came to power."[12]

This sort of history is an outcome of a perverted mind or the result of Pakistani propaganda which does not have an iota of truth.

PARTITION OF BENGAL

Partition of Bengal in 1905 was the most important event in arousing natioal consciousness and mass awakening throughout India. The province of Bengal, at the time, included Bihar and Orissa and presented a lot of adminmistrative problems. In 1874 itself, two frontier districts of Bengal had been transferred to Assam. In 1896, the Chief Commissioner of Assam had proposed that Chittagong division and the districts of Dacca and Mymen Singh should also be transferred to it, but the proposal was dropped. When partition of Bengal was effected in 1905, the motivation was political, rather than administrative. This would be clear from the Note prepared by the Home Secretary, Risley, for Lord Curzon, in December 1904, which stated:

"Bengal united is a power, Bengal divided will pull in several different ways. That is what the Congress leaders feel; their apprehensions are perfectly correct and they form one of the greatest merits of the scheme...One of our main objects is to split up and thereby weaken a solid body of opponents to our rule."[13]

The partition plan of Bengal by which a new province of East Bengal, comprising of Assam, Chittagong and 15 other districts, was created, generated a tempest of opposition and bitterness throughout India. There were protest rallies in every nook and corner. The Swadeshi movement attained an all- India character. The boycott of British goods caused considerable financial loss to the British industrial establishments in Lancashire (England). Initially, the Muslims supported this movement, but later the majority of them, especially in the new province of Bengal, turned against it and pledged their support to the government.[14] The Reverend John Page Hopps, Editor of 'The Coming Day, London', wrote; "The phrase 'Home Rule' is a phrase of ill omen to the ruling classes of Great Britain. This 'Home Rule' was the demand of the Hindus. As against this, the Musalmans had consistently been following the policy of fidelity chalked out by Sayyid Ahmad khan whose complete programme could be summed up in three words, 'Education, loyalty, opposition to the Hindus."[15]

The anti-partition agitation was followed by a reign of repression. Heavy punishments were awarded for small or no fault. The Governor of Bengal, Sir Bamfylde Fuller put all the forces of fury on the Hindu public of Bengal. Even John Viscount Morley said, "He is evidently a shrewd, eager, impulsive, overflowing sort of man quite well fitted for government work of ordinary scope, but, I fear, no more fitted to manage the state of things in East Bengal than am I to drive an engine."[16]

Two boys were fined for singing Bande Mataram in the streets of Mymensingh. Sir B. Fuller issued a circular calculated to prevent the Muhammadans from making a common cause with the Hindus. In it, the Divisional Commissioners and District Judges were asked to "fix a proportion which Mohamedans should constitute in the personnel of each office, and to instruct those who enjoyed the power of making appointments that so long as that quota was not reached they were not to reject Muhammedan candidates merely on the ground of comparative inferiority of qualification."[17] In his zeal for favouring the Muslims, Fuller called the Muslims as his favourite co-wife, a remark that was resented by many self respecting Muslims.[18]Consequently, there were bloody Hindu-Muslim riots in Bengal in which the Muslims committed all acts of brutality on the Hindu population. "At one place, some Muslims proclaimed by beat of drum that the Government had permitted them to loot the Hindus, while at another they publicly declared"that the Government had permitted the Muslims to marry Hindu widows in the *Nikah* form."[19] The atrocities on Hindus of Bengal, both by the British government and the Muslims, were numerous. Naturally, therefore, Hindus took to terrorist methods against the British officials.

The Muslim League, which was then recently formed, followed its chosen way of not making a common cause with the Hindus except under pressure of expediency. While the anti-partition agitationists criticised the Viceroy Lord Curzon, the Muslims as a class eulogised him. The Aligarh Institute Gazette of May 9, 1904, stated, "One community of India deprecated completely the various acts of Lord Curzon...and this, perhaps, because another community regards his period as the best one and Lord Curzon as the best Viceroy."[20] But, despite all odds, the anti-partition movement got stronger year by year till the partition of Bengal was annulled and the decision was announced in the Imperial Darbar held in Delhi in 1911.

REFERENCES

1. B.N. Jog, Threat of Islam, p. 1.
2. Pattabhi Sitaramayya, History of the Indian National Congress, Vol. I, p. 5.
3. Ibid, p. 8.
4. Sitaramayya, History of Indian National Congress, vol. I, p. 8-9.
5. Ibid, p. 15.
6. B.N. Jog, Threat of Islam, p. 41.
7. Ibid.
8. Pattabhi Sitaramayya, History of Indian National Congress, Vol. I, p. 44.
9. B.N. Jog, Threat of Islam, p. 42.
10. B.N. Jog, Threat of Islam (p. 50-51).
11. Dr. Nihar Nandan Singh, Lokamanya Bal Gangadhar Tilak. p.26
12. Micheal Edwardes, Last Years of British India, pps. 35-36.
13. Tara Chand, History of Freedom Movement in India, vol, III, p. 313.
14. Ibid, p. 317.
15. Lal Bahadur, 'The Muslim League (Its History, Activities & Achievements, p. 56.) Agra Book Stores.
16. Lal Bahadur, Ibid, p. 60.

17. Lal Bahadur. Ibid.
18. Ibid.
19. Ibid. p. 61, based on CY Chintamani's Indian Politics since the Mutiny.
20. Ibid. p. 65.

Chapter III

SEPARATIST MUSLIM THOUGHT – FORMATION OF MUSLIM LEAGUE

"Muhammadans may accept English supremacy, because they have been conquered by Englishmen, but who is to make them submit to the supremacy of the Hindus, whom for 700 years they regarded their slaves?"[1]

This was the theme of the Muslim aristocracy led by Sir Syed Ahmed Khan towards the closing years of the last century. This aristocracy was quite distinct in birth and divorced from the interests of the low class Muslim masses on whose numerical strength was laid the foundation of separatist Muslim thought.

Upto the nineteenth century, neither the Muslims formed a compact whole nor were the Hindus an altogether divided house as is generally propagated and believed today. If Hindus were divided into various castes and sub-castes, the Muslims too were divided into many sects, like the Sunnis, the Shias, the Ahmediyas, the Khojas, the Mughals, and so on. Both, Hindus and Muslims, were interspersed throughout India and they lived peacefully side by side, despite minor local clashes occasionally. The nobility, the ruling classes, used to fight political, not religious wars, though sometimes Muslims also brought in their religion only to win the sympathy and cooperation of the Ulemas. Admittedly, ninety to ninetyfive percent of the present day Muslims are descendants of the Hindu converts, but what is significant is that they also carried with them many of their Hindu social customs, superstitions, way of life, and even the evils of caste and dowry systems.

But, since the last quarter of the nineteenth century, sustained efforts were made to unite the Muslims and divide the Hindus. The wonder of wonders is that a large body of the Hindu intellectuals itself joined hands with the British and the Muslims to divide and weaken the Hindu nation, after whom alone the country was named Hindustan, meaning abode of Hindus, the ocean on its shores named 'Bahr-e-Hind', and the mountain on its north-west as 'Hindukush'. (Even the most powerful and fanatic of the Muslim rulers, Aurangzeb, did not think of changing this name). How fast was the decadence of the Hindus can be gauged from the fact that, while through their vigorous campaigns from 1905 to 1911, they got annuled the partition of Bengal effected by the British to appease the Muslims, even when there was no Mahatma Gandhi, but in a period of next 35 years they got so crippled that they helplessly bowed down before the partition plan not only of Bengal in the east, but also of the Punjab in the west.

The first chief minister of undivided Punjab, (after the Montford reforms of 1919) Mian Fazli Husain (then called the prime minister) himself told Durga Das, the famous journalist and author, sometime in 1920-21, how his family had been converted to Islam and how his own marriage was solmenised first by the Hindu rites and then under Muslim law by a Kazi.[2] During his tenure, this very Fazli Hussain created bad blood between Hindus and Muslims of the Punjab by showering all favours on the Muslim community. It was he who converted Lahore into a Muslim majority area by including in it some Muslim dominated villages into the Municipal area. Earlier, the Lahore Corporation had eleven Hindu and Sikh members and eleven Muslim members. With the change made, number of Muslim members increased to eighteen.[3] Indeed, many of the Hindu converts to Islam proved more fanatic than the fanatics of foreign origin.

Many historians, especially the British, have attributed the Hindu-Muslim conflict to their different religious beliefs, for example, "the Hindus worshipped idols, the Muslims abhored them; the Hindus revered cow, the Muslims ate it". This is a very narrow and mistaken belief. There are Sikhs and the Arya Samajists who do not share idol worship, but that has never been a cause of conflict with them. Similar is the case with regard to the Parsees, the Jews and the Christians, who too do not rever the cow. It is very well known that in the revolt of 1857, when Hindus and Muslims fought together against the British, the main grievance of the Hindus was that the British ate beef and used cow fat on the cartridges supplied to the Indian sepoys. It is, however, true that in their hey day earlier, certain Muslims resorted to cow killing and breaking of Hindu idols to tease or mark their imperial authority on the Hindus. But, by the close of the eighteenth century, the *Jazia* had been removed, cow killing banned, and idol breaking made an offence, by the Muslim princes, including Delhi emperor, in their respective areas of influence.

The Muslim invaders who had established their rule in India, appointed their own men on positions of trust and responsibility. The number of this foreign element went on increasing right upto the end of the ruling Mughal dynasty. In Akbar's time, over seventyfive per cent of the mansabdars were Muslims of foreign origin. Even the number of Hindu (Rajput and others) mansabdars was much higher than of the Indian Muslim mansabdars — 47 Hindus against 23 Indian Muslims. The ratio of foreign mansabdars went down during the later period of Aurangzeb, but still they numbered almost equal to the total number of the Hindu mansabdars — 227 foreign Muslims as against 88 Indian Muslims, 81 Rajputs, and 89 Marathas.[4]

> The account of the leading Mughal grandees in Massir-ul-Umara, an eighteenth century work which covers the entire Mughal period, shows that out of 735 eminent nobles, 515 were Muslims of foreign origin and only 61 were Indian Muslims. Such exaggerated importance was attached to non-Indian descent during the Mughal period that if Muslim aspirants for high government office did not have a foreign ancestor, they sometimes invented a fictitious one to improve their chances. Very often they took recourse to marrying Kashmiri girls so that their fair-complexioned progeny might pass as Iranian or Turkish. This exclusive and foreign character of the power group was kept alive throughout the Mughal period. Even the decline of the Mughal empire did not deter the inhabitants of Central Asia and Afghanistan from leaving the inhospitable land of their birth to try their luck in India.[5]

Thousands of soldiers of the army of Nadir Shah (1739) had stayed back in India. Similarly, large numbers of Afghans had settled in India. They became masters of the area known as Ruhelkhand.

It was mostly the Muslim nobility of foreign origin, having nothing in common with the Indian Muslims, who instigated the latter to wage a 'Jehad' (holy war) against their Hindu neighbours, termed 'kafirs'. Besides the nobility, there was the Muslim clergy, the Ulemas, who held a sway on the Muslim rulers and motivated them, in the name of pure Islam, to inflict all sorts of indignities and cruelties on their Hindu subjects and to maintain a safe distance not only from the Hindus but also from the Shias and other sects of the Muslims. They praised the rulers who were cruel to Hindus and denigrated those who treated Hindus with equanimity.

In this atmosphere, the British took over the reins of power in India. From the very beginning, they realised that their own man-power and resources were inadequate to keep them in power for long and that they must resort to the policy of divide and rule, pitting one class of Indians against another on grounds of religion, descent, caste or anything. This is very clear from various communications issued by the British officers of the time. Marginal differences were no doubt there, but the British magnified them up to the hilt. The British rule in India started from Bengal-Bihar-Orissa, in the latter half of the eighteenth century, consequent upon the war of Plassey (1757), which ousted the Muslim rulers. The Muslim aristocracy of Bengal was, therefore, the first to bear the brunt of the despotic and corrupt rule of the East India Company. The Hindus, on the other hand, felt somewhat relieved from the tyranny of the Islamic laws.

The British attitude towards the Muslims, which term should actually mean the Muslim aristocracy, not the Muslim masses, is very well brought out by T.L. Sharma in his well documented work 'Hindu-Muslim Relations in all India Politics (1913-1925)':[6]

"They saw the Muslims as the displaced rulers, whom they had expected to resent the loss of their former power and to be strongest in resisting foreign rule and western civilization. This fear of the Muslims continued to haunt them throughout the nineteenth century. The Wahabis who fanatically opposed everything that British rule represented, were discovered preparing for a revolt. The Mutiny, too, was considered mainly a product of Muslim conspiracy..."

This Muslim phobia bred contempt for them in the English mind. Robert clive wrote in a letter to Lawrence Sulivan on Dec.

30, 1758, "These Muslims! Gratitude they have none; base men of very narrow conceptions... they have adopted a system of politics more peculiar to this country than any other, viz. to attempt anything by treachery rather than force".[7] Henry Martin wrote about the Muslims that human nature in its worst form was a Mohammedan.[8]

Lord Ellenborough wrote to the Duke of Wellington from Simla, on October 4, 1842, after the fall of Kabul and Ghazni, that while Muslims desire the failure of the British in Afghanistan, the Hindus rejoiced over their (British) victory, and then stated "It seems to me most unwise, when we are sure of the hostility of one tenth, not to secure the enthusiastic support of the nine — tenths which are faithful."[9] Again writing...to Wellington on 18 January 1843, Ellenborough said, 'I cannot close my eyes to the belief that (Musalman) race is fundamentally hostile to us, and, therefore, our true policy is to conciliate the Hindus.'[10]

Anti-Muslim and pro-Hindu feelings were further visible during the mutiny of 1857, as British regarded the Muslims as its Chief Instigators. H.H.Thomas (Retired ICS) observed: The Hindus were not the contrivers or the primary movers of the (1857) rebellion...it was the result of a Mohammedan conspiracy. Russel wrote to the Times as soon as the rebellion was suppressed:

> 'Our antagonism to the followers of Muhammed is far stronger than that between us and the worshippers of Shiva and Vishnu. They are unquestionably more dangerous to our rule...if we could eradicate the traditions and destroy the temples of Muhammed by vigorous effort it would indeed be well for the Christian faith and for tthe British rule.'[11]

Lord Roberts wrote to his sister Harriet after the revolt that the British should 'work with their life's best blood...and show these rascally Musalmans that with God's help Englishmen will still be the masters of India.' The Friend of India; the predecessor of the Present Statesman, in its editorial entitled 'The Centenary of Plassey' which appeared after the outbreak of the rebellion of 1857 wrote about Muhammedans thus:

> "Cruel, sensual, and intolerant, they are unfit to rule and unwilling to serve. Claiming to exercise sway as of Divine right and yet destitute of every gift which nature has endowed the races meant by destiny to dominate over the

world, they fell by necessity under the power of a nation replete with energy and resolution."[12]

The British attitude towards the Muslims till 1870 was that of suspicion and repression. With the rising of Indian nationalism, the British started befriending that very same despised lot.

SIR SYED AHMED KHAN (1817-1898)

In this background of the anti muslim stance of the British and the rising Indian nationalism, appeared a towering personality in the form of Syed Ahmed Khan, a descendant of a noble family of Arabia which had come to India during the reign of Shahjahan and served the Mughal court. Born on October 17, 1817, Ahmed Khan took up employment with the East India Company. During the 1857—58 revolt Syed had saved the lives of many Englishmen and their families. He was one of those few Muslim nobles who felt that the revolt against the British was not in the Muslim interest, and so, he had dissuaded many Muslim zamindars from taking part in it. In appreciation of his services, the British government rewarded him profoundly, in addition to bestowing upon him the Knighthood. But the Syed was not content with his personal gains alone. He used all his talent, resources and status to improve the lot of his community. In this direction his first work was to change the British attitude of hosility toward the Muslims into one of friendship and alliance.Through his laboriously prepared pamphlet 'An Account of the Loyal Mohammedans of India' (Risala Khair Khwahan Mussalmanana), listing about 150 prominent Muslims who had helped the British against the 1857 revolt and another pamphlet, Asbab-i-Baghavat-e-Hind (causes of Indian Revolt), the Syed refuted the British allegations that the Muslims had committed acts of barbarity on the British officers and their families. He alluded the cause to the keeping of the members of "two always antagonistic races", Hindu and Muslim, together in military service which, by constant association, removed all differences between them and the soldiers of one battalion regarded themselves as belonging to one brotherhood, that the Muslims sepoys, under ignorance of their true religion, followed their colleagues, the Hindu sepoys. He emphasised that "It is a strict and sacred command of our Prophet to his followers that when they wage a war against their enemies they are not to slay the women nor children, nor the aged, nor the unresisting, nor those who demand quarter, even if they be kafirs." So, according to Syed, the Muslims could not commit the alleged barbarity. Indirectly, the Syed gave the suggestion that the Muslims and the Hindu soldiers should be kept in separate battalions.[13]

Sir Syed Ahmed Khan wrote a commentary on the Old Testament and the Bible showing that there was much in common between Islam and 'real' Christianity and that the gulf between the two had been caused by the prejudice and ignorance of both the parties. He made out that 'if any religion in the world could be an ally and friend of Christianity that was certainly Islam.'[14] The Syed was the first Muslim to make such an attempt and, therefore, his commentary generated a lot of criticism among the Ulemas. Strangely, no such attempt was made by any Hindu leader at the political level though the basic tenets of Christianity are nearer to Hindu religion and in practice too, the Hindu kings had given all freedom and facilities to Christians much before the Muslim rule came to India.

Sir Syed also exhorted the Muslims to get English education. He set up for the purpose Mohammedan Anglo-Oriental College at Aligarh (now Aligarh Muslim University). He lamented that the people who had derived the greatest benefit from the English education were Hindus.[15] Simultaneously, the Syed desired re-interpretation of the Quran and to effect social reforms in the Muslim community of India but he had to face a lot of opposition from the orthodoxy on both these points.

Sir Syed Ahmed Khan was initially a votary of Hindu-Muslim unity but on his own terms. He was an ardent supporter and promoter of Urdu written in Persian script. Till the last days of his life, the Syed opposed the introduction of Hindi in Devanagari script in the United Provinces (now Uttar Pradesh), the very citadel of Hindi. In 1867, Hindus demanded that the Urdu language and the Persian script, as far as possible, be discontinued and that Hindi written in Devanagari script should be adopted in its place. Sir Syed opposed it tooth and nail and went to the extent of saying that Hindu-Muslim unity and co-operation were impossible ideals. He described his feelings in the following words:

> "When all this was going on in Benares, I was talking to Mr. Shakespeare (then Commissioner of Benares) about

> Muslim education. He was astonished when he heard my views and told me that it was the first time he had ever heard me talk in terms of advancement of the Muslims alone rather than in terms of the welfare of the Indian people as a whole. I replied that I was convinced that the two communities were incapable of putting their heart and soul into anything requiring mutual effort, and even though the opposition was not yet as serious as it might be, I thought that would increase...I assured him that anyone who lived long enough would see the truth of my prediction.."[16]

It would be interesting to quote the distinguished Pakistani scholar, Abdul Haque who, speaking on the role of Urdu in the context of the birth of Pakistan, said in Karachi on Feb 15, 1961:

> "Pakistan was not created by Jinnah; nor was it created by Iqbal. It was Urdu that created it. For, the fundamental reason for the discord between Hindus and Muslims was the Urdu language. The entire two-nation theory and all other difficulties of this nature issued solely from Urdu".[17]

Too much importance has been given to Sir Syed Ahmed Khan's occasional expressions of Hindu-Muslim unity. The fact is that, from the very beginning,he was a staunch communalist and remained so upto his last. It is incorrect, as many other writers have alluded, that, before the birth of Congress, the Syed was a nationalist and that he became a communalist only at the behest of the British. The rules of the Mohammedan Anglo-Oriental College, Aligarh, set up by the Syed (1875) of which he was the life-secretary, provided that only the Muslims could be its members and that funds were to be raised from the Muslims and other people of the Book only, namely, Christians and Jews. Others (meaning Hindus) were not to be approached. He raised objections to every book which, according to him, touched the Muslim psyche. At one place he objected to a book which referred to places like 'Mecca' or the Jama Masjid of Delhi, without a complimentary epithet.[18] He jeered at the national agitation for emancipation and called it as 'no more than the cries of Jackals and crows'. The Syed dreamt of re-establishing the lost Muslim power in India with British help and, therefore, his ambition soared higher and higher.[19]

Thus, the Muslims of foreign origin became the self-styled leaders of the Muslim community and were accepted as such by the British. In a letter to the British Government, Sir Syed Ahmed Khan prayed for nomination of only the upper class Muslims, because:

> "You will see that it is one of the necessary conditions of sitting at the same table with the Viceroy, that the person concerned should have high social status in the country. Will the members of the noble families in our country like it that a person of lower class or lower status, even if he has taken a B.A. or M.A. degree and possesses the necessary ability, should govern them and dispose of their wealth, property and honour".[20]

A close associate of Sir Syed and the one who carried Syed's mission in U.K., Sir Ameer Ali, wrote in his 'A cry from Indian Muhammedan' :

> "The waves of adversity, which have one after another passed over the Muhammedans of India, have left the great majority of the leading families stranded,and a large portion completely wrecked...The destruction of the Muhammedan aristocracy has proved as injurious to the interests of the community as to those of the state."[21]

Having so said, Ameer Ali questioned:

> "Was it necessary to deprive them (Muslim aristocrats) of influence and wealth and reduce them to their present impoverished and subordinate condition? Was it necessary to ruin them by taking away the lands and giving them to their Hindu bailiffs?[22]

In fact, all the alleged sufferings and deprivations of the Muslim aristocracy were based on a study of the situation in Bengal, but the data and the information compiled was applied to whole of India. Besides, neither this aristocracy nor their supporters in the British government had any concern for the fate of the Muslim masses.

About the Congress, the Syed said:

> "I consider the experiment which the Indian National Congress wants to make is fraught with dangers and suffering for all the nationalities of India, especially for the Muslims.

> The Muslims are in a minority but they are highly united minority. Traditionally, they are prone to take the sword in hand when the majority oppresses them. If this happens, it will bring about disasters greater than the ones which came in the wake of the happenings of 1857... The Congress cannot rationally prove its claim to represent the opinions, ideals and aspirations of the Muslims."[23]

However, there were also Muslim intellectuals, like M.A.Jinnah, Badruddin Tyabji, Rahmatullah Sayani, who strongly pleaded that though the Indian Muslims followed a different religion from the Hindus, the political and economic needs and aspirations of the two communities were the same. In later periods, the number of such worthy people declined; most of them fell to the communal tanturm. The prophesy of the Syed came true about 50 years later.

BIRTH OF MUSLIM LEAGUE

In the atmosphere stated above, a body of the Muslim aristocracy led by Sir Aga Khan, desirous of carving out separate political niche for themselves, connived with the British officers wanting to curb the national movement gaining momentum under the banner of the Congress and other local Hindu associations and institutions, and the revolutionaries, set up in Dec. 1906 at Dacca, the All India Muslim League, with the blessings of the then Viceroy, Lord Minto. Earlier, in the memorandum submitted to the Viceroy, by the delegation of the founders of the League, on Oct 1, 1906, the following demands were made:

1. Adequate representation in all services- civil and military - and in the High Courts; the appointment to higher posts being made without competitive examinations.
2. Guarantee of a number of seats in the councils of the municipal and district boards and the syndicates and senates of the universities.
3. Election of Muslims to the provincial Councils through separate electorates, and in numbers not in proportion to their population, but in accordance to their political importance.
4. Election of Muslims to the Imperial Legislative Council through a separate electorate in sufficient number so that the Muslims may not be an ineffective minority.

5. Aid in founding a Muslim University which would be a centre of Muslim religious and intellectual life.[24]

In the meeting held on that day at Shimla., Lord Minto addressed the delgates as "the descendants of a conquering and ruling race."[25]

The Muslim complaint that they did not have adequate representations in the services was baseless as revealed by the facts and figures for the period in Tara Chand's "History of Freedom Movement in India," Vol.III, published by the Government of India. While their number in the civil services had decreased during the British time because of their lack of English education, their number in the army, para military forces and the police force was proportionately far greater than the Hindus.

At the time of the formation of the Muslim League, its objects were:

1. Promotion of feelings of loyalty to the British Governement;
2. Protection and advancement of the political rights and interests of the Muslims of India; and
3. Prevention of the rise of hostility towards other communities.

The queer part of the Muslim agitation then and even now is that their leaders claim Muslim superiority in all matters like, religion, martial values, social solidarity based on the principle of equality, and their history of imperial conquests. At the same time they lament their inferiortiy to Hindus in education,intellectual pursuits, wealth, business, industry, trade, services, and political fields. This self contradictory theme held the ground in pre-partition days and is being repeated even now.

Within three years from the birth of the Muslim League, the British Government granted separate electorates for the Muslims, in 1909. Thus the foundation of Muslim separation was well laid. The Hindu Mahasabha was not there. The local Hindu Sabha of Lahore wrote a protest letter to the Viceroy, but it was of no avail. In the Congress session on Dec.1909, some members raised their voices against the grant of separate electorates for the Muslims, but G.K. Gokhale, the then prominent Congress leader and the Political *guru* of Gandhiji, opposed their view-point.

A more astounding feature of the separate Muslim electorate was that the Muslim electors were enrolled if they paid income tax on an income of Rs. 3,000/- per annum whereas the Hindus paying income tax on Rs.3 lakh per annum alone could have the right to vote. Further, a Muslim graduate of 3 years standing acquired the right to vote, but a Hindu had to be of 30 years standing. Apart from these, the Muslims were given direct elections and weightage.[27]

Incidentally, there was no Hindi-Urdu controversy before Sir Syed Ahmed khan. But, it became a major plank in the later day Muslim politics. Language was given a religious overtone. Nawab Mohsin-ul-Mulk went to the length of saying, "Although we have not the might of pen, but our hands are still strong enough to wield the might of the sword."[28]

REFERENCES

1. Aligarh Institute Gazette, dt. 22 Sept. 1893, pp. 947-948, CF Lal Bahadur's Muslims' League.
2. Durga Das, India from Curzon to Nebru and After, p. 111-112.
3. V.P. Bhatia, Organiser weekly, May 28, 1995 Cabbages and kings.
4. T.L. Sharma, Hindu-Muslim Relations, 1913-1925, pp. 3-5.B.R. Publishing Corporation, 29/9, Shakti Nagar, Nangla Park, Delhi-7, 1987,
5. ——do——
6. T.L. Sharma, Hindu-Muslim Relations. p. 10.
7. Ibid—
8. Ibid—
9. Ibid—
10. T.L. Sharma, Hindu-Muslim Relations in All India Politics, p. 11.
11. Ibid—
12. Ibid—
13. Lal Bahadur, Muslim League p. 20-21.
14. Hayat-e-Javed, p. 79.
15. ——do—— p. 99.
16. ——do—— p. 199.
17. Madan Gopal, leading article in Hindustan Times, New Delhi, 28th July 1994.
18. Lal Bahadur, Muslim League, p. 23.
19. Ibid p. 26.
20. T.L. Sharma, Hindu Muslim Relations, p. 17.

21. ——do—
22. ——do—— p. 18.
23. K.P. Karunakaran, Indian Political Thought, 1832-1921.
24. Tara Chand, History of Freedom Movement, Vol. III, pp. 395-96.
25. Ibid.
26. Tara Chand, History of Freedom Movement in India, p. 409.
27. Mohammad Nomani, Rise and Growth of All India Muslim League p. 61.

Chapter IV

LUCKNOW PACT—SURRENDER TO MUSLIM POLITICS

Separate Muslim electorate was granted by the British in 1909, but the national seal of approval to it was given by the Congress in 1916 through the Lucknow Pact. And, this very separate electorate "was to bear bitter fruit in the shape of the demand for Pakistan and its traumatic fulfilment some four decades later."[1]

The first annual session of the Muslim League was held at Karachi on December 29, 1907, under the presidentship of Sir Adamji Pirbhoy. League's choice of this city in Sindh, for its first session was because it was here that Islam registered its first victory as a political force in India. Pirbhoy said in his presidential speech "If a handful of men under a boy (Mohd.-Ibn-Kasim, then 17 years old) could teach Kalima to the territory of Sindh and promulgate the law of Shariat of God and His Rasul; cannot seven crores of Mussalmans make their social and political life pleasant?" The false myth that the Indian Muslims had been the rulers of India immediately before the British rule, was trumpetted time and again. The Congress leaders have always been shy of refuting this false claim. Only M.G. Ranade said, "It should be noted that the immediate predecessors of the British rulers of India were not the Mohammedans, as is too often taken for granted, but they were the Native Rulers of the country who had successfully thrown off the Mohammadan yoke."[2]

The Muslim League was vehemently opposed to the ongoing mass movement to annual the partition of Bengal. In its December 1908 session, Khan Bahadur Ghulam Mahmud said, "It cannot be gain said that Muhammadans have political status, having been rulers... and as such they deserve, in my opinion, larger representation than may appear warranted by an arithmetical calculation of their numerical strength".[3] It was argued that the Muslims should have exclusive electoral colleges so as to avoid the election of a 'non-representative Muslim', a term used for the nationalist Muslims of the Congress. In the next session of the League at Delhi, January 1910, of which the famous Congress leader, Hakim Ajmal Khan, was the president of the Reception Committee, the British government was thanked for granting separate Muslim electorate. Another significant decision was to transfer the League's headquarters from Aligarh to Lucknow.

In the Congress session of the same year, Mohammed Ali Jinnah (later, Father of Pakistan) moved the following resolution, seconded and supported by Harul Haque and Hasan Imam:

"While recognising the necessity of providing for a fair and adequate representation in the Legislative Councils for the Mahomedan and other communities where they be in a minority, this Congress disapproves the regulation promulgated last year to carry out this object by means of separate electorates and, in particular, urges upon Government the justice and expediency of modifying the regulations framed under the Indian Councils Act of 1909 before another election comes on..."

In fact the separate Muslim electorate, which was seen as a direct consequence of the Muslim League's pro-British and anti-Hindu activities, created a lot of resentment among the Hindus. Sir Tej Bahadur Sapru wrote:

"The last meeting of the All India Muslim League at Lucknow, once again demonstrated the utter hollowness of all talk about compromise between the Hindus and Mohammedans in the matter of political representation..Will the Hindus even now awake to their sense of duty towards themselves, towards their past, and towards their future?....Will or Will not they take a leaf out of the book of the Mohammedan aristocracy? Or, are they'leaders' only for the purpose of organizing demonstration of loyalty and leading deputations?"[4]

The editor of a Bengal paper wrote:

"A Pan-Hindu League has become a necessity of the times, forced upon us by the circumstances which are not our creation. If such an organisation is started, we hope it will, its attitude will not be aggressive or militant. Defence, not defiance, be its motto. The great Hindu community has suffered through the want of such organisations, while others have enormously profited by it."[5]

Lala Lajpat Rai, in a letter to the Times, London, wrote:

"...I do not wish to say one unkind word in reply to the argument based upon the so called historical and political importance of the Mohammedans of India, a vast majority of whom are only descendants of the Hindu converts, and are as much divided into castes and sub-castes as the Hindus. But does the All India Muslim League seriously think that backwardness in education, want of organisation, and want of enterprise are substantial grounds for claiming a larger representation than their numbers entitle them?"[6]

Reflecting the sentiments of the Punjabi Hindus, the editor of Tribune commented that the Muslims

"were as unimportant or important as the other communities in this country. The Mohammedan power had almost vanished when the English appeared on the scene. Historically, the English power had not succeeded to Mohammedan...The Sikhs, Marathas and Rajputs are politically important, because they were holding power when the English came."[7]

Lala Lal Chand, a founder member of the Punjab Hindu Sabha, wrote:

"The Secretary of State speaks of the importance of Mohammedans as a community in the U.P., in spite of their minor numerical strength, but he takes it for granted that the Hindu minority in the Punjab is of no importance against the Muhammedan majority so that according to the Secretary of State where the Mohammedans form a majority they must get a lion's share as a matter of course; and where they are in a minority, they will get it on the basis of their supposed importance."[8]

Lal Chand also expressed his anger against the Congress by condemning it as a "self-inflicted misfortune" of the Hindus. He pointed out: "There is one thing that is strictly forbidden within the precincts of the Congress...it is the term 'Hindu'. Resolutions may be passed to favour purely Mohammedan interests but the word Hindu is a taboo here." He blamed the Congress for encouraging the Muslim aggressiveness and said:

"It looks to be very height of folly and absurdity to go on crying for a united nation, when one important community, by its words and actions, makes it persistently and absolutely clear that they do not desire nor seek for union...The method of offering the other cheek for being slapped has now been tried over 20 years. There has been enough of coaxing and fawning which by giving undue importance to the other community, has begotten only insolence and impudence. May we not now try the counter-method and see its results? At least this is a method equally worth trying, and am sure we shall not thereby be worse off than we are."[9]

There was a joint conference of the League and the Congress leaders at Allahabad on 1st January 1911. There were about 40 Muslim and 60 Hindu leaders. Here, G.K. Gokhale, the most prominent leader of the Congress, said that the Muslim fear of being dominated by the Hindu majority should not be lightly treated. Almost every aspect was discussed, including Arya Samaj's religious and cultural activities. The stress of the Muslim leaders was that they being a minority, no matter should be pressed which, in the opinion of the Muslim League, appeared detrimental to Muslim interest. This joint Muslim League-Congress meeting decided nothing. The resolution of M.A. Jinnah against separate Muslim electorate was lost.

Following the joint Congress-League meeting, came the annulment of the partition of Bengal, announced at the Delhi Durbar in 1911. It shook the Muslim loyalty to the British. Added to it was the attack of Italy (1911) on Tripoli, part of the then Turkish empire. Turkey withdrew its forces from the Balkan states to defend Tripoli. This gave an opportunity to the Christian dominated states of Balkan to get rid of Islamic rule of Turkey. British indirectly helped the Balkans to get their freedom. These developments gave another jolt to the Muslim faith in the British. As a result, in 1913, the Muslim League adopted self-government suitable to India as one of its aims. This very factor opened the way to the Lucknow Pact of 1916. But, the League had retained its bargaining power by the qualifying words 'suitable to India' to self government, together with its main object of protecting and advancing the political and other rights of the Indian Muslims.

In August 1912, the British had rejected the longstanding Muslim demand to raise the level of the Muslim-Anglo Oriental College to a university. The Collector of Aligarh had warned the Government that "The Muslims are not thinking of education in itself at all, but of more boys, more subscription, more candidates for government exployment, more lawyers to fill seats in Council, and more political power generally."[10] He had also stated that the Muslims "were organising higher education on a communal basis to enable them to participate on something like equitable terms in the vast process of political and social change which was going on in India".[11]

Then, there was World War I of 1914 in which Turkey fought on the German side against the British. The Muslim League, a pro-British out-fit, was in a dilemma whether to support or oppose the British against Turkey. They feared that in the event of Turkey's defeat, the Christian powers would destroy the sanctity of the holy places of Islam. There was thus all willingness on the part of the larger section of the Muslims to co-operate with Congress against the British. Still they insisted on separate electorate and reservation, which they already had from the British. They argued that these would improve Hindu-Muslim relation. Here was an opportunity for the Congess to secure from the Muslim League:

1. Abandonment of separate electorate.
2. Stoppage of cow-slaughter on religious grounds or other wise.
   (Cow-slaughter is not an essential feature of Islam).
3. Acceptance of Hindi as the lingua franca of India.

But, it could not be done, because most of the Hindu leaders of the time were themselves the descendants of those vested interests who had devoted their lives in the protection of the Mughal empire or were beneficiaries of the British Raj. Moreover, the Congress had "degenerated into mere platform for glib oratory and claptrap declaration by forging a compromise...Many Congressmen became Honourable members of the Council...Congress proceedings came to arouse little interest in the country and the number of delegates to the session dropped considerably".[12] Aurobindo Ghosh, the right hand man of Tilak in Bengal, summed up the situation in the words: "A hush had fallen over the country. No man seemed to know which way to move and from all sides came the question, what shall we do? What is there that we can do? What next?"

While the League Headquarters was at Aligarh, the party was dominated by the orthodox section, but at Lucknow the progressive group, consisting of men like Wazir Hasan, the Ali brothers, M.A.

Jinnah, the Raja of Mahmudabad, Mazhar-ul-Haque, Syed Raza Ali, Hakim Ajmal Khan, Dr. Ansari, became dominant. Of them, M.A. Jinnah, Mohammed Ali, Mazhar-ul-Haque, Dr. Ansari, Hakim Ajmal Khan, and many other Muslim Leaguers also held important positions in the Congress. And yet, the Congress was being dubbed as a Hindu organisation. All the time the refrain of the Congress, therefore, was to remove the Hindu stigma and prove itself a secular body. The Muslims, on the other hand, not satisfied with the League alone, formed in May 1913 another organisation "Society of the Servants of Ka'ba", after the defeat of Turkey in 1912 at the hands of the Balkan states. It was a Pan-Islamist organisation of those prepared to sacrifice their life and property for Ka'ba. Devoted to propagation of Islam in all parts of the world, this society established in different places Muslim primary schools and Muslim orphanages.

Lokmanya Tilak was released in June 1914 with a shattered health. His wife had died when he was still in prison in Burma. The World War I broke out in Agust 1914 when Gandhi was on way to India from South Africa. In 1915 some prominent leaders of the Congress—G.K. Gokhale, Sir Phroze Shah Mehta, Subramanyam Iyer, expired. Tilak was termed as an Extremist. The Moderates in the Congress were very much opposed to him. While he was trying to pick up the old threads of the Congress and working for unity in the two antagonistic Congress camps, he felt the need for a Home Rule League, towards the end of December 1915. The same was set up in Belgaun in April 1916 with the object of attaining self government within the British empire by constitutional means and to educate and organise public opinion in the country for the same.[14] Annie Besant, inspired by Tilak, founded an All India Home Rule League in Madras in Sept. 1916.

Efforts for a rapproachment between the Congress and the Muslim League had been going on since 1913. The initiative came from the Congress. Lokamanya Tilak had a year long discussion and consultation with the Muslim League president, M.A. Jinnah, who was also a Congress leader of repute.

In December 1916, the Congress held its annual session at Lucknow. The Muslim League also held its session there under the presidentship of M.A. Jinnah. The Lucknow Pact was made. It had two parts. It was agreed that there would be separate electorate for the Muslims and their representation in the Provincial Legislative Councils would be as follows:

Province	Percentage of Muslim Population	Percentage of Muslim seats in Legislative Council
Bengal	52.6	40
Bihar and Orissa	10.5	25
Bombay (including Sindh)	20.4	33.30
Central Provinces	4.3	15.00
Madras	6.5	15.00
Punjab	54.8	50.00
U.P.	14.00	30.00

It was provided that no Muslim shall participate in any of the other elections to the Imperial or Provincial Legislative Councils, save and except those by electorates representing special interests. It was further provided that no Bill nor any clause thereof nor a resolution introduced by non-official members affecting one or the other community, which question is to be determined by the members of the community in the Legislative Council concerned, shall be proceeded with, if two thirds (three fourths according to some) of the members of that community oppose the Bill or any clause thereof or the resolution.

The second part of the Pact demanded that in the reconstruction of the Empire, India should be raised from the status of a dependency to that of an equal partner in the Empire as a self-governing dominion. The Provincial Legislative Councils should consist of four-fifths of elected and one-fifth of nominated members.

It would be observed that the Lucknow Pact provided excessive communal representation to the Muslims in the Councils, except for Bengal, and it was all at the cost of Hindus. Hence, while the Muslims, all over the country, were jubilant generally, the Muslim leaders of Bengal showed all resentment alleging that their interests had been sacrificed to promote the interests of minorities in other provinces.

At the time of the Pact, it was believed, both by the Congress and the League leaders, that separate electorate would be a temporary phase and that within ten years joint electorate would be restored. In the League session at Lucknow, M.A. Jinnah said:

"It is a matter of infinite gratification to me as well as to all patriotic Muslims that the Muslim communal position in this matter has been recognised and met in an ungrudging spirit by the leaders of the great Hindu community."[15]

He further remarked,

"Be the time near or distant, the Indian people are bound to attain their full stature as a self-governing nation...If the Indians are not the Pariahs of nature... if their minds can grow in knowledge and power and can think and plan and organise together for the common needs of the present and for the common hopes of the future, the only future for them is self-government... The cant of unfitness must die, the laws of nature and the doctrines of common humanity are not different in the East.[16]

The Hindus of the United Provinces and the Punjab condemned the Lucknow Pact as it gave far greater representation to the Muslims than what they were entitled to. In his presidential address, Sir V.P. Madhav Rao, of the Hindu Maha Sabha, said at Lucknow that the object of Hindu Maha Sabha would be to educate the public mind on the evils likely to follow from a recognition of this principle and giving effect to it in the coming reforms. The local Hindu Sabhas in Allahabad, Benaras, and Kanpur also denounced excessive representation given to the Muslim minorities in U.P., Bombay, Bihar and Madras and the poor treatment of the Hindu minority in the Punjab.[17] Some Hindu leaders in the Congress, like Pt. Madan Mohan Malaviya and Dr. Munje had opposed the Lucknow Pact but, they were overruled.

The very next day, at the convention of the Home Rule League, Lokamanya Tilak said:

"Two most important events have taken place in Lucknow session of the Indian National Congress. We are determined to demand freedom is one and the other that both Hindus and Muslims have come together and jointly made such a demand. As a litigant in a complex property case, seeks help from a competent lawyer and offers substantial part of proceeds to him to win the case, so here concessions are given to Muslim brothers to win their support in fight against British Rule. When the fight is triangular, two sides have to join forces to overcome the third party."[18]

After the Lucknow session, Tilak went to Varanasi. The Hindu leaders there blamed him for agreeing to separate electorate for the Muslims and opening a floodgate of future disaster. Tilak said:

"Nothing more was possible under the present circumstances. This Pact is for a period of 10 year only. After the period, we shall get it changed. If we were to give up negotiations, nothing could have been gained. It would have provided good opportunity to the British to yield nothing."[19]

There was, however, a definite merit to the Lucknow Pact and that was that the two antagonistic factions of the Congress, "The Extremists" and "The Moderates" (Garam dal and Naram dal) got united.

Whatever may be said about the compulsion of Lokamanya Tilak and other Congress leaders in their defence, the fact remains that on the question of communal representation, the Congresss suffered from self-delusion. Nothing could be more foolish than to hope for the disappearance of separate electorate after ten years of its birth. The evil should have been nipped in the bud, but it was allowed to grow, till it served as an easy stepping stone for the demand of Pakistan two decades later. It showed tactical bankruptcy of the Congress leaders and their hopeless handling of the situation. They failed to understand that the undue favours given to the Muslims would tear the national fabrics apart for ever into sharply divided coommunities of Hindus and Muslims. The British Parliament was happy to recognise the Lucknow Pact as the only agreement between the Hindus and the Muslims and it made more elaborate provisions in the Government of India Acts 1919 and 1935. Once the basis of division of the electorate was accepted, there could be no logic in refusing the division of the country on the same basis. The Lucknow Pact took a very heavy toll when India was partitioned 30 years later. Credit goes to M.A. Jinnah and Syed Hasan Imam who had, as early as 1910, opposed the idea of separate communal electorates in the Indian Political system. The Pact itself, not the communal electorate, was bound to be a transitory provision for it was a child of circumstances for the Muslim community. The ideological differences between the Congress and the Muslim League were so wide that the two could not sit together for a long time; they had to part ways at the earliest opportunity. By the Lucknow Pact, Congress only put the fate of Hindus and the Indian sub-continent on ransom into the hands of the Muslim fundamentalists.

When 25 years later, M.A. Jinnah became a staunch communalist and a crusador for Pakistan, he said, "When Hindus have accepted separate identity for the Muslims through the Lucknow Pact in 1916, how can they now object to Pakistan?"[20]

REFERENCES

1. Durga Das, From Curzon to Nehru, p. 49.
2. Lal Bahadur, Muslim League, p. 79-80.
3. Lal Bahadur, Muslim Leauge, p. 79.
4. T.L. Sharma, Hindu-Muslim Relations, p. 35.
5. Ibid, p. 36.
6. Ibid.
7. Ibid pp. 36-37.
8. Ibid, p. 37.
9. Ibid, p. 37-38.
10. T.L. Sharma, Hindu-Muslim Relations, p. 40.
11. Ibid, p. 41.
12. Dr. Nihar Nandan Singh, Lokamanya Tilak, p. 68.
13. Ibid.
14. Ibid. P 71.
15. T.L. Sharma Hindu Muslim Relations, p. 51.
16. Ibid.
17. Ibid.
18. B.N. Jog, Threat of Islam, p. 131.
19. Ibid, p. 133-134.
20. B.N. Jog, Threat of Islam, p. 133.

Chapter V

EMERGENCE OF GANDHI

The hopes of Hindu-Muslim unity and of the Muslim co-operation in the national struggle, generated by the Lucknow Pact, were soon belied. The orthodox section of the Muslims started a campaign against the Pact. In September 1918, the Central Mohammedan Association, submitted a memorandum to the British government, stating:

"For England now to place the Indian Muslims, without proper, definite, and ample safeguards, under the heels of a hostile non-Muslim majority, would, your humble memorialists venture respectfully to submit, be a cruel act of breach of faith and violation of trust."[1]

A news paper from Calcutta, the Risalat, wrote:

"The success of the scheme (Morley-Minto reforms of 1909) will place the Muslims under the thumb of the Hindus, Muslim interests will not be safeguarded unless they get at least equal representation with Hindus in the Councils. This is our and Bengal Muslim League's opinion."[2]

An Alim (a learned man in Muslim theology) in Madras told the Secretary of State for India that there was no sanction in the Quran for an alliance with non-Muslims. Even much before the Lucknow Pact, the tirade of the conservative Muslims against the League had intensified. Syed Husain Bilgrami had said "The stereotyped Congress slogans are a threat to our very existence." Almizan (UP) denounced Wazir Hasan as an opportunist whose ambition was to achieve prominence through alliance with non-Muslims.[3] It needs to be remembered that in 1915 , the orthodox Muslims, opposed to the Congress-Muslim League rapproachment, had held a huge dharna and demonstration in Bombay to prevent the League session being held there simultaneously with the Congress session.

An interesting aspect of the whole matter is that the post independence Indian writers have generally brushed under the carpet all such provocative and divisive statements and seditious writings, but have given exaggerated account of the defensive and mild protestations of certain Hindu leaders against the Muslim outbursts. They hold only the protesting Hindus responsibe for creating the great communal divide. It is conveniently ignored that the Hindu objection to separate electorate was based on sound principle while the one by the Muslims was based solely on their false cry of 'Islām in danger' or illogical claim for a strict parity with the vast Hindu majority.

The intelligence reports of the time show that the British government was really alarmed at the prospect of the Muslim League and the Congress coming together in their demand for self government or Swaraj, putting the goverment in a perilous position in the midst of world war I. It must, however, go to the credit of the British diplomacy that even in such an alarming situation, it kept its cool and, while keeping both the League and the Congress guessing and in good humour, conducted the war effort successfully.

Pursuant to the Lucknow Pact, a large number of district Congress committees and the branches of the Home Rule League came to be headed by the Muslims.[4] At Peshawar, out of regard for Muslim sentiment, the date of Bharat Milap procession was shifted to avoid its clash with the tenth day of Muharram.[5] But the orthodoxy, opposed to the Pact, instigated the Muslims to take provocative actions which included more of cow-slaughter just to tease the Hindus. Maulana Syed Suleiman Ashraf, Prof. of Theology, Mohammedan Anglo-Oriental College, Aligarh, alleged that the Lucknow Pact was a Muslim surrender of their basic right of cow-sacrifice and the like only for the sake of maintaining friendship with the Hindus.[6] Consequently, there were Hindu-Muslim riots in many towns, especially in U.P. and Bihar. Only in Bihar riots, the Muslims suffered more. The whole Muslim press and many Muslim leaders started spewing venom in threatening tones. At the Muslim League session in Amritsar on Dec. 29-31, 1919, Hakim Ajmal Khan, in his presidential speech, exhorted the Muslims to refrain from injuring the religious feelings of the

Hindus and not indulge in cow-slaughter. He explained that the cow sacrifice was not religiously essential and could easily be avoided, that it was only a matter of choice, not compulsion, to sacrifice camel (as done by Hazrat Mohammed himself), sheep or goat, instead of cow.[7] He referred to Umni Salman (one of the Prophet's wives) as saying that the Prophet once observed, "if any of you sees the crescent heralding the month of Zil haj, and desires to sacrifice a goat..." and said that by tradition, Arabs were in the habit of sacrificing goats.[8]

On the part of Hindus, many of their organisations donated liberally towards helping the Muslim victims of the Bihar riots.

MUSLIM ATTITUDE TOWARDS WORLD WAR I

Seeing that the Muslims were drifting towards the Congress, the British government of India sent a circular letter to all provincial governments to elicit support from leading Muslim associations, Anjumans, and individuals.[9] Wazir Hasan, the League Secretary, sent the following telegram:

"Kindly place following resolutions before His Excellency Viceroy- (1) That Council of All India Muslim League gives expression once more to the deep-rooted loyalty and sincere devotion of Musalmans of India to British Crown, and assures His Excellency Viceroy that participation of Turkey in present war does not and cannot affect that loyalty in the least degree and council is confident that no Musalman in India will swerve even to a hair's breadth from his permanent duty to his sovereign; (2) that council of All India Muslim League expresses its deep gratitude to British Government for assurance given to its Muslim subjects as to immunity of holy places of Islam in Arabia and other places from attack and molestation and for obtaining similar assurances from its allies."[10]

Syed Ali Hairi, of the All India Shia Conference, sent the following telegram, on 18 Oct 1914, to the Viceroy:

"The All India Shia Conference, sitting at Lucknow, has requested me to wire your Excellency the following resolution,passed unanimously;

"That this conference assures His Majesty the King Emperor of the real unflinching loyalty and devotion of the entire Shia Community of India and prays for the success of British arms."[11]

There were many others who expressed similar sentiments in favour of the British government.

But, there were lots of other Muslim leaders, religious devouts, who started anti-British campaign. Prominent among them were Mohammed Ali, Shaukat Ali, Maulana Abul Kalam Azad, Hasrat Mohani and Zafar Ali. The Viceroy reported to the Secretary of State on March 3, 1915:

"The pan-Islamic party has naturally been upset by the war with Turkey, and it has been reported that they are working with the Sikh agitators in the Punjab. It is known that the President of the Khuddam-i-Kaba Society (founded by MaulanaShaukat Ali) opposed a movement to issue a fatwa favourable to the British Government on the subject of the war, the Punjab government has had to restrict to his native village, Zafar Ali, editor of the Zamindar; a section of the Mohammedan press noticeably Mohammed Ali of the Comrade and Hamdard, has been conspicuous for pro-German and pro-Turkish writing. Deliberate attempts have been made to preach Jehad, and a curious incident was the disappearance recently of 15 Mohammedan students from various Lahore colleges, of whom 13 have been traced to Wahabi colony across the frontier."[12]

In August 1916, the Government of India unearthed a plot, hatched by the Indian Muslims, notably Obeidullah Sindhi, a converted Sikh, Maulana Mahmud Husain, and others, to overthrow the British government, and establish ostensibly an Islamic rule with the active participation of Turkey and Afghanistan. The first assault was to be launched in the North West Frontier, synchronizing with a rebellion within the country. A declaration of Jehad from Ghalib Pasha, the then Turkish Military Governor of the Hedijaz had been obtained and its copies, known as the 'Ghalib-nama', were distributed both in India and among the frontier tribes.[13]

A provisional government, in exile, was formed at Kabul, with Raja Mahendra Pratap, as its President. One would wonder how a Hindu could become the president of a Pan-Islamic government. The riddle would be solved if one looks at the fact that the Indian revolutionaries, predominantly Hindus, had already formed a party in USA, known as the 'Ghadar Party', for overthrowing the British rule in India. They conspired with Germany the stark enemy of England, to achieve their objective. One of the eminent leaders of the Ghadar Party, Lala Hardayal, a Hindu revivalist, had been to Germany and Turkey for help. The proposed revolution was in fact a reconstruction of 1857 rebellion, this time having international ramification with involvement of Germany, Turkey, and Afghanistan. If in 1857, the Hindu resurgents could make Bahadur Shah Zafar, a Muslim, as their emperor, there ought to be no surprise in the Ghadar Party making Raja Mahendra Pratap president of its government in exile. Just as Azimullah Khan was the Prime Minister of Nana Saheb Peshwa in 1857, Barkatullah, another member of the party, and a friend of the great revolutionary Krishnavarma, was made the Prime Minister. The secret letters written to Turkey, on silk, for Turkish help, were intercepted by the Government, and this revealed the plot. Hence, it got the name 'Silk Letters Conspiracy.'[14]

In all probability, Lokamanya Tilak was aware of the plot before he went in for the Hindu-Muslim co-operation and unity through the Lucknow Pact, at such a heavy cost. At the Lucknow session of the Congress, at the time of the Pact, Tilak had said:

"It has been said that we, Hindus, have yielded too much to our Muslim brethren. I am sure, I represent the sense of the Hindu community all over India when I say that we could not have yielded too much. I would not care if the rights to self government are granted to the Muslim community only... Then the fight will not be triangular, as at present it is".[15]

MAHATMA GANDHI

Mohandas Karamchand Gandhi, popularly known as "Mahatma" Gandhi, Bar-at-law, came back to India from South Africa on 9 January, 1915. He landed in Bombay as a great political celebrity. Gandhiji's great biographer, DG Tendulkar, states:

"The Indian leaders did not wait for him to land but met him on the steamer upon its arrival, and his landing took place, by permission of the authorities, at the Apollo Bunder—an honour shared with Royalty, by Viceroys and India's most distinguished sons."[16]

On way to India, Gandhi had stayed at London for quite some time. World War I had recently broken out. On August 8,1914, a reception had been given to Gandhi at Cecil Hotel by his British and Indian admirers, including Jinnah, Mrs. Sarojini Naidu, and Dr. Ananda K. Coomaraswamy. The Minister, Secretary of State for India, Earl Roberts, Lords Gladstone, Curzon, Lamington, Ampthill, Harris, M/S Gokhale, Keir Hardie and Ramsay Macdonald sent letters of regret for not being able to attend. Soon Gandhi held a conference with some of the Indian students and then a meeting of Indian residents in Great Britain and Ireland was called. Gandhi expressed his political views which were opposed by many others who felt that it was an hour for making a bold declaration of the Indian demands for Swaraj. Gandhi pleaded that England's hour of need should not be turned into India's opportunity.[17]

The circumstances in which Gandhi packed up and left South Africa for India bag and baggage, leaving behind his anti-aparthied struggle half-way, leads this author to believe that the British government itself wanted him badly in India. It contrived to get him here only to put the Congress on the original path of loyalty to the British Crown from which it had been drifting away for quite sometime under the leadership of Lokamanya Tilak, Aurobindo Ghose and B.C. Pal. On coming to India, as stated above, Gandhi neither joined the Congress nor took part in any other political activity. What he did was to throw off his European dress on board the steamer itself and put on the pure Indian Kathiawari dress and head-gear. His first and the foremost task was to take stock of the political situation. He extensively toured India to have the first hand knowledge of the true Indian climate and conditions prevailing in the country of his future political activity. He was cheered by huge crowds wherever he went. Instructions had been issued to Government officials to provide him all facilities and honour. The English news papers gave him full coverage and showered all praises on him. Thus, the British government and the British press played a major role in putting the halo of greatness on Gandhi. Notabely, though Gandhiji was in the country, the Lucknow Pact got through without his participation.

In 1917 and 1918, Gandhi took up the causes of the oppressed indentured labour of India working in British colonies of Africa and the tormented Indigo cultivators of Bihar (Champaran). Under the indenture system, the poor, ignorant labourers of India were enticed away on a five year contract basis, bound to work for their foreign employers. They could not leave the job halfway, however hard and harsh were the conditions of work or living. The indian leaders had been agitating against this system for a number of years, but, thanks to the British government, it went to the credit of Gandhi that the indenture system was abolished from January 1, 1920. Similar were the woes of the labourers in indigo plantations which were all in the hands of Europeans. Gandhi went to Champaran, heard the woes of the cultivators and cruelties of the European masters. He solved the problems to the satisfaction of the indigo labourers. The success of Gandhi in the two complicated cases concerning the poverty stricken Indian masses raised his level to an Avatar, a Messiah, a Prophet. Gandhi's main thrust was on building the Indian nation with emphasis on Swadeshi and propagation of Hindi as a national language. He said that when the Hindus and the Muslims would regard one another without suspicion, the script which had greater vitality would be more universally used and, therefore, become the national script. To him, it was the Devanagari script.

World war I was on. Gandhi, and Tilak too, worked for finding Indian recruits for the British army. But, Tilak was a suspect. He undertook to recruit 5,000 persons from Maharashtra if Gandhi could secure a promise from the government before hand that the Indians would get Commissioned ranks in the army. Gandhi took the position that the help should not be in the nature of a bargain. It would be interesting to note the following appeal of Gandhi an abhorrent of violence, on June 13,1917 from Nadiad in support of Indian recruits to the British army:

"If you want to learn the use of arms with the greatest possible despatch, it is our duty to enlist ourselves in the army. There can no friendship between the brave and the effeminate. We are regarded as a cowardly people. If we want to become free from the reproach, we should learn the use of arms."[18]

Scholars are still groping in the dark to explain as to why Gandhi did not keep the same truth in mind in solving the Hindu-Muslim conflict. Even after a spate of communal riots from 1921 to 1925 in which Hindus were butchered like sheep and goats, he commented that Hindus as a rule were coward, Muslims as a rule were bullies, but advised Hindus to maintain their non-violence as, according to him, non-violence was the essence of the Hindu religion. It is not clear what prevented the Mahatma from telling the Hindus to defend themselves with all their might so that the stigma of cowardice is removed from their heads.

Gandhi started a satyagraha on 6 April 1919 against the notorious Rowlett Act under which the possession of a document, allegedly seditious, was made a punishable offence. It had created a country wide stir. In addition, there was the infamous massacre of Jallianwala Bagh in Amritsar on April 13, 1919 which sent a shock wave throughout the country.

MONTAGUE-CHEMSFORD REPORT—REFORMS ACT OF 1919

In the meantime, following the announcement in the British Parliament on 20 August 1917 about the steps to grant self rule to India, the Secretary of State for India, Edwin Samuel Montague, came to India. Alongwith the Viceroy, Lord Chemsford, he visited several cities and met leaders of various political groups. Their report was published in April 1918. With regard to communal electorate, it stated:

"A minority which is given special representation owing to its weak and backward state is positively encouraged to settle down into a feeling of satisfied security; it is under no inducement to educate and qualify itself to make good the ground which it has lost compared with the stronger majority. On the other hand, the latter will be tempted to feel that they have done all they need to do for their weaker fellow countrymen and that they are free to use their power for their own purposes...

"The give-and-take which is the essence of political life is lacking. There is no inducement to the one side to forbear or to the other to exert itself. The communal system stereotypes existing relations."[19]

But the Muslims had been promised communal electorate/representation by the British in 1909 itself. The Congress had not only endorsed it in 1916 but earmarked exact number of seats in the provincial Assemblies for the Muslims. Hence, the report stated:

"The Hindu acquiescence is embodied in the present agreement (Lucknow Pact) between the political leaders of the two communities. The Muhammadans regard these as settled facts, and any attempt to go back on them would rouse a storm of bitter protest and put a severe strain on the loyalty during a period of very great difficulty and which we know to be feeling no small anxiety for its own welfare under a system of popular Government."[20]

Thus, the Montague-Chemsford Report, called the Montford Report, reluctantly recommended the continuance of the system of separate electorate, sacrificing the sound principle of democracy to expediency. The major compelling factor behind it was that the Congress, claiming to represent the Indian nation, had given 'national' seal to the derogatory system of separate electorate for the Muslims only about a couple of years back.

Yet another dimension was given to "divide and rule" policy. The Viceroy, Lord Chemsford, started mobilising the rulers of the princely States as a counterpose to the nationalist movement. At a conference of these rulers on Nov 5, 1917, Chemsford announced that, instead of "every succession to the throne" earlier being subjected to the approval and sanction of the Government, would now have the recognition and confirmation of Government. It was a great relief to the native rulers.[21]

The British bureaucracy felt that while Muslim separatism could adequately safeguard British interests in the Northern India, the regions beyond the Vindhyas needed much more to divide the people. Hence, an anti-Brahmin movement was sponsored in the South to create caste conflict among Hindus. Moreover, a new thesis, based on the research of a Christian missionary, that the Hindus of the South belong to the Dravid race and those of the North India belong to the Aryan stock, and that the two classes of Hindus were quite distinct and even antagonistic, was vigorously propagated to create a wedge between the Hindus of the South and the Hindus of North India. It was claimed that Tamil was an older and richer language than Sanskrit.[22]

In the Muslim League session of Dec. 30, 1918, Dr. Ansari, the well known 'nationalist' leader of the Congress and president of the then League's Reception Committee, and some other Muslim leaders, though welcoming the recommendations in the Montford Report, castigated the British for passing aspersions on the principle of communal electorate. It was a tactical move, so that in times to come, the British government may not go back or rescind it.[23] Dr. Ansari also expressed his firm conviction that a non-Musalman, however great a well-wisher and friend to them, would never be so able to plead their cause on Islamic problems as a Muslim representative was expected to do.[24]

The Congress was divided in its opinion on the Report. On the whole, it said that the report did not satisfy the expectations of the Indian people and deserved rejection. The report was implemented through the Reforms Act of 1919.

REFERENCES

1. T.L. Sharma, Hindu-Muslim Relations, p. 52.
2. Ibid.
3. Ibid.
4. T.L. Sharma, Hindu-Muslim Relations, p. 63.
5. Ibid, 64.
6. Lal Bahadur, Muslim League, p. 116.
7. T.L. Sharma, Hindu-Muslim Relations, p. 67-68.
8. Ibid, p. 68.
9. Ibid, p. 69.
10. Ibid, p. 69.
11. Ibid, p. 69.
12. Ibid, p. 71-72.
13. Ibid, p. 72.
14. T.L. Sharma, Hindu-Muslim Relations, pps. 72-73.
15. D.G. Tendulkar, Mahatma, vol. I, p. 234.
16. Ibid, p. 193.
17. D.G. Tendulkar, Mahatma, vol, I, p. 187.
18. D.G. Tendulkar, Mahatma, vol, I, p. 280.
19. BN Jog, Threat of Islam, p. 135: Lal Bahadur, Muslim League, p. 127.
20. Lal Bahadur, Muslim League, p. 127.
21. Durga Das, From Curzon to Nehru, p. 59.
22. Ibid.
23. Lal Bahadur, Muslim League, p. 129.
24. Ibid, p. 131.

Chapter VI

KHILAFAT MOVEMENT—A FATAL PLUNGE

The year 1919 was perhaps the most fateful for India in the twentieth century. It was an year of acute suffering from the price rise. Industrial workers were resentful at the appalling working conditions. There was unprecedented outbreak of strikes.[1] Hundreds of thousands of demobilised soldiers and war supply agencies were disgruntled.[2] Unemployment was rampant. A university graduate was unable to find a job of Rs. 20 a month. Over and above, the notorious Rowlette Bills were introduced in the Central Legislative Assembly in February, 1919. The evil effect of the proposed laws were aptly summed up in the slogan "Na vakil, na daleel, na appeal"—meaning, there is to be no pleader, no pleadings, and no appeal—against any atrocity of the government and its agencies.[3] Gandhi had acquired a prominent place in the Indian political horizon. The orthodox Muslims were sore about the treatment meted out to the Sultan of Turkey after conclusion of the first World War. He was divested of his Khalifahood and his empire was dismembered. On April 13, 1919, there was the brutal massacre of nearly a thousand peaceful and unarmed men, women and children by the British army in the Jallianwala Bagh, at Amritsar (Punjab).

The central theme of the Khilafat is that the Muslims of the world, irrespective of their different nationalities and culture, form one single entity under the suzerainty of a religious ruler who, besides being a political head, is the supreme religious authority and protector of Islam. As a result of the Pan-Islamic movement of the nineteenth century, the Sultan of Turkey was conferred the Khilafat (Khalifahood). But not all the Muslim countries recognised his authority, namely, the final authority to interpret the Shariat (Islamic law). Saudi Arabia in particular did not like Turkish authority and wanted restoration to it of the custody of the main Muslim Shrines of Mecca and Medina, from the Sultan of Turkey.

According to Shariat, Khalifa is the successor of prophet Mohammed who maintains the authority of Islam and it is his duty to protect the Muslim community, anywhere in the world and their holy shrines. After the fourth Khalifa, Ali, the Khilafat passed to Muawiyah, the Governor of Syria, from whom this office became hereditary and passed from one family to another with the passage of time.

The Muslim ire against the British arose out of the ill treatment meted out to the Sultan of Turkey, the symbol of Islamic power. After the conclusion of World War I (1914-1919), in which Turkey was defeated alongwith Germany, the British dismembered the Turkish empire and dethroned the Sultan from the pedestal of the Khalifa (head) of the Muslim world. Muslim orthodoxy the world over, especially the Indians, took it as a grave and unpardonable insult to Islam.

It is necessary to know something about the Rowlett Bills which, alongwith the Khilafat question, made such a great impact on the Indian mind and were used as the most powerful and effective weapon in the hands of Gandhi. Why and how did the British government announce constitutional reforms on the one hand to pave the way to self government and, on the other, came out with draconian laws in the shape of Rowlett Bills? The fact is that when World War I was at its final phase, the Government of India started thinking as to how it would, after the lapse of the Defence of India Act and Rules, deal with hundreds of detained men, Hindu revolutionaries and fanatic Muslims fighting for Turkey in the name of Khilafat. It, therefore, appointed a committee, named as the Rowlett Committee, after its Chairman, a British Judge, to study the situation and make appropriate recommendations. The recommendations of this Committee were effected through the Rowlett Bills.

The Muslim ire on the Khilafat was wholly misplaced because the office of a foreign Khalifa had become irrelevant for the Indian Muslims since the Mughal period. Earlier, the Delhi Sultans considered themselves as Viceroys of the Khalifa and used to pay him tributes from time to time. Akbar the Great, stopped this practice. He himself took over the power to finally interpret the Shariat (the Islamic law) through a decree of infallibility prepared by the Ulemas,

In the last quarter of the nineteenth century only, the new pan-Islamic theme influenced Indian Ulemas in a big way. Men like Sir Muhammed Iqbal and Maulana Azad visited Turkey, Egypt and other important Muslim centres and joined the pan-Islamic movement. As a result, at the beginning of the twentieth century, Iqbal changed the famous line of his national song, "Hindi hain ham vatan hai, Hindostan hamaara" (we are Indians and India is our motherland) to "Muslim hain ham vatan hai, sara jahan hamara" (we are Muslims and the whole world is ours) to give the song a pan-Islamic fervour. All Muslim news papers/journals in India, like Al-Hilal (of Maulana Abul Kalam Azad), Comrade (of Mohammed Ali), Hamdard, Zamindar, etc. carried this pan-Islamic message.

Now, Gandhi set out to moblize all this boiling unrest and utilize it against the British government. Preparations were made for a country wide strike (hartal) and satyagraha from the sixth April (initially the date was March 30). In fact, the idea of launching a satyagraha, a non-cooperation movement, had been lurking in Gandhi's mind since July 1917, even before Montford Report came.[4] But, Gandhi waited for an opportunity. A pledge was drafted in Ahmedabad and signed by a small group, which included Patel, Sarojini Naidu and Umar Sobhani, a well known Muslim leader of Bombay; it was later signed by more than a thousand people in Bombay.[5] Durga Das states:

> "To show that they meant business, the Satyagrahis decided to begin by breaking the laws regarding proscribed literature and the publication of newspapers. They publicly sold Hind Swaraj by Gandhi and the biography and addresses of Mustafa Kemal Pasha. They also started a hand-written paper called Satyagraha."[6]

The pledge of satyagraha read:

> "Being conscientiously of opinion that the Bills known as the Indian Criminal Law (Amendment) Bill no. No. 1 of 1919 and the Criminal Law (Emergency powers) Bill No. 11 of 1919 are unjust, subversive of the principles of liberty and justice, and destructive of the elementary rights of individuals on which the safety of the community as a whole, and the state itself is based, we solemnly affirm, that in the

event of these Bills becoming law and until they are withdrawn, we shall refuse civily to obey these laws and such other laws as a committee to be hereafter appointed may think fit, and we further affirm that in this struggle we will faithfully follow truth and refrain from violence to life, person or property."[7]

In Delhi (and also in Amritsar and some other towns), the strike was held on March 30, 1919. Swami Shraddhanand, a renowned leader of the Arya Samaj and of the Congress, addressed a huge audience in the famous Jama Masjid of Delhi. The Police and the military fired at the processionists. "Swami Shraddhanand, tall and stately in his sanyasin's garb, faced with bare chest the bayonets of the Gurkhas in the Chandni Chowk. India was thrilled by this incident."[8] As a result of the firing, five Hindus and four Muslims were killed, about twenty were missing and 13 persons badly wounded were taken to hospital.[9]

At other places, like Bombay, Ahmedabad and others, the hartal and satyagraha started on April 6. For a week, there was unprecedented enthusiasm everywhere. Here and there, acts of violence also took place and the government took all repressive measures to control the tide. The tragedy of the Jallianwala Bagh (Amritsar, Punjab) took place on April 13, 1919. Mass agitation spread like wild fire.

From October 1918 to November (last week), 1919, Lokamanya Tilak had been in England in connection with a legal case in the Privy Council. The leadership of the country fell on to Gandhi. On 20th April 1919, the All India Congress Committee met to demand an inquiry into the Punjab wrongs. Gandhi was pressed to go to the Punjab immediately. He wrote to the Viceroy for permission to visit Punjab on the excuse that if he went without permission, he would be arrested. The permission was not to come and Gandhi did not go; he dropped the idea of going.

On Oct. 7, Gandhi set up his own press in Ahmedabad and brought out 'Navjivan' in Gujarati. The next day he started 'Young India' in English. "These two organs, so quietly and unceremoniously born, became the greatest instruments of the Gandhian revolution and may be said to have a unique place along with their successor, Harijan, in modern journalistic history."[10] At one time, the circulation of each of these journals reached 40,000: Gandhi's articles were reproduced in almost all the papers in India.[11]

In the meanwhile, an all India Khilafat Conference was formed. Its first, a joint Hindu-Muslim conference, was held at Delhi on November 23, 1919, under the chairmanship of Fazlul Haq. Next day, Gandhi was voted to the chair of the Khilafat Conference. He set out the scheme of non-cooperation. Noted journalist, political analyist and author, Durga Das, who attended it, writes:

> "My first direct contact with Gandhi occurred when he attended a meeting of the Khilafat Conference in Delhi on 24th November, 1919. At it, he made an initial attempt to speak in Hindustani and apologized for his *tooti phooti* (broken Urdu). His words touched the hearts of his audience but I could sense that he was struggling hard to be precise and intelligible. He urged the people to withhold co-operation from the Government until Khilafat wrong was righted, and as he faltered for the appropriate word to express his thoughts in Hindustani he coined the expression "non-cooperation" and said it in Engligh. I came away impressed with his zeal and sincerity, but little did I then visualise him emerging as India's man of destiny."[12]

Notably, the Khilafat question had been discussed in the Muslim League session in 1918 at Delhi, under the presidentship of Fazlul Haq, who had said:

> "To me the future of Islam in India seems to be wrapped in gloom and anxiety. Every instance of a collapse of the Muslim powers of the world is bound to have an adverse influence on the political importance of our community in India."[13]

In the Khilafat Conference, Gandhi said:

> "...It has been contended that the Punjab grievance is a good reason too for refraining from the peace celebration.* I differ from that view. However grievous the wrong done in the Punjab, it is after all a domestic affair and it would show on our part a want of sense of proportion to bring in the

---

* After World War I, the British government held peace celebrations for their victory to which prominent Congress leaders were also invited.

> Punjab grievance to justify our non-cooperation in the Imperial celebration. The Punjab grievance does not arise out of the peace terms as does the Khilafat question. We must isolate the Khilafat question if we wish to give it its proper place and value. In my opinion it is not open to us to refuse to share the peace celebrations on grounds other than those which arise directly out of the peace and that touch the vital parts of our national existence. The Khilafat question alone satisfies these two tests."[14]

Touching the Go-raksha (cow protection) issue, Gandhi said:

> "Asaf Ali, the secretary of the Conference, has intimated in the papers circulated by him that the Go-raksha- cow protection-problem and the Punjab matter will also be considered. I submit that the Hindus may not open the Goraksha question here. The test of friendship is assistance in adversity, and that too unconditional assistance. It is the duty of Hindus, if they see the justice of the Muslim cause, to render co-operation. If Muslims feel themselves bound to spare the Hindus'feelings and stop cow-killing they may do so, no matter whether Hindus co-operate with them or not. Though, therefore, I yield to no Hindu in my worship of the cow, I do not want to make the stopping of cow-killing a condition precedent to co-operation. Unconditional cooperation means the protection of the cow. As regards the Punjab matter too, I venture to differ from many of you. They may have deeply distressed others. I will, however, say that they can distress no one more deeply than they do me, and yet I think that we cannot bring in here the Punjab grievance. We cannot say that the Punjab wrong is unredressed. The Hunter Committee is still at work. Our own committee is equally busy. The Khilafat question is serious one, and needs immediate remedies. We must isolate it, if we wish to give it its proper place and value."

These outpourings would show that Gandhi, called Mahatma, bore a greater "Mullah mind set" than the Mullahs themselves. For him the Khilafat was the first and the foremost issue and the matters of cow-protection, the massacre of Jallianwala Bagh and the Council reforms were mere trifles.

Despite Gandhi's advice from the chair not to bring in the cow-protection issue, Maulana Abdul Bari said:

> "Mahatma Gandhi may say anything as regards the bringing in of the Goraksha question. That does credit to him and to our Hindu brethren. But the Muslims' honour would be at stake if they forget the cooperation of the Hindus. I for my part will say that we should stop cow-killing irrespective of their cooperation because we are children of the same soil. As a *maulvi* I say that in voluntarily stopping cow killing we shall not offend against the canons of our relilgion"[15]

In this context, let one recall the assurances which the Muslims secured just three years ago in 1916 in the Lucknow Pact for cooperating with the Hindus in the struggle for self-government that was to be for the benefit of all Indians. And, now Gandhi submitted the most important question for Hindus, namely, the protection of cow at the sweet will of the Muslims and extended unconditional support to a cause which had very little to do with the Indian Muslims, Khilafat, as explained earlier. The natural result was that as soon as the Khilafat movement failed, the Muslims indulged in cow-killing more and more and claimed it as their birth right. The same is continuing in India till today, even after the Muslims have had their Pakistan. Wonder of wonders is that such a foolish course was taken by a 'Mahatma' who claimed to be a worshipper of cow.

The most important point to note is that the Khilafat movement (civil disobedience to right the wrongs done to the Turkish Khalifa) was carried by the Khilafat Conference headed by Gandhi, not by the Muslim League, the party representing the Indian Muslims and recognised as such both by the Congress and the British government. Being the uncrowned king of the Congress, Gandhi made Congress adopt "Khilafat" as the most important issue on its agenda. Thus, not only had Gandhi got converted as the most fundamentalist Mullah of the time, but converted Congress itself into a larger Muslim body than the Muslim League. It can be said that while the Congress surrendered to Muslim politics in 1916, it itself became Muslim three years later. Only it did not change its name.

CONGRESS SESSION, 1919

Congress held its annual session in Amritsar in the last week of December 1919 under the presidentship of Motilal Nehru. It had become a place of pilgrimage for many. The proceedings were conducted mainly in Hindustani.[16] The Moderates or the Liberals as they now called themselves refused to join the Amritsar Congress; they held their meeting in Calcutta. Lokamanya Tilak, who had recently come from England, attended the Amritsar Congress. There were 8,000 delegates including 1500 peasants. Besides, there were over 30,000 visitors. The first resolution thanked the king-Emperor (about the new reforms) and welcomed the announcement of Prince of Wales proposed visit to India.[17]

Gandhi moved a resolution blaming also people of the Punjab and Gujarat for violence committed against certain British and other government officials. He said:

> "Real manliness consists in not retaliating even when under a shower of bullets, to suffer evil patiently. That is the spirit of real heroes. That is why I want you to condemn the excess of mobs. I am glad that I have been the instrument in exhorting you to do this deed of penance. I warn you to appreciate the solemnity of the proposition. The whole key to future work lies in your recognizing the eternal truth underlying the resolution. Do not return madness with madness; return madness with sanity."[18]

Contrary to expectation, Tilak did not interfere with the passage of Gandhi's resolution, but there were many others to oppose Gandhi.

Durga Das who had specially gone to cover the Congress proceedings, states in his memoirs:

"Released from internment under the general amnesty granted by the King's Proclamation heralding the new Reforms Act, the Ali brothers made a dramatic entry into the way in which they cheered when they stole the show, judging by the way in which they cheered when they appeared on the dais with fez-shaped caps bearing a crescent and in dark suits which gave them the look of militant young Turks. Since Khilafat's future was one of the twin battle cries raised by Gandhi, these two symbolised its meaning."

"There were no microphones and loudspeakers. In oratory the Bengalis stole the thunder, especially Bipin Chandra Pal. ...The orations of Gandhi and Tilak were mild. Gandhi, the new star on the horizon, won hearty applause; the delegates were content with his *darshan* (sight of a venerated person)even if they could not hear him."[19]

Tilak believed that through the policy of responsive co-operation Indians could hasten the achievement of Home Rule. He said:

"I may not live to see it, but the next generation will if we work hard and apply our mind to the new task. I recognise, however, that the Punjab disturbances, the martial law regime and the Jallianwala massacre, which have made men like Sir Sankaran Nair and poet Tagore throw up their jobs and honours, have charged the political atmosphere with spirit of revolt, of which Gandhi is the new symbol. I will not stand in his way, even though I feel that responsive co-operation will yield the maximum benefit."[20]

Durga Das adds, "Tilak did not disguise his fear that the British bureaucracy, which had already undone the good achieved by the Lucknow Pact, might intensify its efforts to separate the Muslims and the backward classes from the main current of the national movement. Anyway, he added, he would do nothing to create a division in the ranks of the Congress Party. He did not think that Motilal Nehru or C.R. Das or any other leader had Gandhi's mass appeal. 'These brilliant lawyers,' he added, ' will rue the day they took up an extreme position to defeat my resolution. They will retract their steps one day, but by then Gandhi would have grown too powerful for them. I have done my duty. My faith in responsive co-operation is based on my belief that Montagu means well by India. We can strengthen his hands to get a time-limit fixed for self government, say fifteen years. It is because of this feeling that on my way to Amritsar I sent a cable to the King promising responsive co-operation as a reply to his appeal for co-operation in working the Act which became law on 24th December. I have faith in the Labour Party helping us achieve our goal."[21]

In the off-the-record talk in which the great Tilak was in an introspective mood, he left with Durga Das the impression that his head was not with Gandhi but that his heart was affected by the scenes he had witnessed of the new leader being lionised. He made one more effort to turn the tide. In April 1920, he organised the Congress Democratic Party to fight the coming elections. It envisaged a federation of India fashioned by Indians themselves. It stood for religious tolerance, minimum wage, promotion of national unity by such means as a link language for all India, betterment of inter-communal relations and readjustment of the provinces on a linguistic basis.[22] Durga Das writes:

"But time was not on his side. Gandhi had enunciated his programme of non-violent non-cooperation to right the wrongs of the Khilafat and the Punjab. He had indeed promised Swaraj within a year if the country carried out his programme and raised a Tilak Swaraj Fund of Rs.10 million, enrolled 10 million members for the Congress and introduced 2.5 million spinning wheels in villages to make the boycott of foreign cloth effective."[22]

"Gandhi knew it would not be easy to capture the Congress and bend it to his will. This became apparent to him when the meeting of the All-India Congress Committee (AICC) at Banaras in May did not entertain a proposal for adopting a policy of non-cooperation and decided to call a special session of the Congress to consider Gandhi's programme."[23]

The resolution finally adopted by the Congress included: (1) Reiteration of its earlier declaration of the previous year for full responsible government; (2) adherence to the resolutions passed at Delhi Congress session on constitutional reforms, the Reforms Act being inadequate, unsatisfactory and disappointing; (3) urging the Parliament to take early steps to establish full responsible government ; (4) trust that the people will so work the reforms as to secure an early establishment of fully responsible government.[24]

The Muslim League, the Khilafat Conference, and the Jamiat-ul-Ulema, had also held their sessions simultaneously at Amritsar. Hakim Ajmal Khan was the President of the Muslim League. In addition to adopting a resolution on the constitutional reforms on the Congress lines, Muslim League also passed resolution protesting against the Amritsar massacre and the proposed dismemberment of Turkey.[25] The Hindu Mahasabha, though formed in 1915, had not yet grown into a political outfit.

ULEMAS AROUND GANDHI

The famous biographer of Gandhiji, D.G. Tendulkar, states:

> "Around Gandhi new forces were gathering. The Ulema felt that the Muslim divines of India whose collective power and influence had been shattered after the Revolt of 1857 should again come together. Maulana Abul Kalam Azad entered the field, with his profound learning, his matchless powers of eloquence and persuasion and his modern outlook. He had been released from internment about that time. More than any other Muslim leader, though he was the youngest of them all, he was a tower of strength to Gandhi".[26]

On March 17, 1920, a Khilafat deputation, led by Mohammed Ali, met Lloyd George who said that while Turkey was to be allowed to exercise temporal sway over Turkish lands, she was not to be permitted to retain those lands which were not Turkish. This struck at the root of the Khilafat agitation in India, although logically the Indian leaders themselves struggling for Indian independence should have supported the freedom of non-Turkish territories from the colonial rule of Turkey. March 19 was observed as a day of national mourning of fasting, prayer and general strike. It was a great success. In the Khilafat meeting held that day in Bombay, Gandhi said:

"And it commits the joint movement to a policy of non-violence in the course of the struggle. But Muslims have a special Koranic obligation in which Hindus may or may not join. They, therefore, reserve to themselves the right, in the event of the failure of non-cooperation cum non-violence, in order to enforce justice, to resort to all such methods as may be enjoined by the Islamic scriptures...

"...Some of them (Muslim leaders) have, therefore, insisted upon the insertion of a proviso to the resolution, meaning that if non-violence fails, they are at liberty to resort to other methods enjoined upon them by the Koran.... And so the resolution undoubtedly foreshadows, in the most honourable and unmistakable manner, the stages through which this great movement will pass, the last stage being a bloody revolution. God forbid that this country should have to pass through such a revolution and all its horrors but the feeling of this Khilafat question runs so high and goes so deep that an unjust solution may, if peaceful means fails, land this country in a revolutionary movement, the like of which we have not seen before, and if it comes responsibility will rest with Englishmen, the Hindus and the timid Muslims...."[27]

The same year, Gandhi accepted the presidentship of the All-India Home Rule League, Mr. Annie Besant having ceded it. Tilak did not share Gandhi's views entirely. He tried to hold the country from going on the Gandhian path on the question of Khilafat. He formed the Congress Democratic Party to work for the removal of all civic, secular, or social disabilities based on caste or religion to oneself and the right and duty of the state to protect it against aggression; to lend out side support to the Muslims for the solution of the Khilafat question according to their dogma and beliefs; to help in the integration or federation of India in the British Commonwealth for the advancement of the cause of humanity and brotherhood of mankind; to secure autonomy for India and equal status as a sister state; with equality of citizenship for the Indians throughout the commonwealth; and retaliation whenever it is denied. While he was not oblivious of the inequitous terms sought to be imposed on Turkey and the inhuman atrocities perpetrated in the Punjab, he wanted to absorb all the energy roused over these episodes and direct it into the path opened out by the Reforms Act. Gandhi, on the other hand, did not want to touch the reforms aspect unless the Khilafat wrongs were first righted by the British.[28]

On June 1, 1920, at Allahabad, there was a Hindu-Muslim Conference of three hundred influential representatives. Ms. Annie Besant, Pandit Malaviya, Sir Tej Bahadur Sapru. Motilal Nehru, and others were present. Since the peace offers to Turkey were announced on May 14 last, the Khilafatists were very much agitated and some approaches were being made to the Amir of Afghanistan to attack India. In this background, the Hindu leaders at the Allahabad meeting wanted to know from the Muslims as to what would be their attitude if the Amir of Afghanistan invaded India. The Muslim leaders said that if the Amir invaded India to conquer it, they would stand in defence of the country but if the invasion was with a view to upholding the prestige of Islam it would have their full sympathy. The reply did not pacify the Hindu fear. After all, every Muslim invader in the past came with the declaration to uphold, protect and propagate Islam and occupation of the territory was claimed to be an ancillary requirement or a by-product. No decision could, therefore, be arrived at. The joint conference dispersed without any definite conclusion. "It, however, helped Gandhi to estimate the forces arrayed for or against his own programme. He could no longer wait till the Congress pronounced its decision."[29]

On 22nd June, 1920 Gandhi wrote to the Viceroy a threatening letter conveying that if the peace offers to Turkey were not revised in accordance with the Muslim sentiment "Three courses were open to Musalmans in order to mark their emphatic disapproval of the injustice done, namely, (1) to resort to violence; (2) to wholesale emigration (3) non-cooperation with the government.[30]

As the leader of the Khilafat Conference, Gandhi fixed August 1 to launch his much trumpeted non-cooperation movement in a big way. He, and his Muslim associates, still hoped of getting the peace terms for Turkey revised. Already thousands of Muslims, especially from Sindh, had started on hijrat (migration) to Afghanistan, Soviet Union, and other countries. People wanted to know Tilak's attitude. He said, "My idea is that the Muslims themselves should take the initiative in the matter. After full discussion, they must come to a definite decision and it is for the Hindus to support them in whatever decision they would arrive at."[31]

PASSING AWAY OF TILAK

After a brief illness, Tilak passed away on Ist August 1920, the day Gandhi had fixed for launching his crucial non-cooperation movement. In the words of Gandhi's greatest biographer, D.G. Tendulkar, "(Tilak) dreaded by the Government, hated by Anglo-Indians, feared by the Moderates, was the idol of India. "[32] The last words of Tilak were"Unless Swarajya is achieved, India shall not prosper. It is required for our existence."[33] The death of Tilak meant the end of an era after which India entered an altogether different era from 1920, the Gandhi era.

Truly speaking, in 1995, at the threshold of 21st century, India is yet to attain Swarajya. What we got in 1947 was a surrender of one third of Indian territory to Islamic fundamentalism and continuance in the remaining part of India of the same English rule through Anglicised Indians which gave veto power to the same Muslim lot who had created Pakistan. Swarajya of Tilak's dream and Gandhiji's ideal is still a distant cry.

ADOPTION OF KHILAFAT BY CONGRESS

The Treaty of Sevres (with Turkey) was signed on 10th August 1920. It inflamed the Muslims. Gandhi struck while the iron was hot and, at the end of August, held Gujarat Political Conference under an influential Muslim leader, Abbas Tyabji. The Conference, a constituent of the Congress, passed a resolution favouring non-cooperation with the Raj government. Ahmedabad was Gandhi's home base and it was his strategy to first get a mandate for the non-cooperation movement in favour of the Khilafat and then go to the special session of the Congress to be held in Calcutta.[34]

Lala Lajpat Rai, known as the "Lion of Punjab", who had recently returned from America where he had taken shelter for the duration of the first World War, presided over the Calcutta Congress held from 6th to 9th September 1920 to consider the Hunter Committee report on Punjab, and the Khilafat, and take a final view on political reforms. Lalaji "was shocked at the atrocities of the martial law regime, but he did not feel convinced that the Gandhian policy was the right answer".[35] He, alongwith C.R. Das and Jinnah, were to oppose Gandhi's non-cooperation campaign. Gandhi reaffirmed that if there was sufficient response to his programme, Swaraj could be had in a year. He had the backing of Motilal Nehru, the delegates from the South and the Muslim delegates, except Jinnah. Gandhi won by 1855 votes to 873.

The Muslim League also met in Calcutta on 7th September. Finding it difficult to swim against the tide of the popular opinion, Jinnah conceded to support non-cooperation, adding that he did not necessarily approve Gandhi's programme.

The Nagpur session of the Indian National Congress in December 1920 "turned its back on constitutional methods of agitation and handed over the reins of the freedom struggle to Gandhi. Only Jinnah had the courage to oppose Gandhi."[36] He said, "With great respect for Gandhi and those who think with him, I make bold to say in this assembly that you will never get your independence without bloodshed."[37]

It was urged that the visit of Duke of Connaught to India should be bycotted. He was coming to inaugurate the reformed legislature, after the recent Royal pronouncement. Seeing that the Sikhs were being groomed by the British as a separate and distinguished political entity, the Congress adopted a resolution assuring them the same protection and privileges in the scheme of its Swarajya as to the Muslims.

This session of the Congress was unique in the sense that while in all previous sessions, the Congress president was the first among equals, Gandhi emerged as the supreme leader. Also, the Constitution drawn by him created a mass base and an infrastructure for the Congress. Thirdly, Gandhi made a strong plea to make Hindustani, a mix of Urdu and Hindi, written in Devanagari script, the national language.[38] (At a convention at the residence of the Minister of State for Home, Sibte Razi, New Delhi the Home Minister, Shri S.B. Chavan, said on Nov 25, 1995 that the Hindustani which Gandhi had advocated was nothing but Urdu).[39]

JINNAH'S VOICE OF DISSENT

In his interview with Durga Das, after the day's sitting, Jinnah said, "Well, young man, I will have nothing to do with this pseudo-religious approach to politics. I part company with the Congress and Gandhi. I do not believe in working up mob hysteria. Politics is a gentleman's game."[40]

Regarding Jinnah's views on Khilafat, Durga Das states:

> "Jinnah particularly deplored the Khilafat agitation, which had brought the reactionary *mullah* element to the surface. He was amazed, he said, that the Hindu leaders had not realised that this movement would encourage the Pan-Islamic sentiment that the Sultan of Turkey was encouraging to buttress his tottering empire and dilute the nationalism of the Indian Muslims. He recalled how Tilak and he had laboured to produce the Lucknow Pact and bring the Congress and the League together on a common political platform. The British, he added, were playing a nefarious game in by-passing the pact and making it appear that the Muslims could always hope for a better deal from them than from the Congress. 'Well', he concluded, 'I shall wait and watch developments, but as matters stand I have no place in Gandhi's Congress' ".[41]

Durga Das also met Lala Lajpat Rai who, in private, expressed his diffidence about the Gandhian programme, but he would not go against the current. "Do you realise", he said, "that in our effort to carry the Muslims with us we have adopted the Khilafat programme which, if successful, will make them more fanatical? I have this conflict in mind. We have to get rid of the British; we have to carry the Muslims with us. May be this gamble of the Mahatma will pay off. I shall watch and decide my course of action later. For the present, I go with Gandhi. To the extent it will strengthen the nationalist movement and revive faith in our own culture, I will back it."[42]

The irrelevance of Indians fighting for the Sultan of Turkey or his Khilafat has already been explained from a historical angle in the beginning of this chapter. It may now be added that all this fight did not have even a political or moral justification. The objectives of the Khilafat movement were two, (i) to preserve the Khilafat, and (ii) to maintain the integrity of the Turkish empire of the Khalifa. There was no case for the Khilafat simply because the people of Turkey under the popular leader Kamal Pasha, were themselves agitating to remove that office and to set up a democratic republican type of government. It was, therefore, immoral for the Indians to force the Turkish people to carry the burden of a dictator called the Khalifa. Similarly, the demand by Indians to maintain or restore the integrity of the Turkish empire was ridiculous for it meant denial of the right of self-rule of the Arabs and other non-Turkish nations, a right for which we ourselves were struggling. The only point in favour of Turkey was that Smyrna (Izmir), Thrace, and some other parts of Turkey were placed as 'mandates' under the French, British or Greek control. In world war I both the Congress and the Muslim League supported the British government against the combined forces of Germany and Turkey. The Indian army comprising Hindus and Muslims fought for the British on all fronts. When the British and the Allied forces became victorious, they were to dictate peace terms to Turkey, not *vice versa*.* When the Khilafat deputation waited on

---

* In fact, after World War I, many new nations came up or old ones were revived out of the German, Ottomen and Austro-Hungarian, empires, namely, Poland, Estonia, Latvia, Lithuvania, Finland, Zchekoslavakia, Yugoslavia, Syria, Egypt, Iraq and Palestine. Out of these, the last four were mandatory territories--Palestine, Egypt and Iraq to Britain, Syria to France. Port city of Danziq (Turkey) was made independent.

January 19, 1920, the Viceroy said in emphatic language that "Turkey, when she had her choice, deliberately drew her sword against the Allied Powers and must take the consequence."[43] It should be remembered that Germany was dealt with more severely; it was not only dismembered, but a very heavy amount of war damages was imposed upon it. If Turkey had not been at war with the Allied Powers, the matter would have been different.

SPREAD OF KHILAFAT MOVEMENT

But the tragedy of the whole freedom struggle (and even now) is that though the Hindu leaders had a broader and purposeful outlook, they failed to carry the masses who, enchanted by the tall promises of Gandhi and his dhoti-langoti (loin-cloth) rushed to the path of their own disaster. Perhaps, the greatest and the unique feature of Gandhi was his look of a Hindu sanyasin and mind of a zealous and jealous Muslim. He could be countered only by men who, like emperor Akbar, could have strong Muslim body and a zealous (not jealous) Hindu mind, a theme once propounded by Swami Vivekananda.

Gandhi, along with the Ali brothers, made an extensive tour in southern and northern India to propagate the 'gospel of revolt'.[44] Gandhi's appeal to the parents of Aligarh University students is significant. He said:

> "I share too your concern about your boys who are learning at Aligarh. You will believe me when I tell you, that I do not wish to hurt your feelings. I am, myself, the father of four boys whom I have brought up to the best of my lights. I have been an extremely obedient son to my parents, and an equally obedient pupil to my teachers. I know the value of filial duty. But I count duty to God above all these. In my opinion, the time has come for every young man and young woman in this country to make their choice between duty to God and duty to others..."[45]

Government issued a communique warning the people that while the leaders of the movement had not been touched till then, orders had been given to arrest anyone whose words might stir up revolt or incite the people to violence. Gandhi considered it as the first triumph because it showed that the government was in panic. It had great propaganda value. Gandhi advised the people not to submit to the pressure tactics of the government, nor to panic even if he was arrested and not take to violence as even a small measure of violence on the part of the people would provide an excuse to government to commit greater atrocities, "their aeroplanes will bomb the people, their Dyers will shoot into them, and their Smiths will uncover the veils of our women..."[46]

The atmosphere in the country was surcharged with excitement. The common people thought God had sent a saintly man to lead them to freedom and they followed him with a blind faith. India was in the throes of a mass upsurge, a revolt that spread even to the remotest village. Lawyers suspended practice in their hundreds, along with the sacrifices made by Motilal Nehru and C.R. Das et al. All this added up to a great moral victory for Gandhi. Boys left schools by thousands. Where ever Gandhi and the Ali brothers (Mohammed Ali and Shaukat Ali) went, people–Hindus and Muslims–greeted them with slogans of 'Bande Mataram' and 'Allaho-Akbar'. None raised any objection to 'Bande Mataram', but just three years later, in 1923, Mohammed Ali, presiding over the Congress session at Kakinada, objected to the singing of the song '*Bande Mataram*', alleging that it was against the preachings of Islam. Today again the fundamentalist Muslims suffer from the same paranoid psyche. It is one of many instances to show that Islam can be interpreted in two different,and diametrically opposite, directions.

Incidentally, the Duke of Connaught, uncle of the King-Emperor, whose boycott the Congress had decided upon, came to India in February 1921. Majority of the members of the lower house, the Legislative Assembly, were elected by a franchise which covered just three per cent of the whole population. In his inaugural address, the Duke referred to the shadow of Amritsar (Jallianwala Bagh massacre) having lengthened over the face of India. He read out the King's message declaring that reforms made had the beginning of Swaraj within the empire. The word 'Swaraj' was used for the first time in a royal message.[47]

About the same time, in the municipal elections of Madras, a leading non-Brahmin, Dr. T.M. Nair, was defeated by a Brahmin. Nair started an anti-Brahmin movement, espousing the cause of non-Brahmins. He founded a daily "Justice". His party came to be known as the 'Justice Party' and, as Congress did not take part in the elections, it held its sway upto 1936.

In Bombay and Madras, the non-Brahmins and the depressed classes were encouraged to demand separate representation and a reserved share in the services. In U.P., the British contrived to win over many of the landed aristocracies and prominent lawyers. In the Punjab, the British supported the party of the rich and propertied rural class of the Muslims, Hindus, Rajputs and Sikh Jats. All these were acts of creating dissensions and divisions among the Indian people. (Worst of the kind was done by the Indian prime minister, V.P. Singh, in 1989 by opening the Mandal "pandora's-box").

LORD READING AND VISIT OF PRINCE OF WALES

In April 1921, Lord Reading became the Viceroy. Some instances of his time, though minor, are indicative of the British attitude at the top level. Reading made Sir Tej Bahadur Sapru, an Indian member of Viceroy's Executive Council, his political confidant, and, increased the compensation for the victims of the Jallianwala Bagh. Once, the British Executive Engineer looking after the Viceregal Lodge (now Rashtrapati Bhawan) was going on leave. Lady Reading proposed that his junior, an Indian engineer, should act in his place. The Chief Engineer of the CPWD, brought to Reading's notice an order of Lord Curzon that, for reasons of Viceroy's security, no Indian should be appointed as Executive Engineer of the Lodge. Reading over-ruled it saying, 'If Curzon could lay down one rule for his part, he (Reading) for his part could lay down another'. It was a severe blow to the concept of white man's superiority. Near about the same time, the first Indian Accountant General put up a note proposing that an inventory be made of all the furniture, paintings, carpets and valuables of the Viceregal Lodge to keep a check on misappropriation of government property in future. Indirectly, the note cast an aspersion on the integrity of the Viceroys themselves. To the astonishment of the British bureaucracy, Lord Reading not only approved the note, but reprimanded an officer who resisted its implementation.[48]

For the first time an Indian ICS officer, Sir B.N. Sarma, was appointed in the Central Secretariat, a preserve of the white officers. The news of Sarma's appointment raised a stir among the Europeans. The success, however, went to Sarma's head. He became notorious for his insolence. He made it a habit to raise his walking-stick by way of acknowledgment of a white man's salutation. He did the same thing to Lady Reading's courtly greeting on Simla's Mall. The incident, however, was allowed to pass off with just a polite remonstration communicated through his personal assistant.

In this background, Gandhi met the Viceroy, Lord Reading, on 13 May, 1921 at Simla. The Viceroy sought Gandhi's cooperation in welcoming the visit of Prince of Wales to India scheduled to take place a few months later. Gandhi, who once had told the Hindus earlier not to put up any conditions on the issue of cow-protection, for helping the Khilafat cause, said that, unless a political settlement was made, no cooperation would be forthcoming. It was a condition that was beyond Viceroy's power to fulfil. In fact, the cooperation if given would have strengthened Viceroy's hands to enlarge the sphere of autonomy already granted through 1919 Reforms Act. The talks failed except that when confronted by the Viceroy on the point that Ali brothers had been preaching violence and extra-territorial loyalties, Gandhi "agreed to make the Alis recant publicly."[49] On 21st September, when Durga Das met the Viceroy, the latter told him, "I tell you, if India honours the Prince, Swaraj is within your grasp. The Prince would make his visit memorable."[50]

MOPLAH REBELLION

Inspite of Viceroy's warning to Gandhi, calls to violence and Pan-Islamism for establishing the Nizam-e-Mustafa (kingdom of God, but actually reign of terror continued. In fact, the theme that Muslims should be rulers had been preached by almost every Maulana, including Maulana Abul Kalam Azad, for about past ten years. It only reached its climax during the Khilafat movement, with a slight change in the tone and tenor to get the Hindu support. It would be knavish to think that Gandhi was oblivious to all these happenings or, as some present day Hindutva ideologues lament, that Gandhi had not read the Quran; Gandhi always kept with him a copy of the Quran, the Bible and the Geeta, which made him look as the twentieth century *Messiah* having come to synthesise the three great religions-Hinduism, Islam and Christianity. But none except the gullible Hindus believed in this incarnation. A close study of the Khilafat agitation, whose high mark was the Moplah rebellion, would show that, without changing his name and without undergoing formal conversion ceremony, Gandhi had

Islamised himself, Islamised the Congress and went on a spree of Islamising India.

The inevitable happened. There were Hindu-Muslim riots at many places but the Moplah rebellion in the Malabar area of Kerala surpassed all limits. Throughout July and August, 1921, innumera le Khilafat meetings were held. Knives, swords, and spears were secretly manufactured, bands of desperadoes collected; and preparations were made to proclaim the coming of the kingdom of Islam. On August 20, when the District Magistrate of Calicut, with the troops and police, attempted to arrest certain Muslim Moplah leaders in possession of arms at Tirurangudi, a severe encounter took place. It was the signal for immediate rebellion throughout the whole area. Roads were blocked, telegraph lines were cut, and the railway station was destroyed. The DM returned. Such of the Europeans as did not succeed in escaping, were murdered. With bestial savagery prevailing, Khilafat flags were flown and Ernad and Valluvanaj talukas were declared Khilafat kingdoms. Reinforcement had to be sent. The rebels took to the hills. After quite a long time an appreciable number of the rebels was caught. It took six months to bring the situation well in hand.

An idea of the fierceness of the sitution can be gauzed from the night attack at Pandikad on a company of Gurkhas who suffered about 60 casualties. The Gurkhas retaliated. The hordes of Moplah fanatics lost about 250 men before they pulled back. In the long drawn campaign, government troops had 43 soldiers killed, 126 wounded, while the Moplahs lost over 2,000 lives. On November 19,1921, through the neglect of the guard, 67 Moplah prisoners, who had been stuffed in a goods train wagon, died of suffocation. The Muslim leaders put the number of the Moplah martyrs (?) as 10,000. Statements issued by the Secretary and Treasurer of the Kerala Provincial Congress Committee, Secretary, Calicut District Congress Committee, Secretary Ernad Khilafat Committee, were sent to Gandhi and others, bringing out Moplahs' wanton and unprovoked attack on Hindus; wholeale looting, forcible conversion, even at the very outset of the rebellion. Later on, brutal murders of inoffensive Hindus—men, women and children—took place in cold blood in large numbers. The women of Malabar presented a memorial to Lady Reading, stating how pregnant women were cut to pieces and left on the road side; how they were driven out of their native hamlets, how they wandered, starving and naked, in the jungles and forests. A Conference of prominent men was held at Calicut presided over by the Zamarin. In its sixth Resolution, the Conference viewed with indignation the crimes committed by the rebels, especially the wholesale slaughter of men, women and children, burning alive entire families; forcibly converting people in thousands and slaying those who refused; throwing half-dead people into wells.

Two other forms of torture credibly reported were of skinning men alive and making them dig their own graves before they were slaughtered*.

One might ask as to how and why the Moplah rebels kept on fighting pitched battles for six long months against a well trained army of the British? The answer is that among the Moplahs, there was a large number of recently demobilised Muslim soldiers who had returned from battlefields of Mesopotamia and settled on Malabar coast. Gandhi's chief confidant on the Khilafat movement, Mohammed Ali's speeches in the south and reports of the successes of the non-cooperation movement had considerably inflamed their passions.[51]

When the Moplah rebellion was still at its peak, Gandhi was propagating his non-cooperation and civil disobedience to restore the prestine glory of the Sultan of Turkey. At Madurai on 21st Sept 1921, he got his head shaved and donned the loin cloth for which Churchill called him a 'half-naked fakir'. It was another great honour from Gandhi's point of view.[52] On the Moplah rebellion, the attitude of Gandhi and his followers in the Congress, and all the Muslim political parties, was the same. The Moplahs were hailed as the 'brave' and 'courageous' people who were said to be fighting for their religion while the British action against them was condemned vehemently. The atrocities committed on the Hindus were just played down. They were accused, without any substantial evidence, of helping the British through money and other means. On september 19, 1921, at Trichinopoly, Gandhi said, "My heart bleeds to think that our Moplah brethren have gone mad".[53] Yes, the Moplahs were Gandhi's 'brothers;not their victims. Gandhi added:

---

* These details of Moplah rebellion are from R.C. Majumdar, History of Freedom Movement in India, vol. 3, 1963, pp. 190-200.

"Their acts are not the acts of all the Muslims of India, even nor thank God, of all the Moplahs. Every Mussalman of note that I know has repudiated everyone of their acts. Let our loyalty to Hindu-Muslim unity therefore remain firm and changeless .Our loyalty to that creed may still have to suffer greater shocks, but so long as we are satisfied, that there is nothing in Islam to warrant any of the things that these misguided Moplahs have done, and so long as we are satisfied as I am satisfied that no sensible Musalman approves of these acts or any single one of them our loyalty to the creed of Hindu–Muslim unity need not suffer any shock whatsoever."[54]

In Young India of Oct 20, 1921 he wrote:

"It is quite improper to judge Islam or the Mussalmans of the rest of India by the present counduct of Moplahs",[55]

and rated the Moplahs as "among the bravest in the land" and "God fearing," who went mad because of ignorance. Gandhi advised the Hindus as under:

"The Hindus must have the courage and the faith to feel that they can protect their religion inspite of such fanatical eruptions. A verbal disapproval by the Mussalmans of Moplah madness is not a test of Mussalman friendship. The Mussalmans must naturally feel the shame and humiliation of the Moplah conduct about forcible conversions and looting, and they must work away so silently and effectively that such a thing might become impossible..."[56]

But Maulana Hasrat Mohani, a prominent Congressman, spoke in his presidential address at the Muslim League session at Ahmedabad on Dec 30, 1921:

"The Moplahs justify their action on the ground that at such a critical juncture, when they are engaged in a war against the English, their neighbours (Hindus) not only do not help them or observe neutrality, but aid and assist the English in every way. They can no doubt, contend that, while they are fighting a defensive war for the sake of their religion and have left their houses, property and belongings and taken

> refuge in hills and jungles, it is unfair to characterise as plunder their commandeering of money, provisions, and other necessaries for their troops from the English and their supporters."[57]

In the view of the Maulana, the Hindus having seen sword in one hand and the Quran in the other, should have opted for one and should not have sought protection from the British army. This, he made clear when in the subjects committee of the Congress in the Ahmedabad Session, in Dec. 1921 itself, opposed a resolution that condemned the Moplah atrocities on the ground that:

> "The Moplah country no longer remained Darul-aman but became Darul-harb and as they suspected the Hindus of collusion with the British, enemies of the Moplas, therefore, the Moplas were right in presenting the Koran or Sword to Hindus. And if the Hindus became Musalmans to save themselves from death, it was a voluntary change of faith and not forcible conversion."[58]

Maulana Hasrat Mohani was a prominent Congress leader even when he was the President of the Muslim League. By isolating the Hindu sufferings in Malabar and praising the Moplah's bravery, Gandhi indirectly incited the Muslims in other parts to emulate the Moplahs.

Addressing every Englishman in India, Gandhi wrote in 'Young India, Oct.27; 1921

"...In my humble opinion, no Indian has co-coperated with the British Government more than I have for an unbroken period of twenty-nine years of public life in the face of circumstances that might well have turned any other man into a rebel.."[59]

Then, why did Gandhi so violently turn against the British to the extent of declining every good offer made by the British and array himself with purely anti-Hindu and Pan-Islamic forces, more virulent than the Muslim League? Why did he twist the sermon of the Geeta to suit his perverted notion of non-violence in which violence against non-Hindus alone was violence and the violence against Hindus was an excusable aberration? What was it, if not conversion of Gandhi, without the formalities of conversion, into a fanatic Moulvi? If the Hindus do not understand this simple logic, they themselves are to blame for being a political non-entity in spite of being numerically in a over-whelming majority.

In the abovesaid address to the Englishman, in the 'Young India', Gandhi also wrote:

"The Ali brothers were your friends as I was, and still am. My religion forbids me to bear any ill will towards you. I would not raise my hand against you even if I had the power. I expect to conquer you only by my suffering. The Ali brothers will certainly draw the sword, if they could, in defence of their religion and their country.."[60]

Obviously, Gandhi day-dreamt that he was the incarnation of Lord Krishna of Mahabharata who had, in the great Mahabharata war, not used any weapon, but had made others use all their weapons of war. Be as it may, Gandhi made Hindu religion a mockery and Hindus a herd of sacrificial goats to be slaughtered at will by the Englishmen for their appetite and by the Muslims for Qurbani. It is a mystery as to how and why the Hindu masses followed him so blindly, for so long!

After meeting Lord Reading, as stated earlier, Gandhi had intensified his non-cooperation movement. Now he declared that complete Civil Disobedience would take place from November 17, 1921, the day on which the Prince of Wales was to land in India. On the fateful day, there was a strike in Bombay coupled with riots leading to police firing in which several people died. The human touch in the first speech of the Prince of Wales on Indian soil- 'I want you to know me, I want to know you'- was lost in the din of affray."[61] In the riots, the victims were Parsees and Christians who had gone to welcome the Prince. Gandhi was moved. He went on a fast on Nov 19 and broke it on Nov 22, taking a vow that he would observe a fast every Monday until Swaraj had been attained.

The hostility shown by Gandhi and the Congress towards the Prince only led to strengthening of the anti-reform lobby in England and in the ICS. The Dec 1921 Congress session was held in Ahmedabad under the presidentship of C.R. Das. Pandit Madan Mohan Malviya tried that the Congress should ask for a Round Table Conference to resolve the political demand. But Gandhi, riding the crest of the revolutionary wave of non-cooperation and civil disobedience, insisted on Satyagraha saying that it was the only civilized and effective alternative to an armed rebellion.

Maulana Hasrat Mohani, also the president elect of the Muslim League, "advocated violent methods, including guerilla warfare to win independence." His printed speech was seized by the police. The Maulana was convicted for sedition, and sentenced to three years imprisonment. Gandhi was given the powers of a virtual dictator to lead the civil disobedience movement. Durga Das states:

"The intellectuals in the freedom movement felt paralysed by the new agitational approach adopted by Gandhi and understandably sought escape in the legislative forum. By and large the teenagers who joined the movement abandoned their studies and shut the chambers of their minds to knowledge and blindly followed the leader, sowing dissatisfaction among the masses with their inflammatory charges and going in and out of jail. (This ill-educated element reached the top echelons of the various political parties in the mid-sixties, with deplorable consequences.)"[62]

M.A. Jinnah and Pt. Malaviya, to avert the threatened confrontation with the British government, held an all-parties conference in Bombay on January 14, 1922, attended by 300 delegates, under the chairmanship of Sir Sankaran Nair. Gandhi put up certain conditions for a settlement with the British. Accordingly, Jinnah's proposal urging the desirability of a round table conference on conditions acceptable to Gandhi and the government was adopted.

CHAURI CHAURA EPISODE

On Feb. 8, the police, in trying to halt a procession of satyagrahis, at Chauri Chaura in U.P. opened fire. When their ammunition got exhausted, the police personnel ran to their police station. The mob pursued them and set the Thana on fire. Twenty two policemen were thus trapped and burnt alive. Gandhi, who had remained totally unmoved on the killings of thousands of Hindus in Malabar, had felt a little pain at the sufferings of some Anglo-Indians and Parsees in Bombay recently, was now enraged at the Chauri Chaura incident. He declared the civil disobedience movement withdrawn and fasted for five days. Though the Congress Working Committee approved his action, leaders like Motilal Nehru, Jawaharlal Nehru and others, then in jail, strongly opposed this sudden withdrawal of the movement that had been going on for about two years and in which lots of people had lost their lives and thousands had lost their jobs, property and career.

In the words of Gandhi's greatest biographer, DG Tendulkar:

"The year 1923 was not a happy year. The co-operation between the Hindus and Muslims was on the decline and dissensions grew apace. The issue of Khilafat was solved by the Turks themselves. In November 1922, the Turks under their leader, Mustafa Kamal, rose and deposed the old sultan cum Caliph, putting new figurehead in his place as Caliph only, without temporal power. The old Sultan fled to Malta on a British ship. Mustafa Kamal was elected president and he concentrated all power in himself. The Khilafatists accepted Kamal's decision without protest, for it was now clear to them that nothing that Indian Muslims did was likely to have much relevance or effect. The struggle was almost over, their enthusiasm was a spent force."[63]

Mrs Annie Besant said: "It is the queerest revolution that ever was, since Gandhi replaced Tilak, has had the queerest leader, and has now the queerest collapse."[64]

REFERENCES

1. D.G. Tendulkar, Mahatma, vol. I, p. 292.
2. Durga Das, India from Curzon to Nehru, p. 67.
3. —do— p. 64.
4. Durga, Das, India Curzon to Nehru, p. 67.
5. Ibid.
6. Ibid.
7. T.L. Sharma, Hindu-Muslim Relations, p. 85.
8. Tendulkar, Mahatma, vol. I, p. 301.
9. Ibid, p. 302.
10. Durga Das, India, Curzon to Nehru, pp. 67-68.
11. D.G. Tendulkar, Mahatma, vol. I, p. 323.
12. Durga Das, India, Curzon to Nehru, pp. 66.
13. Tara Chand, History of Freedom Movement in India, vol. III, p. 416.
14. D.G. Tendulkar, Mahatma, vol. I, p. 330-332.
15. Ibid p. 330-332.

    Prophet Mohammed had recommended cow's milk and butter as wholesome but declared beef as unwholesome as containing disease producing bacteria. Citing the Prophet's injunction, Hazrat Abdullah bin Masud stated "Cow's milk is beneficial to you, as its milk and butter act as health-giving medicines. But its meat is a source of ill health". Many other Islamic theologians and physicians have said the same thing. Thus, Islam has not cast any taboo against beef but it instructs its faithfuls to shun it. (Muzaffar Hussain, in Organiser weekly, Dec 10, 1995, p. 15).

16. D.G. Tendulkar, Mahatma, vol. I, p. 335.
17. Ibid p. 336.
18. Ibid, p. 337.
19. Durga Das, India From Curzon to Nehru, p. 69.
20. Ibid p. 69-70.
21. Ibid p. 70.
22. Ibid p. 70-71.
23. Ibid p. 71.
24. D.G. Tendulkar, Mahatma, vol. I, p. 339.
25. Ibid p. 339.
26. Ibid, p. 343.
27. Ibid p. 346-348.
28. Ibid, p. 351.
29. Ibid p. 353.
30. Ibid, p. 358.
31. Ibid p. 368.
32. Ibid, pp. 369-370.
33. Ibid, —do—
34. Durga Das, India from Curzon to Nehru, p. 73.
35. Ibid p. 73.
36. Ibid, p. 75.
37. Ibid p. 76.
38. Ibid.
39. Dainik Jagaran (Hindi Daily) Delhi, Nov. 26 1995 issue, front page.
40. Durga Das, India from Curzon to Nehru, p. 76.
41. —do— p. 77.
42. Durga Das, Curzon to Nehru, p. 77.
43. Lal Bahadur, Muslim League, p. 139.
44. D.G. Tendulkar, Mahatma, vol. II, 1951, p. 27 (Published by Vithal-bhai K. Jhaveri, 64 Walkeshwar Road, Bombay-6), covering the period from 1920 to 1929.
45. D.G. Tendulkar, Mahatma, vol. II, p. 27-28.
46. Ibid, p. 33-34.
47. Durga Das, India Curzon to Nehru, p. 79.
48. Ibid.
49. Ibid p. 91.
50. Ibid, p. 93.
51. Ibid p. 91.

52. —do—
53. T.L. Sharma, Hindu-Muslim Relations, p. 125.
54. T.L. Sharma, Hindu-Muslim Relations, p. 125.
55. —do— p. 125.
56. —do— p. 125-26.
57. —do— p. 124.
58. —do— p. 124.
59. D.G. Tendulkar, Mahatma, vol. II, p. 30.
60. —do— p. 32.
61. Durga Das, India from Curzon to Nehru, p. 93.
62. Ibid p. 99.
63. D.G. Tendulkar, Mahatma, vol. II, p. 154-155.
64. —do— p. 155.

Chapter VII

AFTERMATH OF KHILAFAT—ECLIPSE OF GANDHI

The immediate consequences of the Congress-Muslim League pact and the Khilafat movement spearheaded by Gandhi, in the words of noted historian, Dr. Tara Chand, were:[1]

1. The Indian National Congress which had become united in 1916, was split again. Those who disapproved of the new programme of action seceded and formed the All India Liberal Federation.
2. For the next 25 years the Congress was an instrument of Gandhi's will, and its politics was overlaid with religious (though not denominational) fervour.
3. The Muslim League lost its popularity and Muslim politics came under the domination of the religious leaders. Men like Jinnah, Wazir Hasan, Mahmudabad, Fazli Hussain, Muhammad Shafi, who had been the pillars of the Muslim League were relegated to the background.
4. The Khilafat Committee and the Jamiat-ul-Ulema assumed the lead of Muslim politics.
5. The Hindu and Muslim masses were drawn into the political struggle in increasing numbers.

Pandit Madan Mohan Malaviya, Lala Lajpat Rai and a few other leaders of the Congress had got disgusted with its pro-Muslim and anti-Hindu policies. In 1915 itself, they had formed an All India Hindu Mahasabha, but it did not then have any political agenda of its own, except agitating against the separate electorate for the Muslims. Their petition to annul separate electorate for the Muslims was rejected by the British government. The first political meeting of the All India Hindu Mahasabha took place in 1923.

Gradually, the Muslim League came under the influence of the orthodox Muslim Ulemas who had always been inimical towards Hindus. The Muslim forces earlier gathered around Congress to fight against the British in the Khilafat movement now diverted completely against the Hindus. The same fundamentalist Muslims who dominated the Muslim League also dominated the Congress. Hakim Ajmal Khan, Mohammed Ali, Dr. Ansari, Maulana Abul Kalam Azad, etc. were presidents of Congress at one time and presidents of the Muslim League at another. In addition, there were others, like Maulana Hasrat Mohani, who held top positions both in the Congress and the Muslim League. Thus, Congress led by Gandhi and dominated by Ulemas and orthodox Muslims was practically a Muslim organisation in spite of its numerical Hindu majority.

After the non-cooperation movement in the name of Khilafat was withdrawn, there was gloom all around. The Muslim masses called Gandhi a traitor. He was arrested on March 10, 1922, a few days after the agitation had been withdrawn. Muslims were very angry with Gandhi. Had he not been in jail, some Muslim fanatic might have shot him or stabbed him to death. Though Gandhi was jailed for six years he was released after an year on account of illness.

There was complete lull in political activities of the Congress. On return from jail, Gandhi carried the message of constructive programme of *Swadeshi*, manual spinning and weaving, Hindu-Muslim unity, and uplift of the depressed classes. There were internal dissensions, split, and personality clashes in Congress. After the Gaya session of 1924, Gandhi stopped taking part in active politics. It was a tactical move to let the Congress factions themselves settle scores with each other. One group wanted to cooperate with the government and the other insisted on non-cooperation till self government was fully attained.

Although the Khilafat generated movement had been withdrawn, the bad blood created during the period continued. The period that followed was marked by Hindu-Muslim riots in almost every city of India. Khilafat itself became irrelevant with the establishment in 1924 of a Republic form of government in Turkey and the abolition of the office of the Khalifa. It must be borne in mind that the Muslims in general did not like the leadership of a non-Muslim in a purely Islamic movement. Gandhi's leadership was, therefore, highly resented. Maulana Syed Sulaiman Ashraf, Professor of Theology in MAO College, Aligarh, had criticised the speeches made in the very first Khilafat Committee's meeting in November 1919. On learning that in the fervour of Hindu-Muslim unity, certain Muslims had stopped cow sacrifice, the Maulana said that where cows had been sacrificed in the past, it was a religious obligation to continue the same and those who had abandoned it were sinners. An allegation was brought against Mohammed Ali that he had prostrated before Gandhi and called him God. The charkha and khadi of Gandhi were ridiculed. Some of the couplets of the time were:

> Khaddar se kya kategi, ghulami ki bediyan,
> Gandhi ne kah diya hai, shayad mazak men.[2]

(Khadi cannot cut the fetters of slavery. If Gandhi said it can, it must be a joke.)

> Patloon ko tark karke bandhi sari,
> Ye pahante hain ab bhi jo badhai dadhi;
> Bahroopiye hain ye log, dhokhe mein na aanaa,[3]
> Ḡarhe ke libas mein hai challein gaarhi.

(Having discarded trousers, they (Gandhi's Muslim followers) have worn saree, but still they grow the beard. These men are imposters; they have evil designs under the khadi clothing)

Allegations of financial irregularities were also brought in against leaders of the Khilafat.

Still the Islamic fervour of the Indian Khilafatists did not die. They formed a delegation of three men, Abdul Majid Badauni, Syed Suleiman Nadvi, and Kadir Kasturi, who sailed for Hejaz on 18 December 1924. Thousands of Muslims of Bombay, including office bearers of the Central Khilafat Committee, gave them a hearty send off. But it was a great disappointment for the delegation when the Turkish government refused to receive it.[4] The Khilafatists took the event with a good deal of diplomacy.[5] They admitted that there was no priesthood in Islam. Mohammed Ali, *de facto* author of the movement offered an apology for its failure. It was said that the office of the Khalifa had degenerated itself into a harmful institution and could hardly lay claim to its continued existence. Questions were raised, "What did it do for Islam and the Muslim world outside Turkey? Did it protect the Muslims in Morocco or Algeria or in other parts of Africa against the European Christian powers which have brought them under their sway?"[6]

According to Indian Statutory Commission Report, vol.I, p.27, in the years from 1923 to 1927 about 450 lives were lost and 5,000 persons were wounded in the communal riots.[7] The worst of them were the communal riots of Kohat in Sept 1924 in the North-West Frontier Province. According to official estimates, 155 Hindus were killed, several Hindu temples, vast Hindu properties and houses were burnt, destroyed or looted. Hindu women were molested. The cause of the riots was said to be a poem derogatory to Hazrat Mohammed. The poem was circulated by agent provocateurs.

Sarojini Naidu asked Gandhi to do something effective. Gandhi went on 21 days fast. As usual, the fast resulted in unity conferences and passing of resolutions to maintain communal unity which were forgotten as soon as they were passed. The communal riots spread in many cities of United Provinces (Uttar Pradesh), Central Provinces (MP) Bombay and Bengal. The Kohat riots were jointly investigated by Shaukat Ali and Gandhi: Shaukat was Gandhi's lieutenant in Khilafat movement, but the two held diametrically opposite view. While Shaukat Ali put all the blame on the poem, Gandhi said, "I am prepared to strongly condemn publication of the poem but I am unable to condone the looting and arson. I do not endorse your opinion that the pamphlet was the cause of the conflagration. The ground was already prepared. I cannot treat the conversions as lightly as you seem to do. In my opinion the Khilafatists have greatly neglected their duty".[8] Thus, for the difference of opinions, the Kohat report was not published. If Gandhi, for the first and the last time, took a stand against the Khilafatists, it was only because the same people for whom he had put his every thing at stake, were accusing him of betrayal.

For similar difference of opinion on the inquiry report on Kanpur riots of 1931 in which 400 persons had died (including the famous Hindi journalist, a reputed social worker and Congress leader of Kanpur, Ganesh Shankar Vidyarthi) was first kept in close quarters. When ultimately, Congress decided to issue it, Government confiscated the copies and proscribed it. This author, however, saw it (Roots of Communal Politics), running into 485 pages, prepared by a committee consisting of Dr. Bhagwan Das (Chairman), Purushottam Das Tandon, Khwaja Abdul Majid, TAK Sherwani, Zafarul-Mulk and Pandit Sunderlal. It was published by South Asia Books, Columbia, Missouri. A Summary of its recommendations and Notes of Dissent of Purushottam Das Tandon and Zafarul Mulk are given in Appendix 'A'. It mirrors well the helplessness of Hindus and the aggressive Muslim mind way back in 1931, the former trying to accommodate upto the breaking point and the latter pushing its demands in the name of pure Islam. In the post Partition days, Purushottam Das Tandon was branded a communalist Hindu. Here, it is suffice to say that the Kanpur riots according to the said report were triggered off by the local Congress call for hartal in protest against the execution of Sardar Bhagat Singh with his two associates a day earlier. The Muslims opposed the hartal. Government's hand in starting the riots and escalating them was also seen. The report says that preparations for the riots had been made for about a decade under the Tanzim movement of the Muslims which had taken strong roots in U.P., especially in Kanpur and Lucknow. "The proportion of the Tanzim movement can be gauged from the fact that about 160 Anjumans sprang up in the city (Kanpur). They began daily to parade the city in batches of twenty or more singing anti-national and anti-Hindu songs. These Anjumans had each their volunteers partly in Khaki uniforms and partly without uniforms. Each Anjuman was usually connected with a mosque. The number of volunteers gradually ran up to thousands. Their daily demonstrations assumed a threatening posture and became a menace to the peace of the city. The ostensible object of all these organisations was to persuade Musalmans to say their Namaz five times a day. Parties of volunteers used to go to Muslim houses and forcibly wake up people at four o'clock in the morning to say their Namaz".[9]

The report further states that "Provocative songs against Hindus were also a common feature of these processions. These Tanzim processions were no doubt brought out in answer to the Congress processions organized in connection with the Civil Disobedience Movement. But they differed from the Congress processions in that the Muslim processionists carried arms—

Ballams (spears), Karaulis (daggers), Khantas (axes), and even drawn swords were always in evidence. A few examples of the songs sung are given below:

(1) Musalmano, jigar men dushmanon ke khar ban jao.
Tarap kar Phir Ali ki tegh-i-jauhardar ban jao,
Agar mauqa-i-jihad aye khushi se josh men akar
Katakar sar Khuda ki rah men sardar ban jao,
Mitane ke liye is Kufr ko Islam kahta hai,
Shariyat ki taraf se din ki talwar ban jao.
Qiyamat phat pare in mushrikon par momino gar tum
Alam-bardar ke khadim alambardar ban jao.

(O, Muslims: Be thorns in the hearts of (your) enemies;
Vigorously, you again be the miraculous sword of Ali.
If there be an opportunity of jehad, rejoice, gather your energy,
Offer your head for sacrifice in God's path and gain glory.
On behalf of Shariyat, be the sword of Din (Islam). Islam ordains you to wipe out the falsehood, so
Qayamat will befall on the infidles if only you,
The servants of God, become the protector of the faith.)

(2) Jhagarna marna aur lootna kafir ka jayiz hai,
Zarasi bat men amada-i-takrar ho jao.

(It is lawful to quarrel with a kafir (Hindu), kill or plunder him. On the smallest pretext, you should pick up a quarrel with him)

(3) Ham hasti-i-kafir ko dunya se mita denge.

(We will wipe out the very existence of kafirs from the world.)

(4) Jab josh men wahdat ke ayenge dikha denge;
Butkhano ki diwaren dam bhar men gira denge;
Kufr pe kar denge hamla ab agar milkar,
ham Khoon ke darya alam mein baha denge;
Shariat par raho qayim adu ke qatla karne ko,
An Alamgir, Alamgir, Alamgir ban jao.
Mitaane ke liye is kufr ki hasti ko duniya se
Ali-e-Haidar-i-Karrar ki shamshir ban jao.

(With the religious fervour of devotion, we will show the world
We can pull down the walls of (Hindu) temples in a moment.
Now, if we unitedly declare a war on the infidels (Hindus),
We will run streams of blood in the world.
Be firm on the Shariat (Islamic law) and prepared to slaughter the enemy,

Be Aurangzeb (Alamgir), Aurangzeb, Aurangzeb.
To wipe out this kufr (Hindu religion) from the world,
May you be the sword of Ali, Haidar Ali and Karrar).

The immediate cause of each of the Hindu-Muslim riots might be different, but the under current of every one is the same as in Kanpur or Kohat. A publication "*Sita ka chhinala*" depicting Devi Seeta as a prostitute, also came in circulation from the Muslim side.[10]

After the Moplah carnage of Kerala, Hindus started thinking of organising themselves against such riots. They never had any countrywide or even statewise organisation which could take to fighting or retaliating in an organised manner. So, wherever the riots did start, the Hindus got killed like sitting ducks for the first few days. Then only Hindus could join hands in numbers to defend themselves or retaliate. Faced with a pro-Muslim British government and the pro-Muslim Congress, Hindus were the worst sufferers, especially in areas like the N.W.F.P. where they were in microscopic minority. In frustration, or in retaliation to armed attacks of the Muslims or abusive poems/publications as cited above, some Hindus wrote on Islam or prophet Muhammed showing them the other side of their prophet and their faith, quoting the Quran and the Hadis. This author has had the chance to see a copy of the much maligned booklet 'Rangila Rasool'. It just enumerated the names of the known wives of Hazrat Mohammed who came from different backgrounds and belonged to different age groups, from elderly Khadija Begum to young Aisha. The description, was not in good taste as it presented the Prophet in a poor light in the absence of an explanation of the different political and social circumstances leading to the marriages of the Prophet. But compared with the earlier stated provocative songs and outrageous comments on Devi Sita, the '*Rangila Rasool*' was an amateurish act of retaliation. It should not have made an issue.

Even so, historians have singled it out as one of the major causes of Hindu-Muslim riots. They have conveniently skipped over the derogatory and abusive writings of the Muslims on Hindu gods and goddesses. The obvious inference is that when a people adopt a code of conduct that "Jhagarna marna aur lootna kafir ka jayiz hai, zaraasi bat mein amada-i-takrar ho jao", logic gives way to brutality. Rajpal, the author of '*Rangila Rasool*', although cleared in judicial proceedings, was stabbed to death in his shop on April 6, 1929.[11] In another case, one Nathumal Sharma, author of a book on prophet Mohammed, was convicted under S.195 IPC. He made an appeal in the court of Judicial Magistrate. While Sharma was awaiting the hearing to commence, one fanatic Muslim, Abdul Qayum, murdered Sharma, in Sept 1934 in the court premises. When Qayum was convicted and his appeal was being heard in the Lahore High Court, his counsel, Barkat Ali, argued[12] that Qayum was not guilty because his act was permitted by the law of Quran. The great Arya Samaj leader, Swami Shradhanand was treacherously shot dead in Delhi in 1926, partly in retaliation to the book on Mohammed, objected to by the Muslims, and partly for Swami's work on *Shuddhi*.

C.R. Das, a prominent leader of Congress from Bengal, was very sore about Gandhi's prescriptions. He too felt that Gandhi was leading the country away from the path of constitutional struggle to the wilderness of sterile political agitation and wondered "How can we get rid of the Mahatma."[13] But, Das also had no remedy except to offer more concessions to the Muslims, like 60 per cent job reservation in Bengal services. Das died on June 16, 1925 in Darjeeling. Lala Lajpat Rai and Pandit Madan Mohan Malaviya were disgusted with the Muslim appeasement policy of the Congress and the growing Muslim atrocities on Hindus that went on without even an earnest condemnation from the Congress. When Abdul Rashid, the assassin of Swami Shraddhanand was caught he disclosed that his next target was Pandit M.M.Malaviya. Whether to prove his Sainthood or his true Muslim colour, or both, Gandhi pleaded that Abdul Rashid should be pardoned. How high was the fanatic spirit of the Muslims can be judged from the statement of Mohammed Ali, (Gandhi's main confidant of the Khilafat movement) in 1926, that "conversion of every non-Muslim to Islam is the duty of every Muslim. The day I would succeed in converting Gandhi to Islam would be a golden day in my life. "[14] (Mohammed Ali was Congress President in 1923-24). At another time, he had said that in his opinion even the meanest of a Muslim was superior to a (Hindu) Gandhi. When it was brought to Gandhi's notice, the latter explained that, "What Mohammed Ali said was correct according to his religion".[15]

In the midst of these developments, the idea of a Hindu unity (Sangathan) came into being. In 1923, the Hindu Mahasabha had its session at Gaya and it decided to organise a Hindu Volunteer Corps (Hindu Raksha Dal) to protect Hindus during riots and to look after the interests of Hindu community. The meeting was chaired by Pandit Malaviya. In fact it was the first meeting in which the Hindu Mahasabha took up political questions. A committee was formed to carry out the programme. It included Swami Shraddhananda, Pt. Malaviya, Vijay Raghavachari, Shri Sathyamurthi, N.C. Kelkar, Shankaracharya Dr. Kurtakoti, Kharpade, Lala Hans Raj, Dr. Munje, the Maharaja of Kasimbazaar and Jamanalal Bajaj. Gandhi and C.R. Das were opposed to any separate Hindu party or organisation.

About this period, Lala Lajpat Rai wrote to C.R.Das:

> "...I have devoted most of my time during the last six months to the study of Muslim history and Muslim law and I am inclined to think, it is neither possible nor practicable. (Hindu–Muslim unity). Assuming and admitting the sincerety of the Muhammedan leaders in the non-co-operation movement, I think their religion provides an effective bar to any thing of the kind. You remember the conversation, I reported to you in Calcutta, which I had with Hakim Ajmal Khan, and Dr. Kitchlew. There is no finer Mohammadan in Hindustan than Hakim Saheb, but can any other Muslim leader override the Koran? I can only hope that my reading of Islamic Law is incorrect, and nothing would relieve me more than to be convinced that it is so. But if it is right then it comes to this that although we can unite against the British we cannot do so to rule Hindustan on democractic lines..."

Rabindranath Tagore expressed his views on Hindu-Muslim unity in 1924 to the representative of a Bengali paper which were translated in an article, 'Through Indian Eyes' in the Times of India of April 18, 1924:

> "...another very important factor which, according to the poet was making it almost impossible for Hindu-Muhammedan

> unity to become an accomplished fact was that the Mohammedans could not confine their patriotism to any one country... The poet said that he had very frankly asked many Mohammedans whether, in the event of any Mohammedan power invading India, they would stand side by side with their Hindu neighbours to defend their common land. He could not be satisfied with the reply he got from them. He said that he could definitely state that even such men as Mr. Mohammed Ali had declared that under no circumstance was it permissible for any Mohammedan whatever his country might be, to stand against any other Mohammedan."[16]

Dr. Rajendra Prasad said:

> "The Shuddi movement of Swami Shraddhanand has come in for a great deal of criticism both from the nationalists and Mussalmans. Whatever one may have to say about its opportuneness at that particular moment, it is difficult to understand how Christians and Mussalmans can object to it on merits. They are constantly engaged in their proselytising missions and converting Hindus to their faiths. If Hindus on their side also start converting non-Hindus to their faith, it is no business of non-Hindus, especially if they are themselves engaged in the work of conversion, to object. The Hindus must have the same right of propagating their faith as others have. But men are not always guided by logic nor by a sense of justice and fairness. And there was much bitterness among Mussalmans against the Shuddhi movement and against Swami Shraddhananda personally, as a result of which he fell a victim to a Muslim assassin sometime later. Mussalmans on their side started the Tabligh and Tanzim movements.[17]

Mohammed Ali answered the points raised by Dr. Rajendra Prasad, in the Congress session at Kakinada in December 1923 of which he himself was the president. He said, "Christianity, and Buddhism as well as Islam are known to be missionary religions, but Judaism, Hinduism, Zoroastrianism, are generally regarded as non-missionary."[18] The thrust of Mohammed Ali's argument was that conversion to Hindu religion being carried out by the Arya Samaj was anathema to Hindu religion. Mohammed Ali also ridiculed the *sangathan* work of Hindus and told his Muslim audience "removal of untouchability is not intended to result in the absorption of the suppressed classes into Hindu society, but merely to use them as auxiliaries on the Hindus side in future affrays. Let us befriend the suppressed classes for their own injured sake and not for the sake of injuring others or even avenging your own injuries."[19]

Sheikh Abdullah (later the Prime Minister of J&K in freed India) as Chairman of the Reception Committee of the Muslim League session, December 1925, at Aligarh, castigated the Hindu Mahasabha and said that the real cause of the Hindu-Muslim rift and strife was the concept of false patriotism of certain Hindu leaders. He added that the most harmful and provocative of all the overt acts was the teaching of youngmen among Hindus under the names of jathas or akharas to match their physical strength equal to the members of the Muslim community. According to the Sheikh, this preparation was for a civil war by the Hindu section of the population.[20] (Even now in 1995, this very theme is being spread not only by the fanatic leaders of the Muslim community, but even the so-called progressive leaders, writers and opinion makers.)

In a speech in 1925, Dr. Kitchlew said:

> "The Congress was lifeless till the Khilafat Committee put life in it. When the Khilafat Committee joined it, it did in one year what the Hindu Congress had not done in forty years. The Congress also did the work of uplifting the seven crores of untouchables. This was purely a work for the Hindus, and yet the money of the Congress was spent on it like water. But the brave Mussalmans did not mind... *Listen my dear Hindu brothers, listen very attentively: If you put obstacles in the path of our Tanzeem movement and do not give us our rights, we shall make common cause with Afghanistan or some other Mussalman power and establish our rule in this country.*"[21] (emphasis added)

As a matter of fact, the Khilafat movement united the Muslims as never before. The Muslim leaders, coming from the elite section of the community were now wooed both by the Congress and the British government. The situation gave strength to Muslim separatism. The author of the 'Hindu-Muslim Relations,

1913-1925', has very aptly stated, "With the Muslim masses in their pocket and both the Congress and the British vying with each other to win their support, the Muslim elite was emboldened to look for advantages that would further enhance its political effectiveness." The Lucknow Pact had sown the seeds of separatism, the Khilafat movement germinated those seeds. All the unity moves and unity conferences to bring the Hindus and Muslims together failed. As a last resort, an All Parties Conference was called by Gandhi at Delhi on 23-24 January 1925. It also failed, but made it crystal clear that India's communal problem was insoluble. The conflict between the Ali brothers and Gandhi was revealed to the public for the first time. Gandhi got exhausted. All his appeals fell on deaf ears. At the Khilafat Conference at Patna, on September 22, 1925, Gandhi said that he had lost his hold on both the Hindus and the Musalmans. In a public speech at Calcutta on May 1st 1925 he said that he had been found wanting as a physician prescribing a cure for this malady.[22]

Interestingly, the annual session of the Hindu Mahasabha was held in the Congress pandal at Belgaum on Dec 27, 1924, with Pt. Malaviya as President. Gandhi, C.R. Das, Motilal, the Ali brothers, Maulana Azad, Hasarat Mohani, were among those present. Answering the charge that the Mahasabha was a commual organization, Pt. Malaviya said: "It would be a shame if any Hindu opposed the National Congress. Their object was to supplement and strengthen the Congress. The necessity for organizing the Mahasabha had arisen because the Congress being a political body could not deal with questions which affected various communities in social and other non-political spheres."[23] At the Congress session at Belgaum at the same time, non-cooperation movement was given a good bye.[24]

The foremost question before Gandhi and the Congress was how the Muslims' appetite could be satisfied and how far the Hindu could be bent without breaking. The second question was how soon the British could be made to hand over the political power to Hindu-Muslim combine under the Congress banner. In a piquant situation as above, there were only two possibilities, Islamisation of the whole country or a civil war. Hindus were not prepared for the civil war. Challenge after challenge was thrown from the Muslim side, but replies were always evaded. There had to be a stalemate in the political horizon till the British themselves came forward in 1928 with the proposals for further constitutional reforms, as promised in the 1919 reforms.

While Hindus were raising the slogans of Hindu–Muslim unity and were also getting slaughtered in communal riots like sheep and goats, a large section of the Muslims was drawing up the scheme for a separate independent Muslim state.

In 1923, the Government of India appointed a committee to make recommendations about whether North-West Frontier Province should be maintained as a separate unit or merged with the province of Punjab. Mohammed Gulkhan, President of Islamiya Anjuman of Dera-Ismail-Khan was asked, 'Your Islamiya Anjuman believes in Pan Islamism, i. e. a confederation of various Islamic states. Are you, therefore opposed to the idea of merger of the Frontier Province with Punjab? ' Gulkhan replied, 'It is so. Their idea is that Hindu–Muslim unity will never become a fact. I would much rather see the separation of Hindus and Mohammedans,[23] crores of Hindus to the South and eight crores of Muslims to the North. Give the whole portion from Kanyakumari to Agra to Hindus, and from Agra to Peshawar to Mohammedans. I mean transmigration from one place to the other. This is an idea of exchange.'..It was the dream of many Muslims then to convert the area between Agra and Peshawar as a non-Hindu territory.[25]

Baffled by the failure of all Hindu-Muslim unity moves, Lala Lajpat Rai made a deep study of Islam and the demands being made by the Indian Muslims. In his presidential address at the Bombay Hindu Confernece on Dec 5, 1925, he said:

> "The Muslims are determined to preserve and perpetuate not only their religion but also their political system as far as it may be possible for them to do so. They are not prepared to merge their separate entity into a body-politic which might be a composite entity composed of all the religious communities that claim India as their home. They insist on communal representation all along the political line and also on organising their separate communal entity in India. This is bound to come about if other communities refuse to organise themselves...Those who neglect to organise must give way to the organised..."[26]

In the meantime, when Gandhi and the Congress were engaged in non-cooperation and Civil Disobedience movements, a section of the Congress leaders, led by Motilal Nehru formed the Swaraj Party which fought the first election to the Central Legislative Assembly under the 1919 Reforms Act. Swaraj Party captured a large number of seats. In 1920, Mian Fazli Husain resigned from the Congress and managed, alongwith Lala Harkishan Lal, to get into the ministerial office of the Punjab Governor. Lala Harkishan Lal was also a Congressman who had once been condemned to death under the martial law but got reprieve. Later, Fazli Husain founded the Unionist Party of the landed aristocrats, including Hindus and Muslims. His party won the Punjab elections and Fazli Husain became Punjab's first Prime Minister. In the name of helping the poor and the backward, Fazli showered all favours on the Muslims, and filled all government posts with the Muslims.

The Congress had withdrawn the non-cooperation movement, but could not decide on the question of Council entry. Gandhi was still opposed to it. Following the AICC decision, on March 6, 1926, the Swaraj Party, the largest one in the House, walked out of Legislative Assembly on the ground that its demands had not been met by Government. On March 13, the All India Hindu Mahasabha held its session at Delhi and decided on Council entry. Those attending the Conference included Pandit Madan Mohan Malaviya, Lajpat Rai, Swami Shraddhanand, Bhai Parmanand, Dr. Choithram, Jairamadas Daulatram, Jamnadas Mehta and Dr. Moonje.[27] Motilal Nehru objected to the Hindu Mahasabha holding such a political conference and said that the Mahasabha had deviated from its non-political stance and brought "together under its banner political parties as wide apart as the poles."[28]

Three months later, the Khilafat Conference was held at Delhi. It is strange how the Congress was tolerating and cooperating with this organisation when the Khilafat question had been settled once for all over two years ago. (But, by then the Congress itself had become virtually a Muslim Conference). The Conference President, Maulana Suleman Nadvi, stated that the Muslims in India did not mind *Sanghathan* but they were concerned about *shuddhi*. Maulana Mohammed Ali supported Tablig and said that it was the duty of every Muslim to convert non-Muslims to Islam. Shaukat Ali told the Khilafatists that if the Hindus or any other community attacked them, they should pay back in the like manner. Dr. Ansari announced that he ceased to be a member of the Muslim League, the Khilafat Committee or any other communal organisation.[24]

On April 3, 1926, the Responsivists with Lala Lajpat Rai (who had decided to take part in the next elections for Council) joined hands with the Independents in Bombay and formed the Indian National Party to prepare for the establishment of Swaraj of the dominion type, by all peaceful and legitimate means with liberty to resort inside the legislature to responsive co-operation. Motilal Nehru regarded the formation of this new party as a challenge to the Swaraj Party. The Swaraj Party and the Indian National Party, the two wings, met at Sabarmati on April 20, 1926 where it was decided that there was no need to put further conditions for the Council entry. Later, Motilal Nehru imposed three conditions which were not acceptable to the Indian National Party. Nehru's idea was that the Swaraj Party could by itself win the elections and form ministries. On August 7 Lala Lajpat Rai resigned from the Swaraj Party and helped Malaviya to form a new party, the Independent Congress Party to oppose the Swaraj Party. It represented a more moderate outlook and was a wholly Hindu party working in close cooperation with the Hindu Mahasabha. Gandhi did not like the emergence of this new party. He said,"Lalaji sees no escape from communalism... Panditji cannot brook even the thought of it. I must hold myself in reserve till the storm is over."[30] Thus Gandhi watched from a distance the struggle that went on between the two factions.

The general elections took place in November 1926. The Swaraj Party suffered heavy losses. Some of the Muslim members dropped off and joined the Muslim League or other communal organisations and some Hindu members joined the Indian National Party (Nationalist Party). Lala Lajpat Rai and Pandit Malaviya made a powerful combination and greatly influenced the Hindu electorate. The Nationalist Party had tremendous success. "Not a single Hindu or Muslim seat for the Assembly could be captured by the Punjab Swarajists. Lajpat Rai was returned with an overwhelming majority. In U.P., excepting Motilal Nehru whose election was not contested, not a single Swarajist was elected. In C.P. the Swarajists secured only one seat. The Swarajists were routed and Responsivists had a walkover in all the provinces except Madras."[31] Analysing his defeat, Motilal Nehru wrote:

"It was a fight between the forces of nationalism and those of a low order of communalism reinforced by corruption, terrorism, wealth and falsehood. 'Religion in danger' was the cry of the opponents of the Congress, both Hindu and Muslim. I have been denounced as beef-eater and destroyer of cows, the supporter of prohibitions of music before mosques, and the one man responsible for the stoppage of Ramalila processions in Allahabad. I could only contradict these lies in the public meetings but they penetrated hamlets and villages which I could not reach. Staying in dak and inspection bungalows, and eating food cooked in the European style, was taken to confirm the lying propaganda."[32]

Obviously, this rout of the Swaraj Party in the 1926 elections was not taken in a sportsman like spirit. To say that the Nationalist Party resorted to corruption, terrorism, wealth and falsehood is nothing but to cover up the shame of defeat. Notably, this episode of the freedom struggle is hidden from the public gaze. As expected, the communal riots became more extensive. In 1926 itself, there were thirty five riots. Lala Lajpat Rai passed away On November 17, 1928 on account of police lathi blows received while protesting against the Simon Commission at Lahore.

BIRTH OF RSS

Alarmed by the continuing submissivenss of the Congress to the Muslim bully, increasing number of Hindu-Muslim riots in which Hindus were always at the receiving end, and absence of any Hindu organisation at the grass-root level, Dr. Hedgewar started the Rashtriya Swayamsevak Sangh (RSS) on the Dusshera day of 1925. It was not his idea to make the RSS a fighting force, but to inculcate in men a true sense of patriotism and nationalism, especially in the younger generation, to remove untouchability in practical terms and to prepare the Hindu community to face any challenge, internal or external. He preached non-violence, but did not, unlike Gandhi, abhor violence used for protecting the weak or against a tyrant, when logic or reason failed to yield any positive result. Thus, Shivaji, Guru Gobind Singh, Shri Ram, were his heroes. He did not seek Swarajya straightaway. He wanted to prepare the people for Swarajya and, for that matter, his foremost thrust was on building character both as individual and as a segment of the nation. Swarajya, he thought, would follow by itself. In a way he believed in Aristotle's theory that a people get only that sort of government which they deserve or in the English phrase 'first deserve then desire'. Hedgewar chose young boys for enrolment in his missionary work. This explains why basically the RSS still remains a social and cultural organisation, though expressing its views on political matters also. If he abhored anything, it was untouchability and defeatism that was eating the Hindu society from within. Perhaps, as a reaction to Gandhi's propagandist style, he refrained from publicity saying 'Let your good work itself publicise you'. For this very trait, the RSS has often been branded as a secret organisation. People know RSS more through its opponents' propaganda than through its meagre literature, officials or workers.

REFERENCES

1. Tara Chand, History of Freedom Movement in India, Vol. III, pps. 417-18.

2&3. Lal Bahadur, Muslim League, pages, 143-144.

4. Lal Bahadur, Muslim League, p. 146.
5. Ibid.
6. Ibid, p. 147.
7. Ibid, p. 163.
8. T.L. Sharma, Hindu-Muslim Relations, p. 163.
9. N. Gerald Barrier, Roots of Communal Politics, p. 255-56, South Asia Books, Columbia, Missouri.
10. B.N. Jog, Threat Islam, p. 179.
11. Ibid, p. 184.
12. Ibid, p. 150.
13. Durga Das, India from Curzon to Nehru, p. 116.
14. D.G. Tendulkar, Mahatma, vol. II, p. 307; B.G. Jog, Threat of India, p. 183.
15. Tendulkar's Mahatma, vol. II, p. 252.
16. T.L. Sharma, Hindu-Muslim Relations, p. 151.
17. Ibid, p. 151-152.
18. Ibid, p. 152.
19. Ibid, p. 153.
20. —do— p. 154-155.
21. Ibid, p. 156.
22. Ibid, p. 167.
23. D.G. Tendulkar, Mahatma, vol, II, p. 224-225.
24. Ibid.

25. B.N. Jog, Threat of Islam, p. 177-178.
26. T.L. Sharma, Hindu-Muslim Relations, p. 149.
27. D.G. Tendulkar, Mahatma, vol. II, p. 307.
28. Ibid.
29. Ibid, p. 307.
30. Durga Das, India from Curzon to Nehru, p. 123.
31. D.G. Tendulkar, Mahatma, vol. II, p. 310.
32. —do—

Chapter VIII

RE-EMERGENCE OF GANDHI

After withdrawal of the Khilafat agitation, Gandhi had almost gone into oblivion. In 1927, Government devalued the rupee from 1s. 6d. to 1s. 4d. It created a lot of anti-British feeling. In 1928, there was Katherine Mayo's book 'Mother India' in which India and the Indians were badly maligned. Gandhi called it a "drain inspector's report". It was rumoured that Lord Reading, the then Viceroy, was instrumental in bringing out such an obnoxious stuff on India. Seeing the mood of the people, Vallabhbhai Patel organised a civil disobedience, a no-tax campaign at Bardoli against the increased land revenue assessment. It had a great success. Patel was nick-named Sardar. The campaign which lasted four months resulted in a Bombay government decision to appoint a committee to revise the revenue rates. Patel won nationwide applause and became a hero.

It was time for a review of the working of 1919 Reforms and to draw up new schemes on way to self-government. At the beginning of 1927, Motilal Nehru, Jinnah and Sir Tej Bahadur Sapru started working for bringing about a common scheme acceptable to the British government. The British on their part wanted to create dissensions. They won over a section of Muslims led by Fazli Husain, chief minister of the Punjab and also Dr. Bhim Rao Ambedkar in whom they saw the sole spokesman of the depressed classes. The efforts of Motilal Nehru resulted in the famous Nehru Report by a Committee which also included members from the Muslim League and other parties. Motilal was its chairman. The British appointed the Simon Commission on constitutional reforms for India. As it did not include a single Indian member, protest rallies were held wherever this Commission went.

THE NEHRU REPORT

The Nehru Commitee was composed of Sir Ali Imam and Shuaib Qureshi to put forth the Muslim view point; M.S. Aney and M.R. Jayakar for the Hindu Mahasabha; G.R. Pradhan, for the depressed classes; Sardar Mangal Singh, for the Sikh League; Sir Tej Bahadur Sapru, to represent the liberals; and N.M. Joshi, to look after the labour interest. On March 20, 1927 itself, the Committee had received the "Muslim Proposals" stating that they were prepared for joint electorates both in Provincial and Central legislatures on the following conditions.

(i) Sindh was made into a separate province.
(ii) The N.W.F. Province and Baluchistan were treated on the same footing as the other provinces.
(iii) In the Punjab and Bengal the proportion of representation was to be in accordance with the population of the communities.
(iv) In the Central Legislature, Muslim representation was not to be less than one-third. (Nehru Report p. 17&18).[3]

The Congress Working Committee and the AICC had accepted these conditions.

The Nehru report recommended that all powers of the Government and all legislative, executive and judicial authority should be derived from the people and the same should be exercised within the Commonwealth of India, through the process of law. There would be no state religion. All men and women were to be equal. Everyone of 21 years of age and above would have the voting right. Provinces would be re-organised on linguistic basis on the demand of the majority of the concerned area, subject to financial and administrative considerations. There would be no communal electorate. NWFP would be a full fledged province and Sindh would be separated from Bombay Presidency. Elections would be by joint electorates. The only safeguards for the minorities, mainly the Muslims, would be reservations of seats in proportion to the size of the community. The principle being that "A minority must remain a minority whether any seats are reserved for it or not".

The Nehru report was adopted by the All Parties Conference held at Lucknow in 1928. Among those present were the Raja of Mahmudabad, Sir Ali Imam, Sir C. Sankaran Nair, Sir Tej Bahadur Sapru, Motilal Nehru, etc. Though Gandhi was not present, he hailed the report most enthusiastically.[1] The pleas on behalf of the extremist Muslims for retention of separate electorate and reservation of one-third of seats in the Central Assembly were rejected. Obviously, Hindu sentiments so profoundly expressed in the recent elections were duly taken note of by the members of the Nehru Committee. Maulana Mohammed Ali went to the extent of calling the Report a document of the Hindu Mahasabha. The report was further discussed and adopted in the AICC meeting on 26 December at Calcutta in which Gandhi was present. The Ali brothers (ex-confidants of Gandhi) strongly opposed the Nehru Report. Shaukat Ali declared that he had taken a vow "not to participate in any mixed gathering of Hindus and Muslims for one year unless the present atmosphere was changed", and he would in the meantime devote his time and energy exclusively "to organising Muslims not against Hindus but for the services of the country".[2] The annual session of the Congress was also held in Calcutta in Dec 1928, under the presidentship of Motilal Nehru. Subhash Chandra Bose who had led the Congress procession with Motilal in presidential chariot, opposed the Nehru report. When Durga Das asked Bose the reason for his opposition, he replied, "I do not like Gandhi's appeasement of the Nehrus. We in Bengal represent the real revolutionary force. Jawaharlal only talks. We act".

The most important decision taken in the session, initiated by Gandhi, was that if the Constitutional reforms recommended by the Nehru report were not accepted and dominion status was not granted to India within two years (later reduced to one year), India would seek complete independence.

While discussing the Nehru report in its annual session at Calcutta, the Muslim League got divided into several factions; one faction supported it, one opposed it, and a third favoured a compromise. Yet another pro-British group, headed by the Aga Khan, was on way to chalk out another plan in order to bypass the Muslim League. They held an All Parties Muslim Conference in Delhi on January 1, 1929. It passed a resolution pleading for a federal system of government with complete autonomy, residuary powers being vested in the constituent states. It also demanded continuance of separate electorate and 33 per cent seats for the Muslims in the Central Assembly.

When Jinnah got disillusioned with the Congress at its Calcutta session of 1928 and joined the Muslim League, his first and the foremost task was to bring unity among various factions of the Muslim League and emerge as its leader. In order, therefore, to outwit the All Parties Muslim Conference sponsored by the Aga Khan, Jinnah came out with his 14 point demand (the charter of fourteen demands on behalf of the Muslims). Of these, 13 were drafted by the noted journalist Durga Das at the behest of Jinnah. Only one was added by Jinnah himself to make the number fourteen as number thirteen would appear ominous. Durga Das states:

> "The Government's success in organising the Muslim Conference had led him (Jinnah) to revise his stand, and when I met him to discuss the programme he was to submit to the Muslim League Council that day, he spiritedly remarked: 'Durga, I want your help urgently. Please use your journalistic talent to enunciate our stand by amalgamating our resolutions with the demands made by the All-Parties Muslim Conference. We must appear before the Muslims as the best protectors of their interests".[4]

Durga Das gladly responded and, after scrutinising the various resolutions, reduced them to thirteen points. After a quick glance, Jinnah exclaimed: "Good, but let us make them fourteen like Wilson's fourteen points". So saying, Jinnah added: "No Cabinet, either provincial or Central should be formed without their being a proportion of at least one-third Muslim Ministers." Jinnah, says Durga Das, was not thinking in terms of demands but of tactics, of keepings himself afloat as a political leader. His last point was thus motivated by the desire to champion the cause of the Muslims in areas where they were in a minority. All the fourteen demands are listed in Appendix 'B".[5]

BRITISH CONTRIBUTION TO MUSLIM UNITY

The British were always interested in keeping Hindus and Muslims apart. Their game seemed frustrated with the Khilafat movement jointly launched by the two communities. For breaking this Hindu-Muslim unity, the British took Sir Mohammad Shafi, a member of the Viceroy's Council, the Nizam of Hyderabad and others. The Nizam was the first to declare on 22 May 1920 that since the Khilafat was an anti-Muslim movement, it was henceforth declared illegal. On November 2, 1921, Shafi presented a two pronged scheme to the British:

(i) To weaken the movement for a united India, it was essential to lure away the Muslims which could only be done if the British signed the Peace Treaty with Turkey; and

(ii) An Anglo Mohammadan union in the interest of British empire should be organised.[6]

Both the schemes were implemented by the British.

On 21 September 1922, Viceroy Lord Reading wrote to the Secretary of State for India:

> "I have just sent you a telegram, which will show you, how near we have been to a complete break between Muslims and Hindus. I have been giving the greatest attention to this possibility and I have had the greatest assistance from Shafi on my Council, who is a highly respectable Mohammadan".[7]

But the British got worried when the Muslims got divided into various factions towards the end of Dec. 1928. Curiously each faction was prepared to accept the British leadership, but none was ready to accept the leadership of one of them. The two main factions were, one led by Shafi and the other led by Jinnah. The British were unhappy when Jinnah lent his support for joint electorate. Efforts were made to win him over. On May 20, 1929, the Viceroy wrote:

> "I had a long talk with Jinnah a few days ago, which made it very clear to my mind that he and all the Bombay people, who are not disposed to Congress, are disposed to swing towards our direction if we can give them help later".[8]

On 26 November 1929, the Viceroy wrote:

> "I hear that suggestions are being put out that government should intervene in some way towards raising funds in order to organise proper Muslim representation, and, of course, we should like them to have the best advocacy they can find".[9]

The British government provided all necessary funds to help a strong Muslim party. On 2 February 1931, the Viceroy wrote about Sir Fazli Husain:

> "He (Fazli Husain) developed the view that the only chance of some progress was that a strong party should come into being which should devote itself to fighting the Congress".

The British definitely needed an organisation to fight against the Congress and that organisation was one of the Muslims. Indeed, the Muslim League was playing the role assigned to it by its British patrons. On 9 February 1931, Lord Irwin addressed his party members:

> "I told him (Sir Mohammad Shafi) that I thought they would all have to fight hard and that it was no good supposing that a few packed meetings or newspapers articles would do the job. They must go out as whole-time missionaries and carry the flaming torch throughout the length and breadth of India. They must be prepared to build up a great organisation which might focus all constructive efforts to fight the Congress...and they proposed to get to work, vigorous and comprehensive. This is encouraging and I only hope their good resolutions do not fade away. The League prepared a scheme, the financial aspect of which was the responsibility of the Princely States".[10]

It was the British plan to first unite the Muslims of India under a proper organisation and then tell the world that they were unable to relinquish power because of the hostility between the Hindus and the Muslims. They financed the separatist Muslim movement through Muslim princes and Zamindars. Prominent among them were Nizam of Hyderabad and the Aga Khan. During the first Round Table Conference, the British took maximum advantage of the communal differences. Simulataneously, the British wanted to use the Harijans to divide the Hindus further into the upper castes and Depressed Classes. They were, at the time of the Round Table Conference, very happy to have on their side the Muslims, the Princely States and the Depressed Class leader, Dr. B.R.Ambedkar. The Viceroy wrote on 28 December 1932, "Ambedkar had behaved very well at the Round Table

Conference, and I am most anxious to strengthen his hands in every reasonable way".[11]

Incidentally, the Aga Khan, for his services rendered to the British during the Round Table Conference, demanded to be made a Ruling Prince of some Indian territory. The matter was raised in the Legislative Assembly.[12]

In the meantime, the Simon Commission had started its enquiry by visiting various places in India. There were "anti" Simon Commission demonstrations and rallies wherever it went. Early in 1929, Government introduced a Public Safety Bill to deal with terrorist activities. On 8 April 1929, when the Bill was under consideration, Bhagat Singh and Batukeshwar Dutt hurled a bomb in the Central Assembly. Some papers were burnt, but no one was injured. There was a huge commotion. The report of the Simon Commission was published on September 5, 1929. It was disappointing to all. It gave neither federal constitution nor a dominion status. On the contrary it hinted that the Provinces might develop different constitutional practices in times to come. The Viceroy, Lord Irwin, also got alarmed at this report. He approached his home Government in U.K. and got a statement from Ramsay MacDonald (UK's prime minister in waiting) that dominion status would be coming to India in a matter of months, not years.[13] (It was immediately repudiated by other British leaders) A meeting between Lord Irwin and Gandhi was arranged on 23rd December 1929. When the Viceroy was coming to Delhi on a train, the revolutionaries placed a bomb on the railway track. A bogey was damaged but the Viceroy's compartment remained intact. Gandhi-Irwin meeting took place but no agreement could be arrived at regarding the holding of a Round Table Conference. Gandhi insisted that the proposed Conference should work out a constitution based on dominion status, but the Viceroy would'nt make any such commitment.

Next annual session of the Congress was held at Lahore in 1929. Due to the special efforts made by Gandhi, Jawaharlal Nehru was elected President of this Session. Congress presidentship passed from father to son. Durga Das aptly commented:

> "It is certain that Gandhi's decision marked a turning-point in the history of modern India. A dying man, Motilal was

naturally eager to see Jawaharlal Congress President in his own lifetime. Azad expressed to me the feeling that 'Jawahar would make a great appeal to Muslim youth'. But the effect of Gandhi's decision was to identify the Nehru family with the nation. There is little doubt that this identification was a factor in the choice of Nehru as the first Prime Minister of free India and of his daughter Indira as the third". [14]

Gandhi moved a resolution declaring that Swaraj now meant complete independence. He said that as one year notice to the Government had been ignored, the scheme contained in the Nehru report had also lapsed. At midnight of 31st December 1929 on the banks of the river Ravi, the banner of independence was unfurled by Jawaharlal Nehru in the presence of Motilal Nehru. A Declaration of Independence was adopted at the session and it was ceremoniously read out as a pledge all over the country on 26 January 1930. This document said that the people of India had the inalienable right to freedom which they wanted to promote their growth. This session also caused split in the party and gave birth to the Congress Democratic Party. Its members refused to comply with the call to resign their seats in legislatures. Khan Abdul Ghaffar Khan, later known as the Frontier Gandhi, had attended the Congress session for the first time along with his Khudai Khidmatgars. He joined the Congress.

The Lahore Congress authorised the AICC to launch civil disobedience movement whenever it deemed the time was ripe. "With an unerring instinct for a simple and at the same time dramatic effect, Gandhi chose to inaugurate his Satyagraha campaign with a march to the sea at Dandi, in Gujarat, to break the salt laws. He started from his ashram at Ahmedabad on March 12, 1930 and, after covering 241 miles (410km) distance in 24 days, reached Dandi on April 5. Next day, he made salt out of the sea water in defiance of the salt laws. Simultaneously, he declared a nationwide civil disobedience movement and similar defiance of the salt laws. Though Gandhi had announced his intention two days before starting from Ahmedabad, Government did not arrest him because the legal advice from an Indian member of the Viceroy's Council was that mere intention to break the law was not a sufficient cause to arrest a person. When the movement spread like a wild fire, Government took all repressive measures, like lathi charge and arrests of people and leaders. About 90 thousand men and women, three times more than the number of 1920-21 non-cooperation movement, were arrested and convicted. Gandhi himself was arrested on May 5, 1930, and put in Yeravada jail. A British writer says:

> "The act received great publicity abroad, specially in America where it appeared to have overtones of the Boston Tea Party. The government of India, however, had not sent a single policeman to watch this symbolic act. On the same day, salt was made at about five thousand meetings throughtout India; Congress gave five million as the offical number of those involved, but anything in India can draw a crowd and it is certain that the majority of those who attended the ceremonies did so as casual on lookers".[15]

Thus Gandi re-emerged as the supreme leader of the masses. The Satyagraha had great propaganda value which influenced even the British government. At the same time, unfurling of the Independence flag by Jawaharlal Nehru on the banks of Ravi and the Pledge, together with all the blessings of Gandhi, made him the supreme youth leader.

In the meantime, Fazli Husain got included in Viceroy's Executive Council on April 1, 1930. The Muslim League being a divided house, Fazli Husain followed up the demands formulated at the All Parties Muslim Conference held under the Aga Khan's chairmanship in Delhi on 1st January, 1929. The Nizam of Hyderabad and the Aga Khan provided necessary funds for propaganda and other work. Fazli ensured that only those Muslim delegates were called for the Round Table Conference proposed to be held in London as would support the demands of the Muslim Conference.[16]

While Gandhi was carrying on the non-violent civil disobedience there were others who felt that a general rebellion was the better way of getting rid of the British. They were preparing to strike with guns and bombs. In Bengal, an armoury was attacked and eight men were killed trying to defend it. On the north-west frontier, the city of Peshawar exploded into violence after the arrest of Abdul Gaffar Khan. Troops had to be called in and heavy casualties were inflicted. Two Garhwaļi platoons of the Indian Army refused to go to Peshawar to shoot their unarmed processionists. The scenes of 1857 revolt seemed to be approaching again. In April, 1930, conditions became so bad in Peshawar that the British were no longer in control of the city. Only after the British troops and aircraft arrived twelve days later that the city was reoccupied. It was before Gandhi was arrested on May 5. The same British historian states:

> "The government on the advice of a Muslim member of the Viceroy's council, offered local self-government (to North-West Frontier Province) and secretly encouraged the spread of propaganda which smeared Congress as a Hindu body, so helping to intensify Muslim separatism. The Government...was beginning to see Congress, like the devil, under every stone and behind every disorder. The government even went further; it declared the All India Congress Committee an unlawful association, and arrested Nehru, the Congress president".[17]

The arrests, however, did not halt violence, which continued all over the country, though not on a large scale.

ROUND TABLE CONFERENCE

The first Round Table Conference was opened by King George in London in November 1930. Congress could not participate in it because its leaders were in jail. Some delegates, including Jinnah, Shafi, and Malaviya, worked out a formula for a community-wise division of seats in the legislatures.[18] Later, at the prompting of Fazli Husain from Delhi and the Aga Khan, majority of the Muslim delegates repudiated this communal settlement with regard to Hindus and Sikhs. It meant that reservation of seats agreed to by the Muslims was for the Muslims only. During the proceedings, it was found that it was fruitless to continue the Conference without Congress participation. Viceroy, Lord Irwin, lifted the ban on Congress Working Committee and invited Gandhi for talks. Gandhi's stature rose sky high. On March 5, 1931, there was Gandhi-Irwin Pact whereby Gandhi agreed to take part in the Round Table Conference. However, the Congress being the largest single party, it was claimed that its delegation should also be the largest. Gandhi ji wanted to take two prominent Muslim Congressmen, Dr. Ansari and Ali Imam, to present the view point of its Muslim followers. The proposal was, however, turned down by Lord Willingdon, who had in the meantime replaced Lord Irwin, as Viceroy (April 1931). This was the time when Fazli Husain, member of the Executive Council of the Viceroy, and the Aga Khan had monopolised the Muslim leadership. Willingdon was already hostile to Gandhi but he had to honour the Gandhi-Irwin Pact. Durga Das states:

> "Mitter (another member of the Viceroy's Executive Council) told me that while I was in London Fazli had queered the pitch for Gandhi. The Nawab of Bhopal, he said, had brought together representatives of the Muslim Conference and the nationalist Muslims and they had reached an agreement. But Fazli got it disowned by the Muslim Conference executive. He next persuaded Willingdon to disown Irwin's commitment that Gandhi could take Ansari and Ali Imam or at least Ansari, with him as Congress delegate to London. Thus Gandhi's plan to show that the nationalist Muslims did not agree with the Aga Khan-Fazli group had been frustrated. 'I pity Gandhi,' Mitter added. 'This Fazli is a devil and the Viceroy dances to his tune. Willingdon too acted cleverly. At their meetings in May and July, he was non-committal and almost charged Gandhi with breach of faith by pointing out that the main purpose of the Gandhi–Irwin Pact was to enable Gandhi to participate in the Round Table Conference".[19]

It is difficult to understand as to how a shrewd politician like Gandhi could digest such a remark from Willingdon when it was Irwin who had initiated a dialogue with Gandhi and not the other way round. He could have very well withdrawn from participating in the Conference and agitated against the British policy of giving greater weightage to extremist Muslims. But, it seems, the prospect of going to London as the sole representative of the vast Congress organisation held its sway on Gandhi. So, he went as a single delegate from the Congress to take part in the Round Table Conference (Pandit Malaviya and Smt. Sarojini Naidu went in their personal capacity).

Incidentally, most of the British officers in India considered that the Viceroy had been foolish to parley with an already defeated enemy who was only playing time. They did not realise what a brilliant tactical advantage Irwin had achieved in the results of the parley,[20] says a British historian. The truth of this analysis would be revealed when one would see how a defeated and humbled Gandhi returned to India only to resume his non-cooperation and civil disobedience movement.

The second Round Table Conference was held from Sept 7 to Dec 1, 1931. The communal question remained as tricky as before. There was also no guarantee for a federal constitution for India. Disillusionment came to Gandhi early, when the provisional agreement reached with some Muslim delegates in the first week of Ocotber was disowned by the others under the influence, according to Jinnah, of the Aga Khan and of remote control by Sir Fazli. The effort of a settlement had been trumped with the crescent card. Gandhi realised too well that besides playing the crescent card, the British were out to split the Hindus into caste Hindus and the Depressed Classes."[21] On Nov. 13, Ramsay MacDonald announced that the previous evening an agreed formula embodying the demands of the minorities had been formally presented to him by the Aga Khan and that he would give a Communal Award on his own should the Indian delegates fail to agree by a given date.[22]

On his part, Fazli Husain said that the efforts to find a communal settlement failed because Gandhi wanted the Muslims to present a common demand. This, in his opinion, was like the British wanting the Hindus and the Muslims to prepare an agreed constitution or at least a communal settlement. One dissenting Jinnah, he said, was bad enough, and he did not want the Muslims to speak in different voices in the London conference.

On learning that the Round Table Conference had virtually collapsed, the Congress Working Committee asked Gandhi to come back. Jawaharlal even announced a fresh passive resistance campaign without waiting for Gandhi's return. Gandhi came back on 28 December 1931. Congress was banned. Thousands of its workers and leaders were arrested. Women in thousands came out in the open to offer Satyagraha. Congressmen planned to hold their annual session in Delhi in April 1932 in defiance of the ban. Arrangements were made secretly. On the appointed day, about

1000 participants, including Pandit Madan Mohan Malaviya, Congress President (designate) were arrested.

Here, it will be important to note the submission made by Dr. Dutt, who represented the Indian Christians at the Round Table conference. Opposing the sectarian demands of various other minority representatives, he said:

> "If these suggestions are implemented, India will be splintered into religion-based groups. According to the League of Nation's charter, the minorities can merely demand the right to follow their religion and freedom from coercion by the follwers of other faiths. However, these charters preferred by the parasites growing on the body of Indian nation in the name of community and religion contain such aggressive claims that if they were to be conceded the very name of democracy will cease to exist in the constitution".*

The Third Round Table Conference in November 1932 was a farce as neither the Congress, nor the British Labour Party, nor the Princes attended it. Even here, the communal problem remained unresolved.

COMMUNAL AWARD AND POONA PACT

As no decision could be arrived at about the communal question the British Prime Minister, Ramsay MacDonald, announced his Communal Award. It not only upheld separate electorate and other safeguards for the Muslims but also categorised the Depressed Classes as a separate political entity and granted them a separate electorate. It was too much for Gandhi. He was in Yeravada jail. There itself, Gandhi started his fast unto death on Sept 20,1932. He said if this move succeeded it would be the end of the Hindu community and of nationalism. Hindu leaders from all parts came to Poona to persuade him to give up the fast. Orthodox Hindus threw open the temples to untouchables. On 26 September there was the famous Poona Pact between Gandhi and B.R. Ambedkar, the leader of the Depressed Classes. With this pact, the Depressed Classes remained in the general electorate but were given a larger share of seats and right to choose their

---

* Sandhya Choudhari, Gandhi and Partition of India, p. 20, quoted by BN Jog, Threat of Islam, p. 220.

candidates in the electorates against the seats reserved out of the Hindu quota.

In passing, it must be stated that Gandhi's hold on the Hindu masses, during 1931-32, was so great that his word was treated as the gospel truth. At the time of the first Round Table Conference, Gandhi in the midst of the salt Satyagraha, was in jail. Dr. Munje, the president of the Hindu Mahasabha, went to the Conference and vehemently opposed Jinnah's charter of 14 demands, point by point, but he, along with others who had gone to London was named a traitor. Those who courted arrest in India were treated as patriots. Since the majority of the blind followers of Gandhi belonged to Depressed Classes, the intention of the British Government was to cut Gandhi to size by separating them under B.R. Ambedkar, letting Gandhi to be the leader of only the upper caste Hindus.

However B.R. Ambedkar's views on the communal award may be read with interest. He said:

> "It grants the Muslim minorities in the Hindu provinces the right of self determination in the matter of electorates, but it does not grant the same right to the Hindu minorities in the Muslim provinces. In the Hindu province, the Muslim minority is allowed to choose the kind of electorates it wants and the Hindu majority is not permitted to have any say in the matter. But in the Muslim provinces, it is the Muslim majority which is allowed to choose the kind of electorates it prefers and the Hindu minority is not permitted to have any say in the matter. Thus, the Muslims in the Muslim provinces having been given both statutory majority (in relation to Hindus) and separate electorates, the communal Award must be said to impose upon the Hindu minorities under the Muslim rule, which they can neither alter nor influence."[23]

If Gandhi were really concerned with the Hindu community or the national unity, he would have fasted also against the separate electorate and reservation for the Muslims whose evil effects are given in Dr. Ambedkar's words quoted above. The truth is that Gandhi felt the threat to his supreme leaderdhip which rested on large crowds made up of the huge mass of poor backward, and depressed class people who by a stroke of pen, were sought to move to a different camp.

Thus, the question of the Depressed Classes was settled between Gandhi and Dr. B.R. Ambedkar and it was also accepted by the British Government. But, the part of the communal award relating to Muslims remained yet to be decided. Every national leader, except the Muslims, was against it. Gandhi described it as higly anti-national and grossly unjust to the Hindus. Jawaharlal also said: The communal Award is an utter negation of nationalism and is meant to divide Hindustan into communal compartments and give strength to disruptive tendencies and thus to strengthen the hold of British Imperialism. Rabindranth Tagore felt greatly pained and wrote to Pandit Madan Mohan Malaviya to do everything to hold up implementation of the communal award. The storm of opposition could very well be discerned by the British government. The Secretary of State for India, Samuel Hoare, tutored the Aga Khan to so manage that the Congress did not oppose the Award. The Aga Khan and Jinnah, then at London, wired Dr. M.A. Ansari to persuade the Congress to accept the Award in the interest of Hindu-Muslim unity'. (Indeed, whenever Congress wanted to do something against the Hindu interest it was always justified in the name of Hindu-Muslim unity). Before it, Dr. Ansari since 1928 had been one of the opponents to the separate electorates for the Muslims and that is why Gandhi had proposed to take him to the Round Table Conference. But on receipt of the message from London, Ansari changed his stance. It was pointed out to the Congress leaders that they had to choose between the Muslim support and the national interest. The matter was fiercely debated in the Congress Working Committee held at Wardha on June 12 and 13, 1934 and again on June 17 and 18, at Bombay. Only Pandit Madan Mohan Malaviya and Shri. M.S. Aney kept on opposing the Communal Award and both of them tendered their resignations, Malaviya from the presidentship of the Congress Parliamentary Board and Aney from the Congress Working Committee. They were prevailed upon not to press for their resignations. The Working Committee passed the following flabbergasting resolution:

> "The Congress claims to represent equally all the communities composing the Indian Nation and, therefore, in view of the division of opinion, can neither accept nor reject the communal Award as long as the division of opinion lasts."

What a novel way to let the British government go ahead with its scheme of the communal Award ! Is there still any doubt that the Congress was in no way different from the Muslim League, except that its membership was open to non-Muslims too and,secondly, it was antagonising the British whereas the League was fraternising them, for the same purpose of promoting Muslim interests. The discussions with Pandit Malaviya and Shri Aney were renewed at the Benaras meeting of the Working Committee held from July 27 to 30,1934. All attempts were made to retain the co-operation of Pandit Malaviya and Aney. Gandhi mediated and evolved a formula that even those candidates who had"conscientious objection to the Working Committee's resolution on the Communal Award" would be allowed to contest election on Congress ticket. The formula did not find favour with Malaviya and Aney and both of them resigned from their respective posts. They summoned a conference of Congressmen and others which met at Calcutta on the 18 and 19 August under the presidentship of Pandit Malaviya. The conference decided that a separate party should be constituted with the object of carrying on agitation against the Communal Award. It also requested the Working Committee of the Congress to call a meeting of the AICC with a view to revising its resolution on the Award. The Working Committee which met on 25 September 1934 at Wardha, excused itself from calling the meeting of the A.I.C.C.[24]

REFERENCES

1. D.G. Tendulkar, Mahatma, Vol. II, p. 435.
2. Ibid, p. 439.
3. Lal Bahadur, Muslim League, p. 192.
4. Durga Das, India from Curzon to Nehru, pps. 144-145.
5. B.N. Jog, Threat of Islam, pps. 197-198.
6. Wali Khan, Facts are Facts, the Untold Story of India's Partition p. 6.
7. Ibid.
8. Ibid, p. 7.
9. Ibid, pp. 7-8.
10. Wali Khan, Facts are Facts... p. 8.
11. Ibid, p. 9.
12. Pattabhi Sitaramayya, History of Congress, Vol. I, p. 520 (footnote)

13. Durga Das, India from Curzon to Nehru, p. 133.
14. Durga Das, India from Curzon to Nehru, p. 134.
15. Michel Edwardes, The Last Years of British India, p. 63.
16. Durga, Das, India from Curzon to Nehru, p. 136-137.
17. Michel Edwardes, The Last years of British India, p. 65.
18. Durga Das, India from Curzon to Nehru, p. 137.
19. —do— p. 160.
20. Michael Edwardes, The Last Years of British India, pps. 68-69.
21. Durga Das, India from Curzon to Nehru, p. 161.
22. Ibid.
23. Dr. Rajendra Prasad, India Divided, p. 130.
24. The account is based on Pattabhi Sitaramayya's History of Congress, Vol. II.

Chapter IX

CONGRESS CONFUSION

In 1934, Gandhi resigned from the Congress membership, though he continued to be the remote control of the organisation.[1] About the same time, Jinnah became the supreme leader of the Muslim League.

Jinnah was born on the Christmas day of 1876 at Karachi in a middle class Khoja family. He was first educated at the Gokul Das Primary School, Bombay, and sent to England, at the age of 16, to qualify for the Bar, which he did with distinction. When Gandhi arrived in India in 1915, Jinnah was already one of the leading personalities of the Congress. When Muslim League decided to amend its constitution drastically, in 1910-11, Jinnah was invited to render his expert advice. At his instance, Muslim League adopted self government as one of its objectives, but he was formally enrolled as member of the Muslim League in 1913. As a nationalist Muslim, he had good rapport with Lokamanya Tilak. These two leaders and Ms. Annie Besant played the leading role in bringing about the Lucknow Pact in 1916. Later, after Tilak's demise, Jinnah felt neglected, even humiliated, by the Congress led by Gandhi, especially in the matter of non-cooperation movement of 1920-21 which he opposed from the very beginning. On the sixth anniversay of late G.K. Gokhale on February 19, 1921, Jinnah told his audience of his conviction that Gandhi's programme was taking them to a wrong channel. Jinnah's disenchantment with the Congress grew more and more ultimately he snapped his ties with it. For once, he took sanyas from politics and settled in England as a leading lawyer. He aspired to become a judge of the Privy Council of the U.K. But, after the Round Table Conference, Jinnah was called upon to forge unity among various Muslim factions and lead the Muslim League as the sole representative of the Muslim community. As ambitious a man as he was , he found a great opportunity of avenging himself upon Gandhi and Jawaharlal Nehru by turning himself into a fanatic Muslim,though religious fanaticism was never his nature. In his new role, he was greatly helped by the British. In 1937, Jinnah proclaimed that his enemy was the Congress, implying thereby that his enemy's enemy, namely, the British were his friends. Congress, he said, was a Hindu body championing the cause of "Hindustan for Hindus" and wanted to liquidate the League.[1] The truth, however, is that neither Jinnah was a fanatic Muslim nor Congress of Gandhi a Hindu body; both wore a deceptive mask. If the Congress were a Hindu body, orthodox and fanatic Muslims like Maulana Mohammed Ali, Maulana Hasarat Mohani, Maulana Abul Kalam Azad would have left the Congress, not Jinnah. In fact, Jinnah and Maulana Azad never saw eye to eye. But Congress was an organisation in which neither the nationalist Muslims nor the nationalist Hindus (like Pandit Madan Mohan Malaviya, Lala Lajpat Rai) had proper placement.

It needs to be noted that in the second civil dis-obedience movement launched by Gandhi in 1930, to achieve the goal of independence, the Muslims-except those in the North West Frontier Province-did not participate. The failure of the second Round Table Conference led to the communal award, granting separate electorates not only to Muslims but also to other minorities, like, the Sikhs, the Christians, Europeans, the Anglo Indians. The matter of Depressed Classes was resolved, as stated above, through the Poona Pact.

1935 ACT

After the failure of the Third Round Table Conference, towards the end of 1932, the British Government came out with the Government of India Act, 1935, which incorporated the reforms of the earlier Acts and included some more. It provided for a Federation, taking the Provinces and the Indian States as its units. It was made optional for the Indian States to join the Federation or not. The rulers of the princely states did not give their consent and the Federation envisaged by the Act did not materialise. Legislative powers were divided into three parts, the Federal List, the Provincial List and the Concurrent List, as in the post independence Indian constitution. The executive authority of the Provinces were to be exercised by the Governors who were to act with the advice of the ministers responsible to the Provincial legislatures. The Central legislature was to be of two Houses-the Federal Assembly and the Council of States, like the present Lok Sabha and the Rajya Sabha. Dyarchy at the centre, with the reserved subjects was retained but dyarchy in the provinces was abolished. The overall authority of the British Parliament was also retained. The British thought this scheme as the last stage before granting Dominion status to India.

ASSEMBLY ELECTION, 1937

The A.I.C.C. decided to participate in the elections to the Assemblies. The civil disobedience movement was withdrawn. In the annual Congress session at Lucknow, in the middle of April 1936, Jawaharlal Nehru, in his presidential address, characterised the 1935 Act as a "charter of slavery", and gave vent to his Socialistic ideas. A motion was moved by Nehru's socialist group to wreck the new Constitution and refuse ministerial responsibility, but it was rejected by 487 votes to 255. It was indeed a vote of no-confidence against Nehru. In a special Muslim League session at Bombay, Jinnah opposed the federal part of the Act, but favoured contesting the elections to the provincial legislatures.

Sardar Patel, Rajendra Prasad and C. Rajagopalachari were all opposed to Nehru's socialistic ideas. Patel and Prasad inaugurated the election campaign in Bombay on July 7, 1936. In order to neutralise the Hindu Mahasabha's appeal to the Hindu electorate, the Congress gave up its neutral attitude to Communal Award.[3] In its election manifesto, the Congress stated that it would seek to wreck the Reforms Act. The League on the other hand promised to work towards provincial autonomy for all it was worth.

Interestingly, the selection of the President for the next annual session of the Congress assumed considerable political significance. Majority of the Provincial Congress Committees favoured Patel, but Gandhi decided to give Nehru another term but he also knew from last year's defeat of Nehru's socialist group that Nehru stood no chance. So, using his personal weight, Gandhi persuaded Patel to withdraw in favour of Nehru. Patel, however, made it clear that he did not accept Nehru's ideas of socialism nor of wrecking the reforms Act.[4] In this way, Nehru was again made President of the Congress in its annual session held at

Faizpur in the middle of January 1937. In his presidential address, he conceded that the Congress stood for a democratic state and not socialism and that the issue of office acceptance would be decided after the results of the poll were known. It was decided to observe hartal on 1st April to mark the country's protest against the imposition of the new Constitution on that day. It had a great favourable impact in the election campaign of the Congress. The Hindu electorate enthusiastically supported Congress under the impression that it would get the obnoxious communal award annulled.

Only 27 per cent of the adult population (numbering about 35 million) was entitled to vote. The election results surprised every one. Congress got clear majority in six of the eleven Provinces, namely, Bombay, Bihar, the Central Provinces (MP), Madras, Orissa, and the United Provinces (UP). It emerged as the single largest party in Assam. Gandhi had kept himself aloof from the election campaign. Jawaharlal's position rose to unprecedented political heights, next only to Gandhi's. The Muslim League could not get a majority even in the Muslim majority Provinces. The Krishak Praja Party of Fazlul Haque in Bengal and the Unionist Party of Sir Sikandar Hayat Khan in the Punjab got a majority. In the remaining three, the seats were shared between different parties and independents. Notable features were that, out of a total 836 non-Muslim seats for provincial assemblies Congress won 715 and, out of the 482 Muslim reserved seats, Congress contested 58 and got only 26. The Muslim League got 108 of the Muslim seats. In Bengal and Punjab, Congress failed to win a single Muslim seat. In U.P. Muslim Congressmen, like Khaliq-uz-Zaman, Nawab Mohammed Ismail and others, contested the election on Muslim League's tickets.[5] This is a proof enough that Congress represented only the Hindu community. The Muslims refused to accept Congress leadership. At the same time, it was wrong to believe that the Muslim League represented the entire Muslim community in India. The League got some noticeable success only in U.P. and that too because of the support lent to it by the Congress and its ally the Jamiat-ul-Ulema-i-Hind. It had, in fact, arrived at a political understanding with the Congress. Maulana Azad had assured it of two seats in the ministry to be formed by the Congress after the elections. However, at the time of ministry formation, Jawaharlal had other considerations and he offered only one seat to the League in proportion to the assembly seats it had actually won. Congress also tried defection of certain League members to its own fold. The incident caused a great rift between the two major political parties. Jinnah exploited it to his great political advantage. Maulana Abul Kalam Azad lamented over this act of Nehru and accused him of giving a new lease of life to the Muslim League.[6]

But, Congress confusion showed its ugly face once again. It refused to form its ministries in the Provinces unless an assurance was given that the Governors would not use their special powers or would not set aside the advice tendered by the Council of Ministers. Naturally, the Governors referred the matter to the Viceroy. The Viceroy gave a decision in favour of the Congress, but three months were lost in the process. In the meantime, the Governors had invited the leaders of the second largest party to form interim governments. This afforded a much needed opportunity to the Muslim League to secure a foothold in the Muslim majority provinces by winning over the non-Congress and non-Muslim League chief ministers in Bengal, Sindh and the Punjab.

On assuming office in the Provinces, the Congress started on a programme of subverting the Constitution. In the words of Jawaharlal Nehru, the Congress had joined "for fighting the new Constitution and ending it".[7] The left wing of the Congress in U.P. was more particular in initiating a campaign for a socialistic programme. The League, on the other hand, was fast consolidating its position. In the ensuing byelections, all its candidates were returned.

In September 1939, that is, just about two years after the Congress had formed its ministries, World War II broke out. This time, Turkey was on the British side. The U.K. Government declared war on Germany and appealed to all the members of the British Commonwealth to do the same. Following the appeal, the Viceroy himself declared war on Germany. Taking the excuse that the Viceroy had made India a party to the war without consulting its elected representatives, all the Congress ministries resigned. The Muslim League rejoiced and celebrated the event as 'the day of deliverance'. It remained in office as a staunch ally of the British Government which resulted in a yet stronger British-Muslim League combine. The Congress and Gandhi did not realise the bare fact that the Viceroy had simply done what he should have naturally done under the powers vested in him on the Indian part of the British Empire. India had not yet been granted the 'Dominion Status', like Canada, to make it obligatory on the Viceroy to obtain the approval of the national Assembly. Failure of the Khilafat movement had already distanced a big chunk of the Muslims from the 'Hindu Congress'. Now, the British Government turned totally hostile to it. The Muslim League could now speak with an air of superiority and confidence built up in association with the British.

To fight a war from an Indian base, the British needed both to hold firm at the Centre and to reassert control over the provinces. "With the War on its way, Delhi judged that Congress would demand a high price for its collaboration and might threaten to pull out its provincial ministries. But far from being a frightening prospect, this threat was good news for Delhi, since even collaborating Congress provinces were likely to be more of a nuisance in running India during the war than provinces deprived of their Congress Ministries. By April 1939 Delhi had persuaded Parliament to give it powers to take over and run the provinces if the need arose. So, the Viceroy and his advisors were ready, indeed eager, to ditch the eight Congress ministries."[8]

The stature of Jinnah (one time follower of Lokamanaya Tilak and a staunch nationalist) went on increasing day by day during the World War II in the manner Gandhi's position had risen during Woorld War I. V.P. Menon, the State Secretary during the partition period of 1946-47 remarked:

> "It is supreme example of that unrealistic, negative politics in which we are all too prone to indulge, and the outcome of which is sometimes very disconcerting, and even disastrous. The Congress was controlling eight provinces, covering half the country and it should have thought many times before abandoning such an advantageous position of great strength and bargaining power."[9]

It came out of a bureaucrat who worked with Sardar Patel in integrating the Indian princely states and could not use stronger words to condemn Congress action of resigning from their ministerial posts at the outbreak of the War. The outcome of the resignation was disastrous indeed. The British government, even the Labour members who had been supporting the Congress cause earlier, started hating not only the Congress but the whole Hindu community, for being irrational and irreconcilabe.

Jinnah, on the other hand, had been meeting the Viceroy and the British officers and assuring them of Muslim cooperation at the centre if only the British looked after their interests in the provinces and accepted the League as the sole spokesman of the Muslims.[10]

Congress opposed League's demand for Pakistan. Its own demands were:

(i) India should be treated as a free nation, with complete independence after the war;
(ii) An interim national government should be formed for the duration of the war; and
(iii) A Constituent Assembly should be elected to frame India's Constitution.

A meeting between the Viceroy and Gandhi was held in August, 1940, but failed on the very first point. The British government promised Dominion Status within a year after the end of the war and some immediate changes in the Viceroy's Executive Council. It badly wanted the Congress to resume their ministries in the provinces and support the British efforts in the war. Congress attitude was one of belligerancy. After the negotiation failed, it resorted to individual Satyagraha of which Gandhi was made the leader. In 1941, the USSR (now defunct) was invaded by Germany. Consequently, the Communist Party of India, which had till then been anti-British, also turned pro-British.

As a matter fact, the Congress was fighting a lost battle against the Muslim League. It will be more appropriate to say that the Congress was giving only a mock fight to the Muslim League. Because of its own support to Pan-Islamism and conceding separate electorate for the Muslims the Congress had no ground to effectively oppose the basic theme of Pakistan. Only the Hindu Mahasabha leader, V.D. Savarkar, had the countering arguments, but the Hindu Mahasabha was eclipsed by the Congress. In his view, India was territorially one country and one nation of which about 70 per cent, following the Hindu religion, regarded India as their very mother while she was the motherland of the remaining 30 per cent too; that the Muslims or any other section of the people were territorially Hindus; and that none had the right to seek bifurcation of the motherland.

Historians are unanimous that the rejection of Viceroy's offer of August 1940 was a great mistake. By resuming power in the provinces, the Congress would have gained a lot of strength and even bargaining power as against the British government and the Muslim League. Jinnah rightly felt happy with the Congress dithering attitude even at this stage. The movement of individual Satyagraha (civil disobedience) started by Gandhi, did not evoke much enthusiasm as the earlier ones, 10 and 20 years back.

REFERENCES

1. Gandhi had written a long letter to Congress President, enumerating various cases of corruption and misconduct, contrary to Gandhian ideals, and then stating about his inability to continue Congress membership.

2. Durga Das, India from Curzon to Nehru, p. 182.
3. Ibid p. 175.
4. Ibid p. 175.
5. Ibid p. 181.
6. Maulana Azad, India Wins Freedom, pp. 160-161.
7. B.N. Puri, A Study in Indian History, p. 246.
8. Ayesha Jalal, The Sole Spokesman, Jinnah, the Muslim League. p. 45.
9. B.N. Puri, A Study of Indian History, p. 248.
10. Ayesha Jalal, The Sole Spokesman....... p. 45.

Chapter X

MUSLIM PERSONAL LAW

Political analysts and historians till now have paid scant heed to the part played by the innocuous looking Muslim Personal Law (Application of Shariat) Act 1937 in the creation of Pakistan and the continuing Hindu-Muslim conflict in the truncated India.

The Muslim League had been in existence since 1906. It was getting all encouragement from the British and money from various Muslim princes and nawabs. Still the Muslim unity was only on paper. As earlier explained in Chapter III they were no less divided than the Hindus. All the League's achievements upto 1935 were due solely to the British efforts and patronage on the queer logic of protecting the minorities rights. As shown in the last chapter, the performance of the Muslim League in 1937 general elections was dismal; it did not attract even one fourth of the Muslim voters. How is it that in the next general elections of 1945/46, the same Muslim League swept the polls? It won all the 30 Muslim seats of the Central Assembly and 427 out of 482 reserved Muslim seats in the Provincial Assemblies. What made this tremendous change? The Muslim Personal law, the Shariat Act of 1937, is the answer. The Statement of Objects and Reasons of this Act read as follows:

> "For several years past it has been the cherished desire of the Muslims of British India that Customary Law should in no case take the place of Muslim Personal Law. The matter has been repeatedly agitated in the press as well as on the platform. The Jamiat-ul-Ulema-i-Hind, the greatest Moslem religious body has supported the demand and invited the attention of all concerned to the urgent necessity of introducing a measure to this effect. Customary Law is a

misnomer inasmuch as it has not any sound basis to stand upon and is very much liable to frequent changes and cannot be expected to attain at any time in the future that certainty and definiteness which must be the characteristic of all laws. The status of Muslim women under the so called Customary Law is simply disgraceful. All the Muslim Women Organisations have therefore condemned the Customary Law as it adversely affects their rights. They demand that the Muslim Personal Law (Shariat) should be made applicable to them. The Muslim Personal Law will automatically raise them to the position to which they are naturally entitled. In addition to this present measure, if enacted, women have very salutary effect on society because it would ensure certainty and definiteness in the mutual rights and obligations of the public. Muslim Personal Law (Shariat) exists in the form of a veritable code, and is too well known to admit of any doubt or to entail any great labour in the shape of research, which is the chief feature of Customary Law."[1]

In the above text, while it is correct that the Jamiat-ul-Ulem-i-Hind, patronised by the Congress, and the Mullahs and Maulvis of all hues, wanted replacement of the Customary Law by the Shariat law, it is incorrect to say that there was a pressing demand from the Muslim community or Muslim women. League's charter of 14 demands did include one as "Protection should be afforded to Muslim religion, culture and personal law" but it did not mean enactment of a Shariat Act to replace the Customary Law. The Muslim women had no voice of their own at the time. It is only now that a few of them have come into the open but they have joined hands in the cause of redemption of the Muslim women from the vagaries of the Shariat law.

Indeed, the Customary laws of the Muslims as well as the Hindus had been causing difficulties for the judges. The right remedy was to evolve a common civil code applicable to all.

In fact, the Customary Law of the Muslims was based on Shariat law but it gave recognition to the usage and customs generally followed by the Indian Muslims, on the pattern of their Hindu neighbours, in matters of marriage, inheritance and guardianship. Likewise, the Customary Law of Hindus, originating in the Manusmriti, included the usage and customs which had come up during the intervening period of about 2,000 years. As explained in the introductory chapter, Muslims of India were divided in various groups which broadly came under two main heads, one carrying foreign ancestory and the other of local converts from various Hindu Varnas (Castes) and creeds. All these sections carried much of their native customs which did not strictly conform to the Shariat of Arab origin. Jinnah's own family had been Hindu just one or two generations ago. Similary, Sheikh Abdullah of Kashmir was a descendant of a Kashmiri Brahmin and so was Sir Mohammed Iqbal. Fazli Husain's Hindu ancestory has already been stated in the earlier pages. (It is, however, no matter of consolation because many ambitious Hindu converts to Islam proved more destructive to Hindus and Hindu religion than the Muslims of foreign origin).

The Shariat Act sought to bring all the various categories of Muslims under a single Islamic law (of the Hanifi school), removing all traces of the native Hindu traditions and culture. It was, therefore, more of a political move rather than an act of social reform.

Section 2 of the Shariat Act says that, notwithstanding any customs or usage to the contrary, in all questions (save questions relating to agricultural land)regarding intestate succession, special property of females, including personal property, marriage and divorce, the rule for decision where the parties are Muslims shall be the Muslim Personal Law, i. e. Shariat. In legal terms, the Shariat law is to apply only in civil matters specifically stated in the Act, other matters being governed by general secular laws. But, the matter is not that simple. The Shariat includes the whole of the Quran, the Hadith and the Sunna and it covers almost every aspect of Muslim life, including politics, most of which are beyond the scope of the written constitution of a secular state. Such matters, before the Act, were decided on the principles of equity, justice and good conscience. The Shariat Act bade farewell to these principles.

The Shariat divides the world into two camps, Dar-ul-Islam (abode of Islam) and Dar-ul-Harb (abode of war or enemy country). A country where Muslims reside but are not its rulers, is called Dar-ul-Harb. If the Indian Muslims treat India as a Darul-Harb, on the authority of the Shariat, and make preparations to wage a war to turn it into a Dar-ul-Islam, what would a non-Muslim government that pays all respects to Shariat will do? The attitude of the present Indian Government towards J & K provides a clue to the answer.

Thus, placement of the Shariat directly on the Statute book resulted only in mobilising the Muslims against the Hindu thought and Hindu India and in raising the social, legal and religious status of the Ulema, the Mullah and the Maulvi. Simultaneously, the British Government recognised Muslim League as the sole representative of the political ambitions of the Muslim community. The word spread that those who opposed the creation of Pakistan were traitors or kafirs. Soon, the Muslims started joining the League in large numbers. As soon as the League put up the demand of Pakistan, a Dar-ul-Islam, the Ulemas, the Mullahs and the Maulvis also started joining it. Those who did not join supported it from outside. It was the political fallout, or say "Shararat", of the Shariat. On the social plane, Shariat prohibited the Muslims from adopting the life style or copying the non-Muslim customs. The Ulemas were emboldened to coerce the Muslims, individually and collectively, to shed all signs or beliefs which appeared not to conform to the Quranic injunctions and to use only those marks which would show them distinct from the non-Muslims. Those not falling in line could be penalised or excommunicated through a '*fatwa*' by any Islamic theological institute or a mere Mullah anywhere in India. The extra-judicial authority of issuing '*fatwa*' has been extensively used during the past few years, even on trifling grounds. Under fear of ex-communication or the like, the ordinary Muslim follows the dotted line of the Mullahs on a set pattern. Those who defy, do it at the risk of their life. The law enforcing agencies and the judiciary to protect civil liberties have been mere mute spectators. The improvement in the status of the Muslim women, highlighted in the Statement of the Reasons and objects of the Shariat Act, has remained a far cry.

The general belief that Jinnah re-organised the Muslim League and gave it its strength is erroneous. Though a great orator and schemer, Jinnah did not have the capacity to organise. He was very impulsive and impatient. Following an incident with Lord Willingdon when he was the Governor of Bombay, Jinnah left India for London around 1930. He took part in the Round Table Conference of 1930-32 in his individual capacity. During 1931, in an informal meet with Durga Das, Jinnah said: "The Congress will not come to terms with me because my following is small; the Muslims do not accept my views for they take their orders from the Deputy Commissioner (District Magistrate)."[2] Jinnah also disclosed that, on the communal question, the British heavily relied on Fazli Husain and the Aga Khan. Jinnah came to India around 1935 after Lord Willingdon had left India. On 9 November 1937, Jinnah told the then Viceroy (Lord Linlithgow) that the British were not paying sufficient attention to the Muslims and there was the real danger of the Muslims being driven into the arms of the Congress.[3] Clearly, Jinnah owed his initial political clout to the British but his mass following after 1937 was generated by the Mullahs, Moulavis, Pirs and Ulemas.

At the times elections for the Central Assembly and the Provincial Legislatures were held during Dec 1945-Feb 1946 (which resulted in Jinnah of the Muslim League becoming the sole spokesman of the Muslims on all India basis), the Muslim League did neither have adequate organisational set up in the provinces nor funds as compared with the Congress. Most of the work to bring the Muslim masses in favour of the Muslim League was done by the Mullahs, the Pirs and the religious heads. There were large scale desertions from the Unionist Party of the Punjab and the Praja Krishak Party of Bengal in favour of the League. Ayesha Jalal states:

"Sensational stories of conversion to the League took the provincial League leaders by surprise since their workers had not yet reached the villages in adequate numbers...And since no one could actually specify their reasons for supporting the League, it was right and proper that Jinnah should have the credit...

"Indeed the Provincial League (of Punjab) had no programme for running the elections. Its cover was patchy; its coffers were empty. Yet it had the smell of a party about to have victory thrust upon it...No one denies that the choices of the Pirs mattered; but this was part and parcel of local patronage systems, with Pir and landlords working hand in glove, rather than the profane and the religious in some improbable conflict in the plains of the Punjab...Of course there was an appeal to 'religion in danger'; it was an obvious cry. The League encouraged the prelates to give fatwas in its favour. Some propagandists threatened the voters that if they did not back the League they would cease to be Muslims; their marriages would be invalid and, if this did not frighten them, then they were told they would face 'ex-communication including a refusal to allow their dead to be buried in Muslim graveyards', and be debarred from joining in mass Muslim prayers...Unionists too had to become men of the Book. Khizar peppered his speeches with catchy quotes from the Quran to prove that Allah was 'Rabb-ul-Alammen', the Lord of everything and everyone, not the exclusive commander of the Faithful; a more logical line was that the Unionist party had nothing against Pakistan...

"The voters were told that the choice was simple, between 'Pakistan' and 'Kufristan' (the land of the infidels). ...the League won all three seats to the assembly from Jhelum district. Another example of the way pirs and biraderis worked together to the League's advantage was in Jhang district. With Shah Jiwana Bukhari Sayed Pir's help, two candidates related to pirs won both seats. ...The most spectacular success, however, was in the districts of Multan, Jhelum, Jhang and Karnal, where the League did best because the leading pir families decided to back it.

"While some of the members were men of unquestionable religious authority and power in local and provincial politics, others like the Nawab of Mamdot solemnly took the horrific title of the Pir of Mamdot Sharif; Shaukat Hayat became Sajjada Nashin of Wah Sharif; Firoz Khan Noon became the Sajjada Nashin of Sargodha Sharif and by far the most ostentatious title was appropriated by that worldly figure...Ibrahim Ali Chishti who was designated as Fazl-i-Hind Sajjada Nashin of Paisa Akbar Sharif..."[4]

Similar phenomena worked in Bengal and elsewhere.

Thus, it was the Shariat Act which worked as a strong net to rope in the Muslims to support the Muslim League in the 'holy' cause of Pakistan. The Muslims still remaining in Congress, like Maulana Azad and others, attempted in vain to convince the Muslims that the Congress offered a better scope for them in an united India. Indeed, they believed that through the Congress, they could turn the whole of Hindustan into a Dar-ul-Islam whereas in the League's scheme of Pakistan the Muslims would have to be satisfied with only a small part thereof leaving the greater part of their Muslim brethren in the Hindu part of Hindustan at the mercy of Hindu 'wolves'.

REFERENCES

1. Gazette of India, 1935, Pt.V, p. 136.
2. Durga Das, India from Curzon to Nehru, p. 155.
3. Wali Khan, Facts are Facts, p. 13.
4 Ayesha Jalal, The Sole Spokesman, Jinnah, the Muslim League, etc. p. 145.-148.

Chapter XI

TOWARDS PARTITION OF INDIA

As already explained, the election results of 1937 were very damaging to the reputation of the Muslim League as it could not get a majority even in a single Muslim majority province. Jinnah's main job, therefore, was to discredit the Congress governments in the provinces, especially in U.P. To substantiate his charges, Jinnah appointed a Committee under a Muslim landlord, the Raja of Pirpur, to find evidence of atrocities committed on Muslims. The charges made were false (as later found out), but Jinnah put in all his skill as a lawyer to use the report against the Congress and to stress that the safeguards provided in the 1935 Act were very inadequate. The Congress at the time was also in a bad shape because of the contest for party leadership between Subhas Bose and Jawaharlal Nehru in which Gandhi put his weight on Nehru's side.

All the Congress ministries had resigned soon after the outbreak of World War II. The Viceroy, however, wanting to mobilise all the resources for the war effort, invited Gandhi, Jinnah and the Chancellor of the Chamber of Princes simultaneously. It greatly enhanced the prestige and position of Jinnah as he was seated alongwith Gandhi, a position for which he had waited long. In January 1940,Jinnah made another effort to persuade the Congress to accept him as the sole representative of the Muslims, but he was rebuffed. The Congress elected Maulana Azad as its president for the next annual session scheduled to be held in March 1940 at Ramgarh to show that the Muslim League led by Jinnah was not the sole representative of the Muslims. In spite of yet another effort by the Viceroy in February 1940, the Congress did not agree to cooperate with the Government.

The Viceroy now invited Jinnah on March 13 to procure Muslim League's cooperation, both for fighting the war and for frustrating the Congress. These events during the initial period of the War established that there were four parties to the political power in India; the Congress, the Muslim League, the Indian princely states, and the British Raj (contemplating to gradually transfer its powers to Indians).

Gandhi attended the annual Congress session of Ramgarh in March 1940 after a gap of six years. Gandhi proposed that there should be a Constituent Assembly as a solution to the Hindu-Muslim problem. Gandhi explained that the eight million Muslims of India would have the right to self-determination through their elected representatives to that Assembly based on adult franchise. They could then decide either to remain in independent India as members of a joint family or seek partition if they wanted. By another resolution, the Congress reaffirmed its demand for complete independence and a Constituent Assembly on the basis of adult suffrage. It was decided to resort to civil disobedience for which Gandhi was authorised to choose the appropriate date and time.[1]

PAKISTAN RESOLUTION

About the same time, Muslim League held its session in Lahore on 23 March 1940, under the presidentship of Jinnah and passed the resolution declaring that no constitutional plan would be acceptable to the Muslims without acceptance of the principle that "geographically contiguous units are demarcated into regions which should be so constituted with such territorial readjustments that the areas in which the Muslims are numerically in a majority as in the North Western and Eastern zones of India should be grouped to constitute independent states in which the constituent units shall be autonomous and sovereign."[2] The resolution did not use the word 'Pakistan', but the whole scheme immediately got this name through the press, political leaders, and analysts.

While the Congress adopted a warring attitude towards the British, the Muslim League offered cooperation at an affordable price. The British thus relied on the League. The Viceroy, Lord Linlithgow, invited Jinnah on June 27, 1940. In a statement issued on August 8 next, Linlithgow declared that the British Government could not contemplate the transfer of power to any system of government "whose authority is directly denied by large and powerful elements in India's national life. Nor could they be parties to the coercion of such elements into submission to such a government."[3] It was, on the one hand, rejection of Congress claim to represent the will of the entire Indian population and, on the other, endorsement of Jinnah's view point that the interests of the minorities, especially of the Muslim, were not safe in the hands of a Congress government. In effect, it meant giving a veto power to the Muslims, as represented by Jinnah who, telling Durga Das in confidence, said that the League owed the concession to Leopold Amery, the Secretary of State for India. Jinnah added that "All I have to do now is to wait for the next Congress move and to counter it. I have no doubt that Nehru will play into my hands."[4]

At this time, some Congressmen and others suggested that a national government comprising nominees of the provincial administration should be formed for the duration of war. The idea did not find favour with the British government. In fact the British did not now need it because they were getting all the men and material for the conduct of the war against Germany. Nearly 20 lakh Indian soldiers had joined the Army. Material supply through the Indian contractors was also satisfactory.

The situation at the beginning of 1941 is well described by Durga Das:

> "The civil disobedience movement did not excite much public interest and was at a low ebb by the end of the year. Life moved at a dull pace even as the Government stepped up its repressive measures."[5]

The Congress had opted out of power and the Muslim League came to rule in three Muslim majority provinces. [6] The individual satyagraha launched by Congress since[7] 7 October 1940 did not create any appreciable stir. Till August 1941, only about 13,000 persons were behind the bars, an insignificant figure compared with the total membership of the Congress.

CRIPPS MISSION

Japan attacked Pearl Harbour on 6 December 1941. Consequently, United States of America entered into the war. India was also targetted by Japan. America increased its pressure on

UK to settle the Indian political question to ensure whole hearted support of the Indian people towards the war. Thus Cripps Mission came to India in March1942. President Roosevelt of America also sent his personal envoy, Colonel Louis Johnson, in April 1942, to Delhi to help resolve the deadlock between the British Government and the Indian leaders, which, according to a British author, was more like a "relationship of a long married couple who say they want a divorce, yet who are so used to each other's ways that they are reluctant to part".[7] In a way, Cripps proposals carried the August 1940 offer, meaning grant of freedom to India after cessation of war, through a constitutent assembly for creation of a new Indian Union in which the Indian Princely States also could participate. The provisions for protection of racial and religious minorities and right of the Provinces to stay out of the Union were retained as before. In the meantime, for the duration of the war, Britain was to retain control and direction of the defence of India as part of its responsibility to the global war effort. Jawaharlal Nehru, Maulana Azad and many other leaders, were favourably inclined to these proposals, but Gandhi termed the Cripps offer as "post-dated cheque on a crashing bank", fit only for rejection. On April 10, 1942, the Congress sent a reply to Cripps, stating that "...While we cannot accept the proposals you have made, we want to inform you that we are yet prepared to assume responsibility, provided a truly national Government is formed. We are prepared to put aside for the present all questions about the future, though, as we have indicated, we hold definite views about it. But in the present, the national Government must be a cabinet government with full powers and must not merely be a continuation of the Viceroy's Executive Council".[8] Cripps expressed his inability to grant a national Government during the war time.

RAJAJI'S ACCEPTANCE OF PAKISTAN

The Congress members of the Madras Legislative Assembly, led by C. Rajagopalachari, passed a resolution recommending acceptance of League's demand of Pakistan in principle and starting negotiation with it for the formation of a national government. This resolution created a stir in the Congress circles and it was rejected by the AICC in its meeting at Allahabad just the next week. Rajagopalachari could not bear the humiliation and resigned from the Congress.[9]

Looking at the background, it is difficult to blame Rajaji's resolution. In fact, Gandhi had himself conceded in the Congress session at Ramgarh in March 1940 the right of the Muslims to seek partition as members of a joint family. Further, Congress Working Committee's resolution of 2nd April 1942 had declared that "the Committee cannot think in terms of compelling the people of any territorial unit to remain in Indian Union against their declared and established will".[10] It had been drafted by Nehru himself. Later, on release from jail in 1944, Gandhi himself discussed "Pakistan scheme" with Jinnah. The fact is that there had been a good deal of change of outlook in the Congress camp towards Hindu-Muslim problem and, seeing the meteoric rise in League's popularity after its Pakistan resolution, many Congressmen became mentally prepared to give in, but they were mortally afraid to say so in public. The principle accepted by the Working Committee as quoted above was reiterated and elaborated in the AICC meeting held on 21 Sept. 1945, three months before the general elections. But all these resolutions of the Congress did not reach the common man.

On communal question, the Congress resolution of 2nd April 1942 itself echoed in the statement issued from the British Prime Minister's residence in London on December 6, 1946, at the end of the talks with Nehru, Jinnah, Liaqat Ali and Baldev Singh, in the following words:

> "Should a Constitution be framed by a Constitutent Assembly in which a large section of the Indian population had not been represented, His Majesty's Government could not contemplate as the Congress have stated they would not contemplate forcing such a Constitution upon any unwilling parts of the country".[11]

Seeing the Congress resolution of 2nd April 1942, Jinnah had said that he had won his battle as he saw in it Congress surrender to the concept of partition. Simultaneously, the Muslim League Executive Committee passed a resolution expressing "gratification that the possibility of Pakistan is recognised by implication by providing for the establishment of two or more unions in India" and rejecting the Cripps proposals for the reason that they were not open to modification.[12]

Rejection of Cripps proposals by Congress was hailed by Churchill, the British Prime Minister. He is reported to have danced around the cabinet room, singing, "No tea with treason, no truck with American or British-Labour sentimentality, but back to the solemn and exciting business of war".[13]

The Congress was awaiting orders from Gandhi who held that the British presence in India itself gave provocation to Japan to attack India. He demanded that either the British quit India or face a new civil disobedience. About the Hindu-Muslim question, Gandhi said that it was the creation of the British and once they left, the matter would be resolved between the two communities even if there was bloodshed and anarchy for a temporary period. Regarding Japanese invasion, the AICC at Allahabad in August 1942, passed a resolution that they would be met by non-violent non-cooperation. Government feared that the Congress was preparing for negotiations with the Japanese when they arrived. A police raid on the AICC offices discovered notes, by Gandhi himself, for a draft resolution assuring the Japanese that India bore no enmity to them and that if India were free, her first step would be to negotiate with Japan[14]

Under the leadership of Gandhi, Congress launched the 'Quit India' movement on August 8, 1942, with the slogan 'do or die'. Linlithgow's Government was anticipating it and, just the next morning, arrested Gandhi and all members of the Congress Working Committee. The Congress organisation was banned. With all the important Congress leaders in jail, the 'Quit India' movement turned into a mass frenzy. The Government took all repressive measures to control the upsurge. In a period of two months, the movement almost fizzled out.

Attempts were, however, being made in London to resolve the political stalemate in India. So, Reginald Coupland brought out a new plan which sought to resolve the problem by dividing India into four broad geographical regions—the Indus basin, the Gangetic plane, the delta of Brahmaputra, and the Deccan plateau. Two of them were to have Muslim majority while the other two were Hindu majority regions. This, it was hoped, would keep a balance between the two major communities at the Centre. The plan also wanted a statutory guarantee for continuance of the work of the Christian missionaries in the hill tracts of Assam.

In October 1943, Lord Wavell took over from Linlithgow as the Viceroy. The Muslim League decided to establish an Action Committee to fight against any unitary constitution. Wavell released Gandhi in May 1944 ostensibly on grounds of ill-health, but in fact to use him as a mediator.[15] Shortly after his release, Gandhi went to meet Jinnah at Bombay. Talks between the two lasted for over a fortnight without any positive result. Asked about the meeting, Jinnah said, "What I am being offered is a truncated and moth-eaten Pakistan"[16] Durga Das says that when he met Gandhi in Bombay, the latter emphatically denied he had countenanced vivisection of India. Jinnah on the contrary, was jubilant and told Durga Das in Delhi, "You see, Gandhi has defined Pakistan for me. Gandhi asked me whether it would be a State where policy on defence and external affairs could be in conflict with India? I had only to answer, "yes."[17]

Maulana Azad called Gandhi's approach to Jinnah on this occasion "a great political blunder. It gave a new and added importance to Jinnah which he later exploited to the full".[18] M. Asaf Ali, still in Ahmednager jail, recorded in his diary dated 4 Oct. 1944, after seeing Gandhi-Jinnah correspondence in the news papers, "... Perhaps not until Hindustan and Pakistan have actually worked as free countries for some time will either Hindus or Muslims and others begin to see things in proper perspective. If so, well, let even a divided India begin to function as a cooperative commonwealth of sovereign states."[18a]

WAVELL PLAN (SHIMLA CONFERENCE)

After Gandhi-Jinnah talks had failed, Sir Tej Bahadur Sapru called a Non-Party Conference in November 1944 which set up a Standing Committee to examine the communal and minority questions. Jinnah refused to recognise it. On January 20, 1945, Bhulabhai Desai met the Viceroy and suggested complete Indianisation of his Executive Council by giving the Congress and the Muslim League forty per cent seats each and the remaining to other minorities. Desai assured the Viceroy that the suggestion had the approval of Gandhi and Liaqat Ali Khan, League's leader in the Central Assembly. The Viceroy welcomed it, but the next month Jinnah disowned the pact between Desai and Liaqat Ali.[19] In the meantime a Congress ministry was formed in the NWFP and a coalition government of the League and the Congress was formed in Assam. In the Central Assembly also, the Congress and the League stood together in opposition to a number of government proposals.

On June 14, 1945, the Viceroy (Lord Wavell) announced the proposal to reconstitute his Executive Council from among Indian leaders in equal proportions of "Muslims and caste Hindus".[20] Wittingly or unwittingly, the Viceroy used the terms "Muslims and caste-Hindus" instead of "Muslim League and the Congress". The change made all the difference. Shimla Conference opened on 25 June next.[21] Maulana Azad, the Congress President, put up a list of its nominees among whom there were two Hindus, one Muslim, one Sikh and one Christian, total five. League also gave a list of five Muslim members. Four were to be nominated by the Viceroy–a Sikh, two Depressed Class representatives and Sir Khizr Hayat Khan, leader of the Unionist Party of the Punjab. Thus, in a cabinet of fourteen members, seven were to be Muslims. The whole plan, however, failed because Jinnah insisted that all Muslim members should be the nominees of the Muslim League and that the Congress had no business to nominate a single Muslim. Congress did not accept this position.

A question arises as to why Jinnah, in the hour of his triumph of getting parity with the Congress, backed out from the Wavell Plan? The reason is that another development had taken place by the time Jinnah was to announce his final decision. A few moments earlier, he received a message from the "cell" of the British Civil Servants in Shimla, that if he stepped out of the talks he would be rewarded with Pakistan. When, after the press meeting in Shimla, Durga Das asked Jinnah why he had spurned the Wavell Plan, his stunning reply was, "Am I a fool to accept this when I am offered Pakistan on a platter?"[22] Durga Das adds that, after painstaking inquiries, he learned from high official and political sources that a member of the Viceroy's Executive Council had sent a secret message to Jinnah through the League contacts he had formed.[23]

Though Gandhi did not participate in discussion, he was present in Shimla for consultation. When Durga Das approached him, Gandhi conceded that he had agreed to Desai's formula providing for equal Congress and League representation in the interim Government, but it had been distorted in Wavell's proposals. He lamented that most of his colleagues had come out of jail tired and dispirited and without the heart to carry on the struggle, but hungry for power they might throw to the winds the basic principles for which the Congress stood. Gandhi added that the Hindus were indivisible, India was indivisible and there could be no Swaraj without Hindu-Muslim unity. About Jinnah's objection to the expression 'Ram Rajya' Gandhi clarified that by Ram Rajya he did not mean Hindu Raj but divine Raj, Insaf Raj, where justice would prevail between man and man and, if God gave him strength, he would fight for these principles with his life.[24]

ASSEMBLY ELECTIONS

On 26 July 1945, the Labour Party in England won the general elections and Clement Attlee replaced Winston Churchill as Prime Minister. The war with Japan ended in August 1945. In India, Assembly elections were long overdue. These were last held in 1934 (for the Central Assembly) and in 1937 (for the Provincial Assemblies). Fresh elections could not be held because of the war. Lord Wavell decided to hold them as early as possible. The elections were thus held from December 1945 to February 1946. In the Central Assembly elections, the Muslim League won all the 30 seats reserved for the Muslims. All the non-reserved seats were won by the Congress. Candidates of the Hindu Mahasabha, in most cases, had withdrawn in favour of the Congress candidates. Muslim candidates of the Congress (called the nationalist Muslims) who contested on Muslim seats forfeited their deposits. The final results, alongwith corresponding figures in the dissolved Assembly, are given below:

	Party	Seats secured in the election	Seats in the dissolved Assembly
1.	Congress	57	36
2.	Muslim League	30	25
3.	Independents	5	21
4.	Akali Sikhs	2	0
5.	Europeans	8	8
6.	National Party	0	10
	Total	102	100

The Congress secured 91.3 per cent of the votes cast in non-Muslim constituencies and the Muslim League got 86.6 per cent of the votes cast in Muslim contituencies. Thus only the Congress and the League came out as the principal political parties in India.[25]

In the Provincial Assembly elections, Muslim League got 427 of the 482 reserved Muslim seats. (In 1937, the League had got only 108 seats). Although, in the five Muslim majority provinces, Muslim League captured majority of the Muslim seats, but was able to form its ministries only in two, namely, Bengal and Sindh. Even there, the League had to depend on the support of other parties, particularly that of Europeans.

Needless to say that the Congress fought the elections with the promise of getting independence from the British rule and for maintaining the unity of the Indian Union. The League on the other hand sought election to rid the Muslims from the British Raj and the Hindu Raj of the Congress and to get them Pakistan, instead.

Lord Wavell's reading of the political situation of the time, in the words of V.P. Menon, the Secretary of States, was:

> "The Congress commanded the support of practically all Caste Hindus, and of certain other elements. It had the support of nearly the whole of the Press. It had the best organised — in fact the only well organised — political machine; and it commanded almost unlimited financial support. Almost all educated Hindus, and especially the student class, were its enthusiastic followers. *Indian business magnates, although strongly pro-Congress, were anxious for a solution without conflict and disorder.* Most of the big landowners feared the Congress, and would have liked to support the Government, but few of them could be relied upon to give active aid (to the then government).
>
> "*... generally speaking, there was no organised opposition to the Congress amongst Hindus in British India (except possibly in the Punjab) and nothing to put in its place if the British Government suppressed it.* The Scheduled Castes were divided and many of them supported the Congress. The only real opposition to it came from the minorities, of which the Muslim League was of course the principal party, but it represented entirely sectional and not all-India interests. The League, though strongly anti-Congress, was not pro-Government or pro-British..."[26]

CABINET MISSION

On 19 February 1946, the British Government announced its decision to send a Cabinet Mission to India to resolve the constitutional issue. On 15 March, Prime Minister Attlee clarified in the British House of Commons that the form of Government to replace the present regime was for India to decide, though he hoped that India would elect to remain within the British Commonwealth. In conclusion, he said:

> "We are mindful of the rights of the minorities and the minorities should be able to live free from fear. On the other hand, we cannot allow a minority to place their veto on the advance of the majority".

This evoked severe criticism from Jinnah. He protested that the Muslims were not a 'minority' but a 'nation', and that it was futile to expect co-operation from the Muslim League if the machinery to be set up for the framing of the new constitution was to be a single constitution-making body or assembly.[27]

The Cabinet Mission was in India for over three months, from the last week of March to June 1945. It discussed with the leaders of all political groups and non-political ones, including the Hindu Mahasabha, the Sikhs, the Depressed Classes, and reached the conclusion that there was no meeting ground between the two major parties, the Congress and the Muslim League. It found itself unable to recommend either a united India as proposed by the Congress or partition of India as demanded by the Muslim League. The latter wanted a separate sovereign state of Pakistan, consisting of the six provinces, namely, Bengal, Assam, Punjab, Sindh, NWFP and Baluchistan. Out of these, Bengal, Assam and the Punjab had a large Hindu population which could not be placed at the mercy of the Muslim League. The Cabinet Mission, therefore, made its own recommendation which, in essence, meant:

(a) There would be a Union of India, comprising both British India and the Indian States, having jurisdiction over subjects of Foreign Affairs, Defence and Communication. All residuary powers to belong to the Provinces and the States.

(b) The Union would have an Executive and a Legislature constituted of representatives of the Provinces and the states. But any question raising a major communal issue in the Legislature would require for its decision a majority of the representatives of the two major communities present and voting.

(c) The Provinces would be divided in three zones, A, B, and C so as to give a greater strength of assurance to the minorities. Section A was to consist of Hindu majority provinces of Madras, Bombay, United Provinces, Bihar, Central Provinces and Orissa. Section B of the Punjab, Sindh, the NWFP and British Baluchistan, having clear Muslim majority. Section C included Bengal and Assam, where the Muslims had a thin majority over the rest. Any Province would have the right to secede from the Group.

Maulana Azad was then the Congress President and he negotiated the entire scheme with the Cabinet Mission. After initial hesitation, both the Congress Working Committee and the Muslim League Council accepted the Mission's plan in the last week of June 1946. At that very time, Jawaharlal Nehru was elected Congress President and he took over from the Maulana on 6 July at a meeting of the All India Congress Committee (AICC) which ratified the decision of the Working Committee on the Mission's Plan. On 10 July, in a press conference at Bombay, Jawaharlal said, in reply to a question, that the "Congress had agreed only to participate in the Constituent Assembly and regarded itself free to change or modify the Cabinet Mission plan as it thought best".[28] Jinnah found an opportunity in it to withdraw League's acceptance of the plan. Congress passed another resolution to say that it had accepted the plan in its entirety, but without saying that what Jawaharlal had said was incorrect. Though, the Viceroy accepted the clarification, Jinnah did not relent and held out a threat to take 'Direct Action'.

INTERIM GOVERNMENT

The discussions on the Constituent Assembly being over, the Viceroy came on the issue of forming the interim Government as part of the Cabinet Mission plan. It was proposed that there would be fourteen members in the cabinet—six from the Congress (including a representative of the Scheduled Castes), five from the Muslim League, one sikh, one Indian Christian and one Parsi. The list included the name of Nehru and Jinnah. It was also indicated that in the event of either of the major parties being unwilling to join the coalition Government, the Viceroy intended to go ahead with the formation of the interim government. After getting certain clarifications and assurances from the Viceroy, Jinnah gave his acceptance to join the Government. He thought that Congress reply to the Mission would be treated as rejection of the proposal to participate in Government and he would be invited to form it with the Muslim League's representatives. It was not to be. Jinnah was not satisfied with the reply given by the Congress or the British Government. He said that the League had gone to the limit of concession, but the Congress had shown no appreciation of the sacrifices it had made; the League therefore had no alternative but to adhere once more to the national goal of Pakistan. The League passed a resolution that it had been assured that there would be five members each from the Congress and the League in the interim Government, but the Cabinet Mission had gone back on this assurance; and when the League accepted the Cabinet Mission's proposals and the Congress rejected them, they refused to let the League form the Government thus committing a breach of faith; and therefore, League's acceptance of the Cabinet Mission's proposals should be revoked.[29] In another resolution, the League authorised its Working Committee to draw up a plan of 'direct action' and called upon all its members to renounce any titles which they had received from the Government. Immediately after the resolution was passed, Jinnah declared, "This day we bid goodbye to constitutional methods....the British and the Congress each hold a pistol in their hand, the one of authority and arms and the other of mass struggle and non-cooperation. Today, we have also forged a pistol and are in a position to use it."[30]

The Working Committee of the League called upon Muslims throughout India to observe 16 August as 'Direct Action Day'.

Incidentally, by the end of July1946, elections were completed for the 296 seats assigned in the Constituent Assembly to the British Indian provinces. Congress won all the general seats except nine. The Muslim League won 73 seats–all except 5 allotted to Muslims. 93 seats allotted to the princely states and the Sikh seats remained to be filled. After League's withdrawal from the Cabinet Mission plan, on 12 August, the Viceroy invited Jawaharlal to form an interim Government at the Centre. On Viceroy's suggestion, Jawaharlal personally met Jinnah to invite him to join the Governnment, but Jinnah declined.

CALCUTTA RIOTS

Muslim League had fixed 16 August 1946 for its 'Direct Action' as already declared. The League ministries of Bengal and Sindh declared the day as a public holiday. The Muslim press was flooding the country with propaganda of communal bitterness exhorting Muslims to defy law and authority. Bengal's Chief Minister (called prime Minister), Suhrawardy declared that if the Congress were put into power, there would be a declaration of complete independence by Bengal and the setting up of a parallel Government.[31] On August 15, Suhrawardy threatened riots, "The atrocities of Chengiz and Halaku would pale into insignificance." The threat was carried out literally on 16 August. Calcutta was plunged into an orgy of bloodshed, murder, loot and arson. Within 3 days, according to conservative estimate, 5000 persons were killed and 15,000 wounded (all Hindus). Amidst this bloodshed, Jawaharlal Nehru was installed as the Prime Minister (then called Vice-President) on 2 September 1946. The violence, in the meantime, spread to other cities, like Bombay, Ahmedabad and others in the Punjab and NWFP.

It is strange that Jawaharlal Nehru, supported by Gandhi and the Congress Working Committee, took office unmindful of the large scale massacre of Hindus in Calcutta and elsewhere. Why could'nt they ask the Viceroy to ban the Muslim League, arrest its leaders for the open rebellion, defiance of law and inciting the Muslims to violence? There must have been intelligence reports about the preparations made for the 'direct action'. But no one bothered because the blood shed was that of Hindus. Instead of condemning Jinnah and his League, Nehru agreed to the Viceroy's proposal to invite Jinnah once again to join the interim Government.

A lot has been written by various authors and Congress leaders about how Jawaharlal was made the Prime Minister. Of all of them the description of Durga Das, the foremost press reporter and political analyst of the time, appears the most credible. According to him Patel was the head of the Congress Parliamentary Board and the Provincial Congress Committees had expressed their preference for him as Azad's successor. The office of the Congress president had become most important because in the event of transfer of power, he was to be invited on behalf of the Congress. Considering this aspect of the matter, Gandhi wanted Nehru to be the president. Maulana Azad had been the Congress president since 1939. As a change in leadership had become overdue, the Maulana issued a statement on 26 April 1946 urging all Congressmen to choose Jawaharlal as the next President in order that the policies laid down by him should continue to be followed.[32] Evidently, Gandhi was influenced by Maulana Azad. Many years later, when Durga Das sought Kripalani's explanation of Gandhi's preference for Nehru as against Patel, Kripalani said that, like all saints and holy people, Gandhi wanted 'significant men' among his adherents. Kripalani added "All the P.C.Cs sent in the name of Patel by a majority and one or two proposed the name of Rajen Babu in addition but none that of Jawaharlal. I knew Gandhi wanted Jawaharlal to be President for a year, and I made a proposal myself saying 'some Delhi fellows want Jawaharlal's name'. I circulated it to the members of the Working Committee to get their endorsement. I played this mischief. I am to blame. Patel never forgave me for that. He was a man of will and decision.."[33] But Jawaharlal was ever grateful to Kripalani. As a mark of this gratefulness, he alsways let Kripalani win his Lok Sabha seat as an independent without opposition from Congress.

When on 12 August 1946, the Viceroy invited the Congress President, Jawaharlal Nehru, to form an interim government, most members of the Working Committee wanted Sardar Patel to be the Prime Minister as he would be able to deal better with Jinnah in those critical times. Durga Das asked Gandhi for his reactions to this feeling. The latter readily agreed that Patel would have proved a better negotiator and organiser as Congress President, but he felt Nehru should head the Government. Asked how he reconciled this with his assessment of Patel's qualities as a leader, Gandhi laughed and said "Jawahar is the only Englishman in my camp."[34] He further added that

> "Jawaharlal will not take a second place. He is better known abroad than Sardar and will make India play a role in international affairs. Sardar will look after the country's affairs. They will be like two oxen yoked to the governmental cart. One will need the other and both will pull together."

Durga Das mentioned to Gandhi Rajendra Prasad's agony (expressed to him in person) that Gandhi had once again sacrificed his trusted lieutenant for the sake of "the glamorous Nehru" and the fear that Nehru would follow British ways. Gandhi replied that he appreciated the views of his colleagues but felt that Nehru would see reason when confronted with the problem of improving the lot of the masses.[35] The future events showed how miserably had Gandhi's speculation about Nehru failed. Firstly, Nehru just could not contain Jinnah that was the primary need of the hour. Secondly, after the Partition, Nehru spoiled everything that he laid hands on, be it Kashmir, a common civil code, the economic policy or even foreign policy that left India friendless in the comity of nations and at the mercy of the Soviet Russia in the matter of defence. It was a queer logic of Gandhi that a person uprooted from the realities of his own country would make an impact in world affairs. But far more intriguing is the fact that other important leaders of the time blindly followed Gandhiji's dictat.

Jinnah saw clear disadvantages of not joining the Government. He sent feelers to the Viceroy who, after consulting Jawaharlal, allowed the Muslim League to join the Government. The League chose to nominate four Muslims and one scheduled caste Hindu, Jogendra Nath Mandal, to be the members of Viceroy's Executive Council, on 20 October 1946. But the League joined only to act as a brake on the Congress. There was continuous tussle between the Congress and the Muslim League. Earlier, in February 1946, there was a naval mutiny. The British Government could no longer depend upon the Indian army. Due to this and due to pressure from the USA and the Soviet Union, the British made up their mind to leave India in Indian hands. The only question was how to go about this process.

REFERENCES

1. Durga Das, India from Curzon to Nehru, p. 194.
2. Ayasha Jalal, The Sole Spokesman, Jinnah, the Muslim League and the demand for Pakistan, p. 58. (Cambridge University Press, London, 1985–South Asian Studies); Durga Das, India from Curzon to Nehru... p. 195.
3. Durga Das, India from Curzon to Nehru, p. 195-196.
4. —do— p. 196.
5. —do— p. 199.
6. —do— p. 207; Michael Edwardes, The Last Year of British India, p. 82.

7. Michael Edwardes, The Last Years of British India, p. 80.
8. BN Jog, Threat of Islam, p. 276.
9. Durga Das, India from Curzon to Nehru, p. 203.
10. Durga Das, -Ibid-, p. 205.
11. —do—
12. —do— pps. 205-206.
13. Michael Edwardes, The Last Years of British India, p. 90.
14. —do— p. 91.
15. Michael Edwardes, The Last Years of British India, p. 97.
16. Durga Das, India from Curzon to Nehru, p. 213.
17. —do—
18. Maulana Azad, India wins Freedom, p. 93.
18a. GNS Raghavan, M. Asaf Ali's Memoirs, p. 286.
19. H.V. Hodson, The Great Divide, second print, 1988, pp. 117-119, Oxford University Press, Karachi.
20. —do— p. 120.
21. In this Conference, Hindu Mahasabha was refused permission to participate because the Congress itself was treated as the representative of Hindus. The Mahasabha, however, passed a resolution against parity between the Muslims and the caste Hindus. It also staged some public demonstration and declared hartal on 8 July 1945.
22. Durga Das, India from Curzon to Nehru, p. 216.
23. Ibid —do—
24. Ibid p. 216-217.
25. V.P. Menon, Transfer of Power in India, pps. 228-234. According to 1935 Act, the voting right was extended to about 35 million people which meant about 10 percent of the population, As the Muslims League got 87 per cent of the votes cast, some Muslim scholars have argued that not more than 7-8 per cent of the Muslims voted for Pakistan and that the partition was imposed on the Muslim community by the British government and the Hindu Congress.
26. Menon, VP., Transfer of Power in India, p. 234.
27. —do— p. 237.
28. Maulana Azad, India Wins Freedom, p. 155.
29-30. VP. Menon, Transfer of Power in India, pp. 286-287.
31. —do— pp. 297-98.
32. Maulana Azad, India Wins freedom, p. 153.
33. Durga Das, India from Curzon to Nehru, p. 229.
34. —do— p. 230.
35. —do— pp. 230-231.

Chapter XII

JINNAH'S PISTOL POLITICS

Muslim League's first demand was for separate electorates. It was granted by the Minto-Morley Reforms of 1909. Congress, supposed to represent the vast majority of Hindus, also put its seal of approval to it through the Lucknow Pact of 1916 hoping that in a period of ten years or so, Muslim leaders would see the reason and opt for joint electorates. Belying the hope, the League increased its demand to one-third share in Central Assembly seats in the local bodies and government jobs. This was a heavy price for the Hindu sentimentalists who had made great sacrifices during the Khilafat movement which was absolutely a religious matter of the Muslims alone. By 1928, it was found that the separate electorate to Muslims itself was wrong and the Nehru Committee composed of members of all political parties and shades recommended its abolition and, instead, recommended other safeguards in the proposed constitution for India. Before it, Jinnah himself was against separate electorates. He had also opposed the Congress move to adopt Khilafat on the ground that it was a purely religious matter of the Muslims. But suddenly, Jinnah's mind changed. He became the most fanatic among the fanatic Muslims. He adopted such ways and means which made partition of India the only possible alternative. While Congress wanted that the British 'Quit India', the League wanted them to 'Divide and Quit'.

Jinnah raised his demand for Pakistan in 1940, shortly after the start of World War II. The Congress had adopted a non-cooperative attitude towards the British war effort. The British leaned on the League. Jinnah found a golden opportunity of blackmailing the British and went on increasing his demands. He himself was not clear about his own scheme of Pakistan. Whenever his alternative demands, like parity with the Congress in Viceroy's Executive Council and special safeguards amounting to a veto power to Muslim League were not agreed to, he revived his demand for Partition. To discredit and defeat the Congress, he stirred the Muslim community by every possible way and contrived with various power groups. He conceptualised that the Muslims were not a mere minority, but were a nation just like the Hindus; and thus the Muslims represented by the Muslim League and its leader, called "Qaid-e-Azam" (Jinnah) must be treated at par with the Congress in all matters, namely, parity in Provincial Assemblies and the Central Assembly, services, and in the authority and control of the Government.

Jinnah argued that the Parliamentary form of democracy, proposed by the Congress was based on numbers-universal adult franchise-and was, therefore, an evil for the Muslims in India where Hindus would always be in a majority. It was, according to him, the surest way of subjugating the Muslims to a Hindu Raj. Jinnah said in Delhi in 1943, "Not only have we evidence, but we have suffered and experienced that. When you talk of democracy, you mean Hindu Raj, to dominate over the Muslims, a totally different nation, different in culture, different in everything. You yourself are working for Hindu Nationalism and Hindu Raj....One society and one nation will by its permanent majority destroy another nation or society in permanent minority—and all that is dear to the minority."[1] Therefore, he argued that only Partition of India on the basis of Muslims and non-Muslims, could assure security and dignity to the Muslims. Creation of Pakistan, he said, was not a device to divide India, but a device to obtain freedom from the British, to ensure peace and Hindu-Muslim unity, and was in the interests of the Hindus themeselves. In League Legislators' Convention in Delhi in April 1946, Suhrawardy, the Chief Minister of Bengal who had organised the mass massacre of Hindus in Calcutta in August, the same year, said that Pakistan was not the last demand of the Muslim League, but only the latest demand.[2] Jinnah aroused a total separateness among the Muslims and a sense of alienation from the rest of the people by repeatedly stressing that:

1. A Hindu is always a Hindu and will act as a Hindu, very much against the sensibilities of the Muslims.

2. Hindus are already organised into a murderous monolith; the Hindu Mahasabha, etc. are themselves strong. The only difference between the Hindu Mahasabha and the Congress was that the Congress masquerades under the slogan of nationalism, whereas the Hindu Mahasabha does not mince words. Thus, the Congressmen are nothing but Hindu Mahasabhaites in disguise.
3. Everything that the Congress does has one singular and exclusive objective-that is, to fulfil the Hindu dream of annihilating the Muslims and to establish the Hindu Raj.
4. The Hindus are already subjecting the Muslims to unspeakable atrocities, suppression, discrimination and one can imagine what will happen when they acquire absolute power in a united India.
5. Singing of Vande Mataram, the efforts to propagate Hindi or Hindustani, the Wardha Education Scheme, etc. were the schemes to finish off the Muslims.
6. The very demand for freedom for a united India was just a euphemism for establishing the domination of Hindus over Muslims.
7. The Congress,no doubt, is the largest single party, but it does not represent the Christians, the Sikhs, the Scheduled Castes, and many others.
8. The Muslims who were with the Congress were dupes of the Congress, the betrayers, careerists, traitors, cranks or lunatics.

To Gandhi, Jinnah said:

> "Why does not Mr. Gandhi honestly now acknowledge that the Congress is a Hindu Congress, that he does not represent anybody except the solid body of a Hindu people? why should not Mr. Gandhi be proud to say, 'I am a Hindu, the Congress has a solid Hindu backing?' I am not ashamed of saying that I am a Musalman. I am right. I hope, and I think even a blind man would have been convinced by now, that the Muslim League has a solid backing of the Musalmans of India. Why then all this comouflage? Why all these machinations? Why not come as a Hindu leader proudly representing your people and let me meet you proudly representing the Musalmans."[3]

The Congress could not effectively counter the arguments of Jinnah for the Muslim League had secured nearly 87 per cent of the Muslim votes and Congress had got 91 per cent of the general votes, which were practically Hindu votes. The allegation against Congress and stories of atrocities on the Muslims were based on the Pirpur Report, the Shareef Report and various pamphlets which were created by the Muslim League earlier in 1938 in order to malign the Congress govenments in the provinces, especially U.P. and Bihar. In these reports, the singing of '*Vande Mataram*' before the Assembly proceeding, adoption of Hindi for transaction of legislative business, banning of cow-slaughter, were also quoted as instances of atrocities on the Muslims. Stories of physical subjugation were also invented. Dr. Rajendra Prasad observed that the League had adopted Hitler's tactics of inventing false charges and of exaggerating small ones into Himalayan blunders and, by incessant repetitions, it made lies appear as truth.[4] When Dr. Prasad offered that the Congress was willing to have the allegations investigated through Sir M. Gwyer, Chief Justice of the Federal Court or some person of similar status, Jinnah dithered and said that the Viceroy had been asked to consider the matter, thus closing the door for a judicial inquiry.

Irony of fate is that the allegations then made by Jinnah and the Muslim League against the Congress are now being made by the present Congress against its rival, the Bhartiya Janata Party and the Rashtriya Swyamsevak Sangh (RSS). The Congressmen themselves are lining up with the fundamentalist Muslims in the matter of 'Vande Mataram', propagation of Urdu and denegrating Hindi, banning cowslaughter, and in framing false charges of intimidation of Muslims in BJP ruled States. Indeed, they have assumed the role of Jinnah and the erstwhile Muslim League! They see Hindu chauvinism in the demand for removal of Article 370 in the matter of J & K, adoption of Hindi as the official language, making a common civil code for all, stoppage of allocation of huge amounts of state funds for Haj pilgrimage, and the like.

It would, however, be childish to think that Jinnah's success lay in his false propaganda and political threats extended from time to time. He had the backing of the British bureaucracy, Mullahs and Moulvis, and, in addition, he had raised the Muslim 'National Guard', a militant organisation having large quantities of arms and ammunition and Muslim ex-servicemen of World War

II. There were 60 to 70 per cent Muslims in the Police force and almost all of them were pro-Pakistanis. They either kept silent or helped the Muslim hooligans when the latter attacked Hindus. Over and above, Jinnah had his men in all departments, especially in the Intelligence Bureau and Viceroy's Executive Council, who gave Jinnah minute to minute information on all important matters, including the discussion held by Congress leaders with the Viceroy. Jinnah always ascertained Congress views on a proposal before disclosing his own mind.

REFERENCES

1 Arun Shourie, Religion in Politics, p. 180

2 -do-

3 Arun Shourie, Religion in Politics, p. 185-186.

4 Atma Katha, Rajendra Prasad, quoted by Lal Bahadur, Muslim League, pp. 250-51

Chapter XIII

MOUNTBATTEN—LAST PHASE

The organised massacre, arson, and loot of Hindus started in Calcutta on August 16, 1946 went on unabated for three days. The police, mostly consisting of Muslims, were silent spectators and, at times, abettors to crimes. In desperation, Hindus stood up on the fourth day and started retaliating and only then the communal riots in Calcutta could be brought under control. At the time, a reporter asked Gandhi, "Sermons on non-violence from afar are of little use. To have offered non-violent resistance would have meant allowing all property to be destroyed and every Hindu to be killed. What is our duty in such circumstances?" Gandhi replied, "....Fratricide will not abate by intimidation and violence...If through deliberate courage the Hindus had died to a man, that would have been deliverance of Hinduism and India and purification for Islam in this land. As it was, a third party (British) had to intervene...Neither the Muslims nor the Hindus have gained by the intervention."[1] The Viceroy (Lord Wavell), not Gandhi, visited Calcutta on 25 August when the signs of massacre, looting and arson were still clearly visible. Instead of taking the Muslim League Government of Bengal to task and punitive action against the trouble mongers, the Viceroy said, "We must involve Muslim League in the Interim government to avoid incidents like calcutta". Surely, this kind of reaction from the Viceroy resulted from the impotence of the Congress (and the entire Hindu mass which was rallying behind it)and was in keeping with Gandhian attitude of always submitting to the Muslim bully. During its four day meeting from 27 August 1946, the Congress Working Committee expressed its views on the Calcutta carnage in the words, "Communal problems are not resolved by violence. They can be resolved only through mutual understanding and impartial arbitration".

NOAKHALI

After Calcutta, the Muslim League chose the districts of Noakhali and Tippehra to commit mass scale murder, rape, arson loot and forced conversions. In the words of Pyarelal, Private Secretary of Mahatma Gandhi:

> "On the 29th August, 1946 there was a sudden flare-up in Noakhali. It was Id-ul-Fitr, a Muslim festival. A rumour had been set afloat that Sikhs, hired by the Hindus were killing the Muslims an masse. Infuriated crowds of Muslims poured into the town...armed with whatever weapons they could lay hands on. Some Hindu fishermen were man-handled. The next day came news of harm done by similar rumours throughout the district. The son of an important Congressman of Babupur village was murdered in broad daylight and the Congress house set on fire.
>
> "A joint meeting of the Ulemas (Muslim divines) and the Muslim League was announced by Mian Ghulam Sarwar on the 6th September by beat of drum to 'devise ways and means to wreak vengeance for the great Calcutta Killing'....It was impressed upon the gathering that the time was now ripe for fabricating weapons and wielding them against the Hindus..."
>
> "The next day, another meeting was held at the village of Dasgharia....Breaking of idols and desecration of Hindu places of worship was openly preached at this meeting..."[2]

Pyarelal states that there was a well-defined and uniform pattern of Noakhali carnage, namely, first extortion in the name of the Muslim League, promising that those who paid would be spared, next demanding surrender of all arms against threat of killing the whole family of the defiant, followed by plunder and setting houses on fire with kerosene and petrol. This process went on for days together. The survivors were asked to accept Islam if they wanted to live. As a proof of the genuineness of conversion, the victims were sometimes required to give their unmarried, widowed, or even married daughters, in marriage' to Muslims selected by the mob. The village Maulavis acted as hooligans and priests at the same time. There was systematic attempt to exterminate the intelligentsia and in the case of well-to-do families all the male heirs. Among those who took part in the carnage, figured presidents and members of the Union Boards, Muslim National Guards, Muslim school masters and students, local criminals, and a sprinkling of ordinary Muslim village-folk including women and children.[3] There was a notable case of conversion of Haren Ghosh, Secretary of the Congress Committee, Raipur. On October 14, a crowd of 500 armed ruffians shouting slogans of Allaho-Akbar and Pakistan zindabad attacked Raipur. They first took away all moveable property, then destroyed Hindu temples and idols and then set fire to the village with kerosene and petrol. Harendra Ghosh escaped and hid himself in jungles during daytime. At night he reached the house of two Muslims who told him that the only way to save him was conversion to Islam. Ghosh agreed. Next day he was brought to Raipur mosque. He was made to sign two pamphlets which were printed in the local press in thousands and distributed amongst Hindus and Muslims. Ghosh was kept confined for twelve days. His daily food, as he later told, was rice and beef which he was forced to eat. He was taught Namaz and made to give lectures on Fridays in front of the Muslims on the Islamic creed and culture. Among the leaders of the frenzied mob were a local MLA, Secretary of the Thana Muslim League, two Secretaries of the Union Peace Committee, two Presidents of Union Boards and a Zamindar.[4]

It is noteworthy that, out of 22 lakh of the total population of Noakhali, 18 lakh or 81.33 per cent were Muslims, 4 lakh being Hindus. It is not well known that one of the products of Noakhali and a principal item of its export was theologians and divines. There was a larger number of Maulanas and Mullas here than in any other part of India. Almost every sizable village had one or two Hajees. The number of Hafeezes (those who have the whole of Quran by heart) was also very large in the district. The bulk of the students that crowded the theological academies at Deoband and Azamgarh in U.P. hailed from Noakhali.[5]

RATALIATION IN BIHAR

Among the victims of Calcutta carnage, there were hundreds of men from Bihar who had gone there for earning their livelihood. On hearing the news of their massacre and looting and the atrocities committed on Hindus in Noakhali, the Hindus of Bihar started retaliating in a big way by burning Muslim villages and killing the Muslims indiscriminately. Now Gandhi rose to the occasion. He told Jawaharlal to act swiftly to stop Bihar riots. He threatened to go on fast unto death. (Why he did not hold out a similar threat earlier at the Calcutta riots is a matter which the reader must ponder). Army was deployed on the rioters in Bihar with the orders to shoot at sight. According to press reports of the time, over five hundred Bihari Hindus were shot dead. One salutary effect of Bihar retaliation was that the Muslim attacks on Hindus in Calcutta and Noakhali came down heavily. Gandhiji proceeded to Noakhali in November 1946, two months after it was ravaged. The mediamen and politicians have written volumes on Gandhi's contribution to bring peace in the devastated areas of Calcutta and Noakhali, but the real contribution had been made by the Bihari Hindus who showed that the Hindus could also use brute force and pay in the same coin.

The surprising aspect of the whole episode is that even in such a gruesome atmosphere, men being slaughtered like sheep and goats and women being raped and dishonoured, Gandhi got a fit of Brahmacharya. He sent for his 19 year old grand-niece to sleep naked with him. When some people came to know of it and questioned Gandhi, he excused himself saying that he was playing mother to his grand-niece.[6] His private secretary, Pyarelal, and others have laboured hard to philosophise and justify this peculiar sex behaviour, but they have completely ignored the permanent damage done to the girls whom Gandhi used as guinea-pigs to test his Brahmacharya for all of them had to pass their lives as spinsters.[7]

LEAGUE JOINS CABINET

Muslim League joined the Interim Government on October 26, 1946, when Noakhali was burning and bleeding under the fire of its 'direct action'. "It was an organised attack engineered by the Muslim League and carried out with the connivance of the administrative officials. The attacks were made by people armed with guns and other deadly weapons; roads had been dug up and other means of communications were cut off to prevent ingress and egress; canals had been blocked and strategic points were being guarded by armed insurgents. Two of the Muslim League members of the Interim Government were openly indulging in belligerant speeches. One even went as far as to declare that the events in East Bengal were but part of all-India battle for Pakistan."[8]

The Muslim League started violent agitation against the Khizr Hayat Khan's coalition ministry in the Punjab in order to replace it by a purely League ministry. Communal riots were also engineered in Lahore, Gujarat, Amitsar, and Jullundur. Khizr Hayat Khan resigned on March 2, 1947. The province came under governor's rule. The riots spread in other towns of Multan, Rawalpindi and Amritsar and also in the NWFP.[9]

In this state of anarchy, the British Government announced on 20 February 1947:

(a) that the British rule in India would in any case end by June 1948. after which the British would certainly transfer authority to Indian hands;

(b) that if by that time, a fully representative Constituent Assembly failed to work out a constitution in accordance with the proposals made by the Cabinet Delegation, His Majesty's Government in British India should be handed over, on the due date, whether as a whole to some form of Central government or in such other way as seems most reasonable and in the best interests of the Indian people.

In March 1947, the British government sent Lord Mountbatten to replace Lord Wavell as Viceroy and to give a practical shape to the intentions of the British Government. He reached Delhi on 23rd March and was sworn in the next day. Immediately, Mountbatten set out on his mission.[10] He had far greater powers and freedom to act than any other Viceroy before him. The only guidelines to him were that he should avoid partition: honour the pledges made to the Muslims and the Princes; secure agreement to the Cabinet Mission Plan without coercing any of the parties; try to keep Indian army undivided; and retain India within the Commonwealth.

Under pressure from the Muslim League's organised massacre of Hindus and Sikhs and its continued obstacles in Governmental work from inside, as an equal partner of the Interim Government, the Congress felt that there was no alternative but 'Partition'. It was, however, not ready to cede to Pakistan large areas of the Punjab and Bengal having Hindu majority. Mountbatten discussed the matter with Jawaharlal and Sardar Patel and got their approval for the Partition. Learning that the two top leaders of the Congress had succumbed to Mountbatten's plan, Maulana Azad went to Gandhiji on March 31. The latter said:

> "What a question to ask? If the Congress wishes to accept partition, it will be over my dead body. So long as I am alive, I will never agree to the partition of India. Nor will I, if I can help it, allow Congress to accept it."[11]

In his prayer meeting on 31st May 1947, Gandhi said, "Even if the whole of India burns, we shall not concede Pakistan even if the Muslims demanded it at the point of the sword."[12] the fact is that Gandhi had accepted the Partition Plan in April 1947. Why did he make a contrary statement on 31st May, has been a subject of considerable speculation and debate.

When Gandhiji was still in the riot affected areas of Bihar and Lord Mountbatten was yet to reach India, the Congress Working Committee (CWC) decided on 8 March 1947 in favour of partitioning the Punjab. The immediate compelling reason was Liaqat Ali Khan's Budget presented just a week before which contained very harsh measures against the industrialists and big business houses on the plea to avoid tax evasion but really meant to demolish the financial base of the Congress. Gandhi reached Delhi in the last week of March when Maulana Azad met him and sought his help to stop Partition. Gandhi discussed the matter with Congress leaders and met Mountbatten a number of times without success. When Durga Das alongwith Devadas met Gandhi, the latter was bitter and accused his followers of betraying him for the sake of power. He said that he would make one final bid to retrieve the situation. Next, Durga Das met Patel who said that Gandhi must bear part of the blame as it was he who had conceded the right of self determination to the Muslims and had made a hero of Jinnah. Gandhi's last bid to avoid Partition was his proposal that the Interim government be dismissed, Jinnah be invited to form government at the centre by choosing his ministers even if all of them be Muslims. Mountbatten wanted the approval of the CWC, but the CWC rejected the proposal. Gandhi withdrew it. All this happened before 15 April 1947. On April 28, Dr. Rajendra Prasad, as President of the Constituent Assembly, read out a Congress statement announcing not only partition of the country but division of certain provinces. From 15 April onwards, only details of the Partition plan were worked out.

It ought to go to the credit of Lord Mountbatten for cornering Jinnah to either agree to a united India with Bengal and Punjab remaining united or to have Pakistan with both the provinces partitioned to allow Hindu majority districts to remain in India. Jinnah argued at length that the partition of Bengal and the Punjab for creating Pakistan would be disastrous to the life and culture of the people in the two provinces. Mountbatten silenced him by saying that the same argument applied to partitioning the whole of India. Jinnah had to reconcile to a Pakistan with a partitioned Punjab and a partitioned Bengal, which he later termed as moth-eaten Pakistan. Taking a cue from Jinnah's opposition to the partition of Bengal and the Punjab, some historians in India and abroad have tried to show that it was not Jinnah or the Muslim League but the Congress and the British who forced Partition on the Muslims.

In May 1947, Mountbatten went to London and got UK Government's approval to his Partition Plan. Coming back to India, he announced on June 3, that the British Government had accepted the principle of partition and had resolved to withdraw its authority from India on August 14, 1947; the provinces of the Punjab and Bengal were to be partitioned provided their Legislative Assemblies asked for it; the boundary commission would determine the dividing lines; British treaties with the princely states would come to an end, leaving them free to remain independent or join either India or Pakistan.

The Congress Working Committee approved the Mountbatten Plan on June 3 itself. The All India Congress Committee considered it in its meeting on June 14. In this meeting, Gandhi strongly pleaded for its acceptance, conveniently forgetting that only two months ago he had declared that India's partition would take place only on his dead body. The AICC approved the Plan with a majority vote, 157 to 29.

Both India and Pakistan came into existence, freed from the British rule on August 15, 1947, but not from the imperial politics of the British Raj. At the request of the Congress, Lord Mountbatten agreed to become India's Governor General. Jinnah himself took over as the Governor General of Pakistan. While Jawaharlal Nehru became the Prime Minister of India, Liaqat Ali Khan, hailing from

U.P., became the Prime Minster of Pakistan. A fury of murder and arson, rape and pillage swept across the country, especially in the provinces which were partitioned, Punjab and Bengal. A convoy of fifty-seven miles long was journeying towards India from West Punjab. Thousands of innocent men, women and childrem were killed and property worth hundreds of crores of rupees was destroyed. Over 20 million people had to abandon their hearths and homes in search of new ones in unfamiliar lands on the other side of the borders. This enforced two way migration was unparalleled in human history. August 15 was thus a day of mourning for those who had been struggling for an independent united India. It was a day of rejoicing for those who had, in the name of Pakistan, been committing wholesale murders, arson and rape throughout the country.

The foregoing account of Gandhiji's plunge into the Khilafat movement and his soft peddling towards the acts of violence committed by the fanatic Muslims, surrender to the Partition Plan after a show of shadow boxing. *et al*, have led many to suspect that underneath his dhoti langoti (the lion cloth), Ram-Nam, and selective non-violence, lay a sinister design to confuse the disillusioned and distraught Hindu masses and to bring them under the crescent flag. The conversion of his own elder son, Hari Lal Gandhi to Islam is symbolic of Gandhi's well guarded attempts to promote Islam. Perhaps, that is why the prominent Khilafatist, Mohammed Ali, ventured to say that it would be a great day when Gandhi himself would embrace Islam. (Hari Lal later came back to Hindu religion).

In a recent issue of the noted English weekly from New Delhi, 'Organiser', Oct. 29, 1995, a reader stated:

> "A lot has been written in Organiser, 1-10-95, about Gandhiji, depicting him as a true Hindu and a pious man. Gandhiji committed a big sin by doing injustice to the Hindus, and we the Hindus are committing a greater sin by tolerating it and still accepting him as our leader and a great man. Gandhiji yielded Pakistan exclusively for Muslims, but denied India to Hindus, and bitterly opposed Hindu Rashtra. He made India a dharamshala, and accepted all Muslim Leaguers responsible for killings of Hindus into the Congress fold.

"He talked of Ramrajya, Gita, Sanatanadharma,brahmacharya, to befool Hindus and get their support, but quietly thrust upon us a person like Nehru, who hated Hinduism and ridiculed the concept of Ramrajya."

The following news item appeared in the famous English daily of New Delhi, the Hindustan Times, Aug.3, 1995 (p.12):

US TABLOID CALLS GANDHI SPY, DEBAUCH

" Kalki P.K. Gaur of Murray Hill Station, New York, who claims to have launched the inaugural issue of Times of America, a new monthly newspaper on South Asian, Central Asian and West Indian politics, dated Aug.2, made a series of outrageous assertions (many of them unprintable) in a statement he mailed IANS with a copy of his eight-page tabloid:

-Mahatma Gandhi doesn't deserve to be put on a pedestal but denounced for his sexual misdeeds and his involvement in espionage for the British in order to sabotage the freedom movement;."

There can be nothing more outrageous and seditious than calling names to the most venerated man of India, whom a large section of the people call 'Father of the Nation', and to brand him a debauch and a spy. But, far more astonishing is the fact that there was no protest or reaction against it from any quarters. Prima facie, the allegations are wild, hyperbolic and malafide. However, certain political moves of Gandhi and some of his experiments on Bhrahmacharya defy all logic.

REFERENCES

1 BN Jog, Threat of Islam, p. 313. and p. 314.
2 Pyarelal, Mahatma Gandhi-Last Phase, vol. I, pps. 301
3 -do- p. 307.
4 Pyarelal, Mahatma Gandhi- Last Phase vol.I, pps.297-298
5 Pyarelal, Mahatma Gandhi- Last Phase Vol.I, p. 308-309.
6 Pyarelal, Mahatma Gandhi-Last Phase, Vol.I, Chapter on Brahmacharya, P. 575.
7 Analysing Gandhiji's experiments with sexual abstinence, Bhikhu Parekh states, "Undeterred by the campaign, Gandhi not only

continued his close associations with women but also embarked upon a most unusual practice. For the past few years he had slept with them in the same room at a respectable distance, and of late he had begun to 'sleep together' with some of them. He now decided to take the next step of sleeping naked with his naked female colleagues as part of a new experiment. He seems to have started doing this after his wife's death on February 22, 1944. His reference to 'women or girls who have been naked with me' in his letter to Birla in April 1945 indicates that several women were involved. It would appear that in addition to Sushila Nayar, Prabhavati Narayan, Abha Gandhi and Manu Gandhi also formed part of the experiment. Lilavati, Rajkumari Amrit Kaur, Antussalam and several others also seem to have been involved, although it is not clear whether they simply 'slept together' with him or did so as part of the experiment. "When some of Gandhi's close friends and colleagues came to

When some of Gandhi's close friends and colleagues came to know about it, they expressed strong disapproval...He was not, therefore, going to bow to social pressure on an issue of such vital importance as his sexual experiment...".

In defence of Gandhi's sexual experiment, Bhikhu Parekh says: "He was determined to control the violence raging all around him... He was also convinced that all violence ceased in the presence of non-violence... He associated sexuality with violence and aggression. So long as he was conscious of himself as a male, elements of aggression and violence were bound to remain even if he was not conscious of them. The only way out was to cease to be a male, to become a woman.

was an attempt to become, and to test that he had succeeded in becoming a woman. This was why he said that he wanted to become a 'mother to Manu'."

(Excerpts from Bhikhu Parekh's Colonialism, Tradition And Reform, Sage Publications India Pvt. Ltd. 1989, Greater Kailash I Market New Delhi-48–published in Times of India, Sunday Review, June 18,1989)

8 VP Menon, Transfer of Power, p. 322-323.

9 -do- pps. 349-351.

10. Ayesha Jalal, the Sole Spokesman Jinnah, the Muslim League, and the Demand for Pakistan, p. 250.

11 Maulana Azad, India Wins Freedom, p. 186.

12 Michael Edwardes, The Last Years of British India, p.179.

Chapter XIV

WHO IS TO BLAME FOR PAKISTAN?

A lot has been said and volumes have been written on the question as to who actually caused the Partition of India or created Pakistan. Some accuse Gandhi, some Jawaharlal, some Patel, some Jinnah and his Muslim League, some British government, some Hindu Mahasabha and the RSS. There is yet another group who blames the whole of Congress and the British Raj. The debate is still giong on.

The British view is rightly expressed by H.V. Hodson, the Constitutional Advisor to the Viceroy in 1941-42 and author of several books on Commonwealth, etc, when he states:

> "Between 1935 and 1946, even between 1942 and 1946, much had happened to make the task of holding India together by national government with Dominion powers much more difficult. The way in which the Congress exploited its electoral success in 1937 was the first blow. Next, the war and all its consequences were a disaster for India's progress to a united independence. The withdrawal of the Congress from provincial governments, its rejection of the Cripps Offer, and its Quit India campaign, set its cause back by years and gave an immense advantage to its opponents, exploited by Mr. Jinnah. The wartime inertia of British policy (except abortively in 1942) and the negativism of the Congress left a vacuum for Muslim separatism to expand. Never was the Gandhian leadership less relevant to practical politics, never did the Congress need more to recognise its own shortcomings. Had it perceived the new Political realities, it might have made a better bargain with the League and the British over sharing central power at

Simla in 1945 than it could have made in any later negotiation; for on his side Mr. Jinnah had not yet found and tested his full strength. And the chance of forming a genuine all-community Government of a united India was never again so strong."[1]

Truly speaking, no single individual or a group of individuals is to blame. It was a nabulous idea of Sir Syed Ahmad Khan in the later part of the nineteenth centurary that the Muslim constituted a separate nation. At that point of time, it was intended to alientate the Muslim elite from the Hindu mainstream which was struggling for Swarajya, self government. The Syed felt that the interests of the Muslim elite, of which he was a member, would be best served by closely aligning with the British Raj. The British needed the Muslim support but they recognised the Muslims as the largest minority, not a nation, and granted them separate electorate.

In 1940, the Muslim League passed the resolution to segregate the Muslim majority areas to be ruled by Muslims. The word Pakistan was not yet used. The resolution had been moved by Sir Sikandar Hyat Khan then Premier of the Punjab. Replying to various queries about the Pakistan scheme, he told Punjab Legislative Assembly on March 11, 1941 that he had not framed any Pakistan scheme. He said that such a scheme had been first formulated by one Maulana Jamal-ud-din, followed by Sir Mohammed Iqbal whose writings and poems gave a ground to think in terms of establishing some sort of Pakistan. Later, a concrete scheme of Pakistan was formulated by Rahmat Ali. According to him Pakistan was to be made up of the Punjab (P), Afghanistan, including NWFP, (A) Kashmir (K), Sindh (S) and Baluchistan (TAN). Perhaps he intended to include Iran (I) also in his scheme. This scheme was widely circulated. In conclusion, Sikandar Hyat Khan said:

> "A vast majority of educated Muslims, however, do not believe in any of these schemes. Take the President of the League himself. He is not a believer in any extra-territiorial scheme. He stands by the Lahore resolution to which our Hindu friends have given the name of Pakistan. Mr. Jinnah naturally, like everybody else, sees the advantage in adopting a catch-phrase which apeals to the masses. If the Hindus

and Sikhs can exploit it why not the Muslim League? The Muslims like it; so it is a convenient slogan to sway the Muslim masses..."[2]

In Sept 1944, after his release from jail Gandhi held seventeen days discussion with Jinnah at Bombay, without any result. But, a few days later when Durga Das met Jinnah at Delhi, the latter jubilantly said. "Gandhi has defined Pakistan for me"[3]. In fact, Jinnah had revived Sir Syed Ahmed Khan's contention that the Muslims were a separate nation, distinct from Hindus, but he had no clear idea of having a separate homeland for the Muslims. Gandhi and the Congress, though opposed to the two nation theory, never once refuted Jinnah's arguments in support of the Muslims being a separate nation. This lent support to Jinnah's basic point. Over and above, Gandhi clearly said that as a member of a joint family, the Muslims had every right to seek partition and that the Congress had no means to retain anyone against his wishes. This contention gave a popular sanction to League's demand for Partition. In a way, Gandhi, not Jinnah, may be called the 'Father of Pakistan'.

Smt. Aruna Asaf Ali, the celeberated freedom fighter states, "The Mountbattens came to India only in 1947,whereas the seed of the sub-continent's partition had been sown in the first decade of the century when the British rulers partitioned Bengal in 1905 and created separate electorates for Muslims under the Indian Councils Act 1909".[4]

The matter would have been different if the Congress had rejected the very idea of the Muslims forming a separate nation and of India being a joint family property. It was not done. On the contrary, Congress conceded that the Muslims had a different language of their own, namely, Urdu, that they had their separate Muslim culture; and that they had a separate set of laws, namely, the Shariat. The only tenuous common factor between the Hindus and the Muslims, according to the Congress and the Muslim League, was that both were bound by the British rule. Even now, the Congress continues to harp on those very differences of the Muslims in India. With all these differences continuing Hindu-Muslim unity in impossible. On the contrary, there is every possibility of the twelve crores of Indian Muslims seeking yet another partition. There is also the danger of other religious, linguistic and ethnic minoritics advancing similar demands for autonomous/ independent pockets within India. Granting autonomy to the Muslim majority State of Jammu & Kashmir, as vehemently suppported by a number of noted journalists and Congress leaders, will not solve the Kashmir problem but will make a strong precedent for granting similar autonomy to other Muslim majority districts and areas. Indeed, Congress always claimed to represent the Indian people as a whole and working for the freedom and welfare of all without distinction of caste, class, or religion, but it always talked in terms of Hindus, Muslims, Sikhs, Harijans, Christians, and so on. For a party engaged in the cause of all, it should have been an anathema to talk in such separatist terms.

At the same time, Hindus as a nation or even as a community showed utter lack of political wisdom. In spite of all their alleged caste and creed differences they got together in the fight against the mighty British empire, braving bullets and bayonets, but they miseraby failed against the Muslim dagger. They failed to see the noose of *Ahimsa* tied around their neck by Gandhi. In every town, in every mohalla, the Hindus were left to fend for themselves whenever they were attacked by well organised and well equipped Muslims. It was because the Hindu elite who should have guided and mobilised the Hindu masses against the fanatics of the two nation theory favoured soft options and rallied around Gandhi and the Congress with an eye on their share of booty in the event of transfer of power from the British to Indian hands. There was no identity of purpose or interest between the elite Hindus and the poor, semi-literate, Hindu masses. As a result, in the midst of the worst kind of blood-shed, arson, and loot, the rich and the influential Hindus (barring exceptions) came to India safely from the West Punjab and East Bengal. (This also applies to the Muslims who migrated to Pakistan). This aspect of the tragedy which accompanied the Partition remains unwritten because all the writers, authors, and politicians who have dealt with the subject belonged to the elite classes.

The elite class of Hindus, consisting of lawyers, professionals, civil servants and big business houses, generally looked down upon their less privileged classes as a despicable lot of men and women, ignorant, illiterate, deep-rooted in superstition. The price for a united India asked for by the Muslim League was 33 per cent of government jobs and equal number of seats in the Central

Assembly, equality with Hindus in the Executive Council (Council of Ministers) against a total Muslim population of 24.28 per cent according to 1941 census, right to secede, and above all a virtual veto power in the Legislature. The Partition was accepted with the sole aim of avoiding a bloody civil war, but the blood actually spilt in consequence thereof was far greater than it would have been in a civil war. Still Partition was perferred because a civil war would have threatened and destroyed many of the privileged ones, the aspirants of power. This divergence of interest persists even today.

The Congress itself was a divided house. Its strength lay in its huge financial resources, well-knit organisational set up going right upto remote villages, its propaganda machine and the press support; and populist slogans, promising everything to every organised group. Since Hindus never came up as an organised lot, they were always treated as the sacrificial goats. For that very reason, Hindus were always the victims of false hopes and false propaganda. One of the false hopes held was that the Partition would finally, and for good, settle the ever agonising Hindu-Muslim question. It persists even today and is taking an alarming proportion day by day. The fact is, that neither was the Hindu-Muslim problem solved nor did India get freedom. What India got in 1947, whether through the labours of Gandhi or other factors, was ceding one third of Hindustan to Islamic marauders and transfer of the reins of power from the rational Whites to irrational and unscrupulous Browns. The new Brown Sahibs completely forgot, and strived to make Hindus forget, the Muslim League's slogan, *'Hans ke liya hai Pakistan, lar ke lenge Hindustan'* (We have won Pakistan with all ease but we will take India through war). They also forgot the parameters within which the League and its sword arm, the Muslim National Guard, carried out their 'Direct Action' as brought out by Justice G.D. Khosla in his 'Stern Reckoning':

1. All the Muslims of India should die for Pakistan.
2. With Pakistan established whole of India should be conquered.
3. All people of India should be converted to Islam.
4. Until Pakistan and Indian Empire is established, the following steps should be taken:

(a) All factories, and shops owned by Hindus should be burnt destroyed, looted and loot should be given to League office.
(b) All Muslim Leaguers should carry weapons in defiance of order.
(c) All nationalist Muslims, if they do not join League, must be killed by secret Gestapo.
(d) Hindus should be murdered gradually and their population should be reduced.
(e) All temples should be destroyed.
(f) Karachi, Bombay, Calcutta, Madras, and Visakhapatnam should be paralysed by December 1946 by Muslim League volunteers.
(g) Hindu women and girls should be raped, kidnapped and converted into Muslims from October 18, 1946.
(h) Hindu culture should be destroyed.
(i) All Leaguers should try to be cruel at all times to Hindus, and boycott them socially, economically and in many other ways.

People wonder as to why the Indian Muslims rejoice on seeing Pakistan cricket or hockey team winning over the Indian team and lament on seeing it losing. The reason is simple. They are counting the day when Pakistan will overtake India and establish Islamic rule here. The insurgency in Jammu & Kashmir and in the North East kindles their hopes. The true face of the Muslim psyche can be seen in the Urdu news papers and journals. Time and again Hindus are challenged to come out and fight on the streets without the intervention of the police and the army. Since ninety five per cent of the Muslims in the police force before 1947 and all Muslim units of the army went to Pakistan, the Muslims feel themselves at a loss and are clamouring for proportionate share in the police and armed forces. The Congress, the Communist Parties and their off-shoots forming the "National Front" are lending support to their demands.

In fact, the Partition as envisaged by its founding fathers has not yet taken place. Perhaps, it augurs well for it raises the hope of some day annuling the great artificial divide of a compact whole and India reverting back to one nation and one country. The Partition was thrust on the Indian people on the sole premise

* CF BN Jog, Threat of Islam, pp. 356-357.

that the Muslims formed a separate nation and could not live in peace with the Hindus on terms of equality. Fired with this religious frenzy, Pakistan, the land of the 'faithfuls,' killed or pushed all its Hindu population (except the scheduled castes) to India. The Indian government, on the other hand, thwarted with an iron hand, every attempt to similarly push the Muslims to Pakistan. As a result, the overwhelming majority of the Muslims, including many ardent members of the Muslim league, the propounders of the two nation theory, chose to live in Hindu India. Instead of effecting a cultural integration of these Muslims with the Hindu majority, and others, the Congress government created further dissensions and created all conditions of the pre-partition days which encouraged the fundamentalist Muslims to reorganise, rejuvenate and resurrect the Muslim League with its old separatist thought. They are now nourishing the fond hope that, sooner or later, the existing Hindu India would also become a greater Pakistan or another bigger Islamic state. Their leadership opposes each and every move to integrate and make a common cause with the rest of the Indian people. Such Muslims may be in the Muslim League, in the Congress, in the Communist Party, or the "National Front", their common aim is to establish the hegemony of Islam and the Shariat. This is more pronounced when, on the eve of every parliament session, all Muslim members of Parliament, irrespective of their party affiliations sit together at the official residence of one of the Muslim minister at the Centre and chalk out a common strategy in furtherance of their Islamic goal in a secular polity. On the other hand, Hindus in the Communist Parties are ranegade, in the Congress they are opportunists, in the BJP they are nationalists, and in any other party, they are a rolling stock. Exceptions may be there. Naturally, Hindus have always failed to make a common cause effectively. This weakness of Hindus adds to the strength of the Islamic fundamentalism.

REFERENCES

1 H.V. Hodson, The Great Divide, p. 526.
2 V.P. Menon, Transfer of Power in India, pp. 451-453 (Extract from Punjab Assembly proceedings).
3 Durga Das, India from Curzon to Nehru p. 213.
4 Aruna Asaf Ali, Private Face of a Public Person (Jawaharlal Nehru), Radiant Publishers, E. 155 Kalkaji, New Delhi-19, 1989, p.89.

Chapter XV

ISLAMISATION OF INDIA

The Partition meant dividing India into two independent units so that in the part called Pakistan Muslims would have their say without interference of Hindus and in the other, called India, Hindus would have their say unhampered by Muslims. The Muslim minority in India and the Hindu minority of Pakistan were to have their rights and safeguards as per minority rights recognised by the United Nations.

Originally, Jinnah himself was not a religious bigot nor did he stand for a Muslim theocratice state. As President of the Pakistan's Constituent Assembly, he said on 11August 1947:

> "You are free; you are free to go to your temples you are free to go to your mosques or to any other place of worship in this State of Pakistan. You may belong to any religion or caste or creed-that has nothing to do with the fundamental principle that we are all citizens and equal citizens of one State. Now, I think we should keep that in front of us as our ideal, and you will find that in course of time, Hindus would cease to be Hindus, and Muslims would cease to be Muslims, not in the religious sense, because that is the personal faith of each invididual, but in the political sense as citizens of the State."[1]

In his speech on Pakistan Radio on August 15, 1947, Jinnah said:

> "...the creation of the new State gave the citizens of Pakistan an opportunity to demonstrate to the world how a nation containing many elements could live in peace and amity and work for the betterment of all its citizens, irrespective of

caste or creed. Their object should be "peace within and peace without."[2]

In the first year of Pakistan, a rumour spread in Karachi about Jinnah's Id prayer speech. He had memorised a passage in Arabic from the Quran. After the prayer on the Id grounds, Jinnah addressed the huge gathering and recited the Arabic passage. After the speech, Jinnah turned to Pakistan Minister, Abdur-Rab Nishtar, sitting nearby and asked him, "Have I done that damned thing correctly?" As the mike was on, the whole audience heard it but fortunately nobody knew that the "damned thing" was the Arabic passage Jinnah had recited.[3]

Jinnah assured the minorities that so long as they fulfilled their duties and obligations as loyal citizens of Pakistan they had nothing to fear. He declared "We have no ambitions beyond the desire to live honourably and let others live honourably."[4]

As a matter of fact, Jinnah considered himself in no way inferior to Jawaharlal Nehru or Mahatma Gandhi, but during his long stay with the Congress he had always felt neglected and humiliated at the hands of both. His ego was satisfied only when, at the outset of World War II, the Viceroy invited him and Gandhi together and treated them on an equal footing. Thereafter, it was only Gandhi and Nehru who called on Jinnah and Jinnah rebuffed them each time until he got Pakistan. If Gandhi was hailed as the Father of the Indian nation, Jinnah was hailed as the Father of Pakistan and 'Qaid-e-Azam'. After getting his Pakistan, Jinnah tried to revert back to his old self, a secularist. But it was too late. In the last phase of his struggle against the Congress and the British Government, Jinnah had virtually become the mouthpiece of the bigot Mullahs and the Ulemas. A country which had come up on the strength of religious frenzy alone together with a bloody hate-Hindu campaign could not proceed on a secular path. Jinnah died a neglected and a disheartened man. It did not take long for Pakistan to say 'good bye' to secularism and declare itself an Islamic state to be governed by the Shariat Law.

In India, Gandhiji was assasinated on January 30, 1948. After his ashes were immersed in the Triveni at Parayag (the confluence of Ganga, Yamuna and the underground Saraswati), Jawaharlal, Sardar Patel and Rajendra Prasad addressed a mass meeting. When the meeting was over, Rafi Ahmed Kidwai whispered to Durga

Das, "Jawaharlal has performed the last rites not only of Gandhi but of Gandhism as well. Now that the master has gone, there will be no one to discipline the crowd. The High Command is dead".[5] The fact however, is that since 1920 Gandhi himself had gone on compromising his ideals of a Ram Rajya before the whims and fancies of the Islamic fundamentalism. In his 'Young India' in January 1921, Gandhi wrote:

> "I want to warn the readers that they should not form an idea that I am, today, engaged in establishing the Swarajya of the kind described in the book (Hind Swarajya). I know India is not yet ready for it...The aim of all my collective efforts today is to get a Parliamentary form of Government."[6]

Interestingly, Gandhi had, in his 'Hind Swarajya', named the British parliament, a prostitute and a barren. He had given elaborate and cogent reasons in support of his contention.[7]

In spite of all his brave front, Gandhi always suffered from a Muslim phobia which he carefully concealed under his philosophic jargon of Hindu-Muslim unity, the cherished mission of his later life. While Gandhi always adopted a confrontationist attitude towards the British, he went on succumbing to each and every demand of the Muslims, howsoever irrational. The Muslims said that Urdu was their religious or cultural language, Gandhi conceded and shifted his stress from Hindi to Hindustani. Whenever he faced Muslim audience he tried to speak in chaste Urdu. A section of the Muslims objected to singing of '*Vande Mataram*', and Gandhi relented. His confidant, Mohammed Ali, said that even the most characterless Muslim was superior to Gandhi, Gandhi defended Mohammed Ali's statement saying it was in accordance with the Islamic tenet. Even as early as 1909, when Gandhi was in South Africa and the Muslims had demanded separate electroate, Gandhi said, "There is mutual distrust between Hindus and the Muslims. If Muslims demand certain rights from Lord Morley why should Hindus object to it? If Hindus don't object, the British would be non-plussed and Muslims would gradually start trusting Hindus."[8] Gandhi had, however, a godly gift of philosophising away all his views and actions which, though far removed from the realities of life, made a great impact on the gullible and ignorant Hindu masses. It was the Muslim phobia which led Gandhi to suggest to Lord Mountbatten, as a last resort to avoid

Partition, to invite Jinnah to become the Prime Minister of undivided India and to choose his ministers from any source. Lord Mountbatten had agreed to proceed on this line but wanted that the Congress should also accept Gandhi's proposal. As expected, Jawaharlal and Patel did not agree to it.[9] Gandhi's Muslim phobia would be evident from his observation on cow protection made as early as 1909:

> "I worship cow which means reverence. Cow is the protector of India because agriculture, India's life-line depends on cow progeny. Cow is useful in many ways. Even our Muslim brothers will agree to it.
>
> But as I rever the cow I rever the human being. Just as cow is useful so the man is also useful, whether he be a Muslim or Hindu. Should I, then, fight with a Muslim to save cow. Should I kill the Muslim? By doing so, I will be an enemy of both the Muslim and the cow. Therefore, I say, the best way to save cow is that I should, with folded hands, make an appeal to the Muslim brother to save the cow for the cause of the country. If he does not agree, I should let the cow be killed because it is not in my power to save her. If I extremely feel for the cow, I should lay my own life but should not take the life of a Muslim. That is the law of religion, according me."[10]

In promoting Nehru, instead of Patel, to the Prime Ministership too, the prime consideration with Gandhi was appeasement of Muslims. At the time, Maulana Azad and many others were dubbing Patel as anti-Muslim. They told Gandhi that only Nehru commanded the confidence of the Muslim youth and was fit to lead the country. Had Gandhi cared for his ideals of "Hind Swarajya", he would have favoured Patel, not Jawaharlal. He was fully aware of Jawaharlal's socialist ideology, atheism, and anti Hindu/Hindi stance, love for English and Western culture, and industrialisation, all vertically opposed to Gandhi's professed ideology. The fact as already stated is that Gandhi himself had moved far away from Gandhism which had by now been reduced to a matter of table talk or a mere slogan for mass consumption. Gandhi's pro-Muslim policy of pre-partition days was adopted as a political strategy by the Congress in post-partition period, under the guise of secularism and socialism. Jawaharlal Nehru's anti-Hindu stance was well known. Patel sometimes called him the only nationalist Muslim in the Congress cabinet. In close concert with Maulana Azad, an orthodox Muslim, Nehru systematically established the hegemony of Islam and Urdu and set out on a path that virtually meant Islamisation of India. Prominent among the steps taken in this direction are enumerated in subsequent paras.

MEDDLING WITH CONSTITUTION

Throughout the freedom struggle, Congress was hammering on two points. Firstly, that the constitution of India should be made by a body elected through universal adult suffrage, and secondly, that the Provinces (States) would have the maxium autonomy. Both these assurances were brushed under the carpet. The Indian Constituent Assembly consisted of the members elected on the old pattern of limited franchise. Moreover, most of the 93 seats allotted to the princely states remained vacant. The present Constitution cannot, therefore, be said to represent the popular will of the Indian people. It is a Congress document tilted towards establishing Muslim hegemony in the guise of minority rights. The popular demands for banning cow-slaughter and making Hindi the official language of the Indian Union were incorporated in such a treacherous phraseology that both the objectives were rendered impracticable. In the past 47 years, the Congress governments at the Centre and in the States have encrouaged the anti-Hindi lobby and promoted the slaughter of animals.

It was Jawaharlal Nehru himself who got Article 370 incorporated in the Indian Constitution by which J & K, the only Muslim majority State secured the right to have its separate Constitution, though forming part of the Indian Union. It is a classic example of a State within a State. Dr. B. R. Ambedkar, Chairman of the Drafting Committee and the Law Minister, was not in favour of such a separatist provision. Sardar patel wanted J & K to be fully integrated to India, like other princely states. The Cabinet was divided over the issue. The trend in the Congress Legislature Party favoured Patel's stand. But "Patel put the unity and solidarity of the Government before everything else and backed Nehru formula".[11] It may be stated that, in their discussions with the Cripps Mission, the Cabinet Mission and Lord Mountbatten, the Sikh representatives had been asking for the rights and privileges as given to the Muslims. When a semi independent status (Article 370) was granted to the Muslim majority State of J & K, the Sikhs in Panjab, being in majority, got a strong point to agitate for an autonomous Punjabi Suba. Thus, the Panjab problem is a direct consequence of Article 370.

Maulana Azad wanted reservation of seats for the Muslims and other minorities. Patel was opposed to it. Nehru, a close ally of the Maulana, excused himself and asked Patel to resolve the matter with the minority representatives. Fortunately, two women members of the Advisory Committee on Minorities helped Patel. Raj Kumari Amrit Kaur, speaking for the Indian Christians, strongly opposed reservation of seats on the basis of religion. Begum Aizaz Rasul of Lucknow, an erstwhile staunch Muslim Leaguer, said that the Muslims left behind in India, were an integral part of the nation and needed no safeguards. Patel seized this crucial moment to declare that the Muslims were unanimously in favour of joint electorates.[12]

Due to Jawaharlal and his cohorts, lots of difficulties were placed in the way of adoption of Hindi as the national link language. Throughout the freedom struggle, leaders of every province, especially those from Maharashtra and Gujarat (besides U. P., Panjab, Bihar, Madhya Pradesh, and Rajasthan), had zealously pleaded for Hindi as the symbol of nationhood. In fact, though English was the link language of the elite, the language which linked the masses of the country was invariably Hindi. Nehru made it incumbent on the promoters of Hindi to work out a formula that would be acceptable to the non-Hindi regions, especially Madras (Tamilnadu) and Bengal. Finally, the formula providing for replacement of English by Hindi in fifteen years was incorporated in the Constitution. With the reorganisation of States in 1956 on linguistic basis, regionalism and fanaticism for regional languages pushed Hindi aside. Amidst the controversy between Hindi and the regional languages, the roots of English went on getting stronger and deeper. In the meantime, the Muslims were encouraged to raise the question of promoting Urdu, which got all support from the Congress and other anti-Hindi parties.

A greater mischief was played in the part relating to the Fundamental Rights. The tragedy is that, even after 45 years of the Constitution, the intelligentsia is ignorant about its evil effects.[14] Article 14 guarantees to every citizen, irrespective of religion, race, caste or sex, equality before law and equal protection of law; Art. 15 prohibits discrimination of any citizen on any ground; Art. 16 guarantees equality of opportunity for all in matters of public employment; Art. 17 abolishes untouchability; Art. 19 guarantees to all citizens the freedom of speech and expression, to peaceful assembly, form association, move freely throughout the territory of India and practise any profession; Art. 25 guarantees freedom of conscience and the right to profess, practise and propagate religion (subject to public order, morality and health); Art. 26 gives the right to every religious denomination to establish and maintain its religious and charitable institutions and to own and acquire moveable and immovable property (subject to public order, health and morality).

In view of the fact that all the fundamental rights, conforming to UNO's declaration on human rights, were included in the Constitution, it is difficult to understand what prompted the learned Constitution makers to confer additional rights and guarantees in Articles 29 and 30 to all minorites whether based on religion, language, script or culture. Art. 30 empowers the minorities to establish and administer their own educational institutions and also enjoy grants-in-aid from the State. By an amendment of 1978, the right to property in Art. 31 ceased to be a fundamental right in general but its provision were added to Art. 30 in respect of the minority institutions. With these two Articles, the minority communities, meaning practically the Muslims and the Christians have been given a superior position with an unhindered right to force their distinctiveness in language, script or culture according to their whims and fancies and at the same time receive financial aid from the Govetnment. It is a subtle way of granting a superior status to the Muslims and the Christians which they enjoyed during the Muslim rule and the British Raj. India makes a unique case of democracy where the will of the minorities prevails over the majority. Notably, the special minority rights are not subject to public order, health and morality. Thus, the Muslims insist that polygamy and cow slaughter being part of their culture are their fundamental rights.

The overriding nature of Articles 29 and 30 can be gauged from the Supreme Court judgment in the State of Bombay versus Bombay Education Society, (1955) SCR 568, which *inter alia* held:

> "Even though Hindi is the national language of India and article 351 provides a special directive upon the State to promote the spread of Hindi, nevertheless the object canot be achieved by any means which contravenes the rights guaranteed by Articles 29 or 30...."

The special provisions of Articles 29 and 30 meant to be a shield for the minorities have now turned into a sword. Indeed, the concept of religious minorities in the Indian Constitution is repugnant to the basic concept of secularism. It can be valid in countries, like U.K. or the USA, where Christianity has been made a state religion. But, in India where no religion is a state religion, secularism being the State motto, any special right to religious minorities is destructive to the very root of secularism. Article 17 has abolished 'untouchability' from the Hindu society. The use of the word 'Harijan' to a person of the Scheduled Caste is a punishable offence. But, in the case of Muslims, the Ulemas, the Qazis and the Muslim religious institutions enjoy an extra-legal authority of declaring any one as an apostate and issue fatwa against him on the slightest pretext. They also have the right to teach their students in their Madrasas that Hindus are 'Kafirs' which is a far more derogatory term than 'Harijan' or 'Untouchable'. The victim has no legal remedy whatsoever against such excommunication and use of abusive words for Hindus and the resultant damage.

Thus, the Indian constitution, though pretending to be secular in shape is communal in content, tilted towards Islam. It provides for all kinds of differentiations and prescriptions for various types of people in the name of religion, language, culture, caste, tribe, majority, minority, backward or forward.

Apart from the above, the Shariat law of the Muslims that has been allowed to continue is a big wedge between the Muslims and the Hindus. In the famous Shah Bano case, a five judges Constitution Bench of the Supreme Court had held, 1985 (2) SCC (Cr.) 556, that Section 125 of the Criminal Procedure Code was applicable to all communities, including the Muslims, and thus a divorced Muslim woman was also entitled to maintenance from her ex-husband. This judgment was initially hailed by the Congress leaders. Its one of the Muslim ministers in Rajiv Gandhi's cabinet, Arif Mohammed Khan, strongly defended it in Parliament. In fact, even before the Supreme Court judgment, certain High courts and lower courts had held the same view and granted maintenance to divorced Muslim women. But the Supreme Court judgment caused a stir among the Muslim Ulemas. Succumbing to their wishes, the Rajiv Gandhi government amended Section 125 of the Cr. PC to make it inapplicable to Muslims and thus the Supreme Court judgment was rendered ineffective. Arif Mohammed Khan resigned from the Government. Emboldened by this success, the Muslim Personal Law Board adopted still a greater militant attitude. The real damage in amending Section 125 of the Cr. PC lies in the fact that the Islamic fundamentalism made a dent in the Indian Criminal Law which had hitherto been uniform for over a hundred years. Now a number of Ulemas have started saying that the Muslims are not bound by such of the provisions of the Indian Constitution which go against the law laid down by the Shariat.

In 1994, in a landmark judgment in one Khatoonisa talaq case, Justice Hari Nath Tilhari of Allahabad High Court held that the tripple talaq (divorce in one sitting by pronouncing 'talaq' thrice) was invalid and also that in a conflict between the customary law and the Fundamental Rights/Duties, the latter shall prevail. A lot of hue and cry was raised on behalf of the Muslims. Members of the Muslim Personal Law Board and a number of Parliament Members (MPs) cried out that the Indian courts had no right to interfere with the Muslim Personal Law. Going a step further, some zealots asserted that only the Muslim Personal Law Board and 'the Shariat courts' established by it were competent to pronounce judgment in relation to Muslims' presonal matters. The editorial of the Indian Express daily of April 21, 1994, rightly observed "these Muslim leaders are making out a plea for removing India's largest minority from the purview of parliamentary legislation and judicial review. In blunt terms they are demanding a system of dual sovereignty for the Muslim community." Protesting against these remarks, Syed Shahabuddin, MP, stressed that since the time of the freedom stuggle, the Congress had been assuring the Muslims of non-interference in the Muslim Personal Law. According to him, what the Muslim Personal Law Board wanted was not sovereignty, but only the authority to interpret the Shariat law. What a novel way of seeking an Islamic state within a secular Indian State!

Time and again, it is said on behalf of the Muslims that the Quran is the word of God and no one has the power to chage a word of it. They conveniently ignore the fact that the Vedas and the Bible too are the words of God. India had adopted secularism, placing the Quran, the Vedas and the Bible on an equal pedestal. The Muslims must follow this creed like all others. If the Muslims leaders feel that it would mean Hinduisation of the Indian Muslims, let it be so. They are already Hinduised in the matter of criminal law (IPC), and most of the civil laws and continue to be Muslims. Why then, the Indian Muslims would cease to be Muslims by adopting a common civil code? They need to be told that those who had thought in terms of the Shariat alone and wanted that the Shariat should precede every other law have already got Pakistan. A demand for placing the Shariat law over and above the Indian constitution virtually means seeking conversion of India into another Pakistan, a theocratic Muslim state. The more astounding fact is that the Congress and other political parties (except BJP) are supporting the Muslim demand on Shariat law. In this situation, the liberal and free thinking Muslims find themselves very insecure. The Supreme Court, in May 1995, in the case of Sarla Mudgal versus Union of India, had suggested to the Central Government to enact a uniform civil code in implementation of Article 44 of the Consititution. However, there were clear indications that the then ruling Congress government was in no mood to oblige the Supreme Court. The then Prime Minister, Shri Narasimha Rao, assured the members of the Muslim Personal Law Board that, unless a contrary demand came from the Muslims themselves, the Shariat law would continue. The successive 'National Front' government has assured the Muslim Ulemas of its policy of non-interference in Muslim Personal Law.

The Muslim Personal Law board is a self appointed body. It is funny that the government of India treats it as a body representing the whole Muslim society just as the British government did for the Muslim League in pre-Partition days. Interestingly, the 'Times of India' found after conducting an opinion poll among 2330 men and women of voting age in the cities of Delhi, Bombay, Calcutta, Madras, Bangalore, Ahmedabad, Lucknow, Hyderabad and Cochin, that 84 per cent of the respondents wanted a uniform civil code for all irrespective of their religion. Those who agreed with the view that a uniform code should be introduced only if the minorities (meaning the Muslims) demand it are mostly concentrated in Hyderabad.[13] It needs to be recalled that when the Congress Government introduced the Hindu Code Bill in 1953, it did not wait for a demand to come from the Hindu religious institutions or Hindu social organisations. Again, when it brought the Terrorists and Disruptive Activities Bill (TADA) in 1985 against the Sikh terrorists, it did not seek prior public opinion. How is it that it now insists on a demand to come from the Muslim organisations before introducing a common civil code? Article 44 of the Constitution was adopted by a Constituent Assembly which had Muslim members also.

The fact is that the Congress party and all the thirteen political parties who jointly make the 'National Front', currently ruling at the Centre with the Congress support, are committed to support the Shariat law. Intentionally or foolishly, they are making way for India to become a theocratic Islamic country. This thought very much coincides with the Congress claim time and again that India is the second largest Muslim country in the world. During the tenure of Smt. Indira Gandhi as Prime Minister, attempts were made at the ministerial level to obtain for India the membership of the Organisation of the Islamic Countries (OIC). The OIC did not, however, oblige.

The British considered India as a country of Muslims and non-Muslims and, after a hundred years of political struggle, partitioned it on the same basis. For the last 50 years, the ruling Congress has again been considering the truncated India in terms of Muslims and non-Muslims. 'Hindu' factor was almost non-existent for the British and so has it been for the Congress. The outcome can better be imagined than described.

CONGRESS ADMINISTRATION

The administrative policy of the Congress has been in no way different from that of the British from whom it received the reins of power. The British justified their continued rule in India to protect the minority communities, the Scheduled Castes and the Scheduled Tribes. The Congress adopted this very principle. To it, Jawaharlal Nehru added his own anti-Hindu bias. He was a known atheist. But, while he saw no evil in Islam and was largely dependent on Maulana Azad, one of the most orthodox Islamic zealots, Nehru saw every evil in Hindu religion. He assiduoulsy kept himself away from any religious Hindu or Hindu organisation, and was always apologetic about his Hindu birth. So, it was his mission to abolish all Hindu sentiments from India. M.J. Akbar, an MP and a noted historian of the Nehru family, writes:

> ".....*He (Nehru) regarded the perennial threat of Hindu dominance as a major danger to the unity of India which could survive only through a commitment to secularism... What worried him even more than the official parties of Hindu revivalism—the Hindu Mahasabha or the Jan Sangh —was the possibility of Gandhi's Congress being usurped by such elements.He could not drive this element out of Congress for that would then have driven them straight into the Jan Sangh. But he kept them under strong check. As his own influence increased, theirs (meaning Sardar Patel and his supporters like P.D. Tandon and K.M. Munshi) were slowly weeded or put into the limbo....* A little before the Bhubaneshwar Congress (in January 1964 when he had a stroke from which he could never recover), remembers Gundevia (a former Secretary General of the External Affairs Ministry), Nehru had joined one of the Friday morning meetings at the Foreign Office where all the senior and junior bureaucrats gathered for a general free-for-all...The topic shifted to the professed neutrality of the Indian Civil Service.
>
> "Gundevia asked, 'Well Sir, this being the case what happens if tomorrow, shall we say the Communists come into power? We have had a Communist government in Kerala. But what happens to the services if the Communists are elected to power, tomorrow, at the Centre, here in Delhi?
>
> "Nehru pondered before answering. 'Communists, Communists, Communists! why are you all so obsessed with Communists and Communism? What is it that Communists can do and we cannot do and have not done for the country? Why do you imagine, the Communists will ever be voted into power at the Centre?' A pause and then the words came slowly and deliberately: 'The danger to India, mark you, is not communism. It is Hindu right wing communalism.' Before the meeting closed he repeated those two sentences..."[14]

Gandhi murder (Jan 30, 1948) gave Nehru the much wanted opportunity. The assasin was a Brahmin and he had killed Gandhi in the cause of Hindus. Thus, the whole Hindu community and all those who talked about Hindus were put in the dock. The Rashtriya Swayamsevak Sangh (RSS) was banned even after knowing that it had no hand in the Gandhi murder. On the other hand, the Muslim League who had caused the Partition and which had direct hand in the bloodshed throughout the country since 1946 was allowed to reorganise and grow. Later, Jawaharlal even blessed the Muslim League by giving it a secular certificate and forming a coalition government with it in Kerala. Thus, the first act of Islamisation of India (after Partition) was banning the RSS and allowing the Muslim League to continue its Islamic politics.

The Hindu community was infected with a false guilt complex of the Gandhi murder. At the same time, an army of British oriented historians, Marxist scribes, artists, singers, playwrights, were employed to highlight the plight of Scheduled Castes allegedly caused by the priests and upper caste Hindus. The fact that the Scheduled Castes were badly treated had been recognised in the nineteenth century itself and a number of Hindu leaders and organisations, like the Arya Samaj, had been engaged in removing untouchability and caste distinctions much before the Congress was born. But, the renewed thrust of the Congress government was primarily intended to organise the Scheduled Castes and the Scheduled Tribes against the upper caste Hindus and thus divide Hindus into two ever warring sections. Language was another weapon used to divide Hindus into two camps, one speaking the Aryan languages in the North and the other speaking the Dravidian languages in the South. So long as Jawaharlal was alive, he repeatedly told the people of the South that Hindi would not be 'imposed' upon them unless they themselves wanted it. It was similar to the assurance given to the Muslims that their Shariat law would not be touched unless they themselves wanted it. Both these assurances were against the Constitutional provisions, but Jawaharlal was always in the habit of exceeding his brief even before he became the Prime Minister. The funny part of the whole affair is that he recognised Urdu as the common language of all the Muslims in India, whether in the North, South, West or East. He gave Urdu all encouragement and facilities to come up and be a challenger to Hindi. Urdu, it ought to be remembered, was one of the main rallying points in the demand for Pakistan. Falsehood of this point became evident in 1971, when East Pakistan became Bangladesh mainly on the ground that it had a separate language, Bengali, and a different culture from West Pakistan. Presently, in Pakistan, Urdu is being vehemently opposed by Sindhis, Baluchis, and certain other sections, but in India the Indian Government is engaged in opening a Urdu University. In fact, for about a century, Urdu had been the larguage of Islamic politics in the Indian sub-continent as the English was and continues to be the language of the British and American imperialism.

All actions of the Congress governments, or the governments formed by its splinter groups in the States, have been actuated by the same British policy of dividing Hindus into various categories (Dalits, non-Dalits, Dravids-Aryans, Hindi speaking-non-Hindi speaking, etc.), destruction of Hindu culture, twisting Hindu history and propping up Islamic fundamentalists. In pursuance of this very policy, about 20 million Bangladeshis have been allowed to infiltrate and settle in various parts of India. Under this very policy, the Mullahs and Maulvis have become the pampered lot and no notice is taken even when they solemnise the marriage of under age girls of 10-12 years with the rich Arabs of over 50 years age, in violation of the Child Marriage Restraint Act 1929 (amended by an Act of 1949) which prohibits the marriage of a girl below 15 years of age. Then, there is Indira Gandhi's 15 point programme and subsequent schemes fromulated by the Government of India intended to benefit the Muslims in getting public employment, government loans and free education while large numbers of Hindus below the poverty line, have to fend for themselves.

A number of books and pamphlets have come up during the past few years lamenting over the plight of Hindus in Hindu India, namely;

(i) reduction in their numerical strength from 85 per cent in 1951 to 82 per cent in 1991 (leaving the Sikhs, Bouddh & Jains) and corresponding increase in the Muslim population from 10 per cent in 1951 to about 13 per cent in 1991.

(ii) Segregation of districts having 15 per cent or more of Muslim population and branding them as minority dominated districts, numbering 40, and giving special banking and other facilities to the Muslim inhabitants.

(iii) Special drives to recruit Muslims in the Provincial police, Central Reserve Police Force, Border Security Force, and so on, by relaxing educational and other qualifications to bring a parity between Hindus and Muslims.

(iv) At the time of Partition, the Hindus in West Pakistan were 22 per cent, but their number by 1981 was reduced to less than 2 per cent. In East Pakistan, Hindus were 33 per cent but their number by 1981 came down to 10 per cent. Inspite of these figures, it is propagated in the world that Hindus in India are persecuting the Muslims and the Indian Embassies in foreign countries are not contradicting this false propaganda.

(v) Almost every communal riot is triggered off by the Muslims returning from the mosques after the Friday namaz, but propaganda made through the mass media is that every riot is caused by Hindus.

(vi) In whichever Indian State the Muslims or the Christians are in a majority, they have overriding special powers like Article 370 and wherever they are in a minority they enjoy special minority rights of Art. 29 and 30. Thus, Hindus are at the receiving end whether they be in a majority or minority.

One would not be surprised at the above situation if one were to know that the Indian rulers since 1947, though bearing Hindu names, are actually a band of Hindu-apologists, or anti-Hindu chauvinists who, swayed by the material prosperity of the West, have indulged in self-negation. Even in the later part of the nineteenth century, Smt. Annie Besant had described the conduct of such people in the following words:

> " Scepticism and materialism had eaten out of the life of the nation. The crowds of the so-called English educated class were followers of Huxley, Mill and Spencer and had entirely forgotten their own literature; were contemptuous of the past and hence hopeless for the future; they were copying English furniture to the destruction of Indian arts and crafts. They had lost all national spirit.

De-spiritulisation had brought about national degeneracy. There was no activity of national life, no pulsing of the national heart...."[15]

In the twentieth century, the tribe of English educated modernists, drowned deep into the Western culture and Marxist thought, expanded by leaps and bounds. It was this tribe to whom the British handed over the political power. The modernists' view has been that Hindutva and Islam were both outdated and India had to come up as a new nation with a 'scientific outlook' towards life and a political thought of the West. They have continued their tirade against Hindus, Hindu thought, and Hindu religion, but have made compromises with the Islamic zealots as a matter of political expediency, only to counter the possibility of Hindu revival. Like the British imperialists, they have engineered communal riots as and when their position is seriously threatened. After the riots , these very modernists rush to the rescue of the Muslims and call names to Hindu leaders and Hindu organisations.

Jawaharlal Nehru always gave false hopes to the nation that, with the economic and educational development, the Muslims would shed their religious bigotry and love for Pakistan. It served his two pronged purpose, of enlisting the Muslim support and of pacifying the Hindu susceptibilities. At the same time, he did everything to promote Urdu and protect the Shariat law, the two major rallying points of the fundamentalist Muslims which once culminated into the creation of Pakistan. It is surprising how did Jawaharlal Nehru forget the recent history of the Muslims before Partition when the Muslim League raised another demand as soon as one was accepted? Following the same pattern, the Muslims have been going on adding to their ever increasing demands. A time has now come when the Congress is unable to rally the Muslims behind it even after providing huge financial assistance to their madrasas, their mosques, their pilgrimage to Mecca, their Islamic studies, Urdu academies, various schemes of granting them bank loans, free coaching for competitive examinations for public services, and so on. It is all because the Muslim leadership had now come to realise that with the financial aid coming from the Arab countries and military support from Pakistan, they need not play a second fiddle to the Congress, but should be the direct rulers of India. For that matter they first shifted their allegiance to the

Janata Dal and later to a combination of the Dalits, the Christians, the Sikhs and the Muslims, called the Bahujan Samaj Party (BSP). A news item in the Times of India, New Delhi, June 23, 1995 reads:

> "Muslim political parties in Uttar Pradesh are working on a strategy by which they can share power in the State on the basis of what they call the 'Bahujan Samaj Party (BSP Model)' in the state.
>
> "The plan is to forge a Muslim collectivity which can then bargain with any major political party for a share in power in exchange for votes—to be a 'bhagidaar' (shareholer) in power rather than a 'tabedar' (servant).
>
> "To this end, the leaders of the state units of the Indian Union Muslim League (IUML), the Indian National League (INL), Muslim Majlis and the Insaf Party, are meeting in Meerut on June 25...."

Their plan is, however, jeopardised by the wave of Hindutva launched under the banner of the Bharatiya Janata Party, about a decade ago. The Congress composed largely of modernist elite has, of necessity, to proceed on its old policy of Muslim appeasement because of the fear of being swept by the wave of Hindutva. So, in the States where the Congress is in a weak position, it goes with any party or parties which is opposed to the BJP or the like.

A classic example of the Congress dilemma can be seen in the conduct of Jawaharlal Nehru towards Sheikh Abdullah. In a meeting held on 15 April 1962, in the presence of late Lal Bahadur Shastri and other dignitaries, Jawaharlal candidly spoke about the stark communal stance of the Sheikh. In the words of B.N. Mullick:

> "He continued his talk against the Sheikh and mentioned all his communal activities throughout the period he had acted as the National Conference leader. It was the Pakistani aggression which had mellowed him a little for a short time, because the tribals had committed gruesome atrocities on the Muslim population in the Valley. But, as soon as he became the Prime Minister, he came out in his true colours once

> again and started his anti-Hindu activities...The Sheikh always talked about the rights of the Muslims forgetting that the Hindus also formed 35 per cent of the population of the State and he never showed any consideration for them...".[16]

But Jawaharlal got the Kashmir Conspiracy case against Sheikh Abdullah withdrawn in 1964 and, after his release, the Sheikh was invited by Jawaharlal to live with him in the Teen Murty House as a family member. The Congress has not changed its course till today.

SHADY SECULARISM

While the administrative policy of the Congress Government was modelled on the pattern left behind by the British, its religious policy was patterned on the lines of Aurangzeb, that is, giving supremacy to the Sunni faith of Islam. The Congress and the Marxist historians patronised by the Congress laboured hard to glorify the Mughal rule of the medieval period and to prove that Aurangzeb was a secular emperor. Aurangzeb had re-introduced jazia (religious tax) on Hindus, but the jazia levied on Hindus by the Congress Government had been indirect. It is the Hindu tax-payers' money from which the Congress Government had been spending Rs. twentyfive to fifty crores annually on Muslim pilgrimage to Mecca (Haj) and which largely benefits Saudi Arabia's economy. On the other hand, it does not spend a single penny on the Hindu pilgrims to Kailash-Mansarover. It makes liberal grants to Islamic institutions and the study of Islam. The status of Sanskrit, the link language of ancient India and the mother of all Indian vernaculars, has been reduced to one of a foreign language, like Persian and Arabic. Aurangzeb is known to have made grants to some selected Hindu temples or institutions which supported his policy. In the same way, the Congress Government has bestowed favour on a few selected Hindu godmen, institutions, and temple heads who toed its 'secular' line and helped in its money making and vote catching programmes.

During an official visit of the Indian Prime Minister, Shri P.V. Narasimha Rao, to Uzbekistan, in 1993, the Uzbek President,in his address at the State reception, referred to the age old ties between India and Uzbekistan and said that Babar was the first cultural ambassador of Uzbekistan to India. The Indian Prime

Minister did not dare to refute this outrageous observation though knowing well that Babar was a barbarious invader even in the words of Shri Nanak Deva, the first Sikh Guru who was a contemporary of Babar. In a similar situation in an Arab country, Mohammed-bin-Kasim, the Arab invader of Sindh in 712 AD, was termed as an ambassador of peace.

Aurangzeb had the distinction of causing the maximum conversion of Hindus to Islam. The Congress did not lag behind. During its regime, the Muslim population of India went up from 10 per cent in 1951 to nearly 13 per cent in 1991 and the Hindu population correspondingly went down from 85 per cent to 82 per cent during the same period. As a result of the massive illegal migration of Muslims from Bangladesh, ten districts of Assam (out of 23) have become Muslim majority districts; in West Bengal almost all the nine border districts except two or three have become Muslim majority or near Muslim majority districts. In 56 constituencies of West Bengal, Muslims have a decisive voice.[17] In fact about 20 million (2 crore) Muslims have infilterated in to India from Bangladesh and comfortably settled themselves in various states of India. The Congress and the Communist Parties of India have encouraged this migration in the same way as the Muslim rulers of the medieval period encouraged Muslim migration from the Central and Western Asia. Urdu is recognised as the religious language of the Muslims. In U.P. and Bihar where Muslim population was just 16 and 14 per cent respectvely[18] Urdu was declared as the addditional official language. While Hindus (including Sikhs, Jains and Bouddhas) have neen brought under a unified civil code, called the Hindu Marriage Act, Hindu Adoption and Succession Act, etc., by abrogating almost the entire Hindu Shastric law, the Shariat law has been recognised as the law for the Muslims. The earlier Hindu law (based on Hindu Shastras) validated polygamy, did not allow divorce, permitted marriage only outside one's '*gotra*' did not allow equal share to girls in family property. All these provisions have been reversed in the new codified Hindu law. The term 'Hindu law' is a misnomer because it is largely based on the English law. The Indian Constitution lays down (Art. 13) that all earlier laws, in force which are inconsistent with the fundamental rights would, to the extent of inconsistency, be void. But the Congress Government has made an exception to the inconsistencies of the Shariat law (A case whether the inconsistent provisions of the Shariat law are void or not is presently pending a final dicision in the Supreme Court).

Even when 84 per cent of the Indian population consists of Hindus, Sikhs, Jains or Bouddhs (all of the same Hindu stock), the Congress Government proudly proclaims that India is the second largest Islamic country. On the other hand, it is blasphemous to call India a Hindu State (Hindu Rashtra). The Congress Government has passed the places of worship Act to preclude the Hindus from claiming any right on their most sacred places of worship, namely, the Krishna Janmabhoomi temple in Mathura and Kashi-Vishwanath temple of Varanasi, both destroyed by Aurangzeb, and the Ramajanmabhoomi temple in Ayodhya demolished by Babar. The hegemony of Islam and a second class status to Hinduism is fortified by Article 30 of the Constitution by which Islamic and Christian institutions are placed at a higher pedestal. The Hindu institutions are always open to Government interference and encroachment and are ineligible for Government grants. Its recent example is the forcible acquisition of 12.19 acres of temple land of Shri Ramanujacharya, founder of the Bhakti cult. The land was acquired in 1992 disregarding vehement protests from His Holiness Shri Varada Ethiraja Jeer, the resident custodian of Sriperumbudur temple land, to erect a memorial for Rajiv Gandhi. Had it been a Muslim Wakf Board land or a land dedicated to a mosque, Government would not have touched it and erected the memorial somewhere else.

Aurangzeb wanted that Muslims should not mix up with Hindus and even the Muslims of non-Sunni faith. Incidentally, upto the reign of Akbar, inter-religious marriages between Hindus and Muslims were prevalent in the Punjab and Kashmir. These were prohibited by the successive orders of Jehangir and Shahjahan. The Congress Government has taken all action to keep Hindus and Muslims in separate and ever fighting camps. This is a natural consequence of the Shariat law and the Congress Government is vehemently opposed to replace it by a common civil code. However, while Aurangzeb proudly called himself a Sunni Muslim and swore by the Quran and the Shariat, the Congress leaders are hypocrites. They call themselves Gandhian and swear by secularism and democracy.

In January 1995, the BJP Government of Delhi submitted two models of tableaux for the Republic Day Parade on the 26th

January. Model-I showed the coronation of the Pandava king Yudhishthira of Indraprastha, the ancient name of Delhi. It was rejected on the ground that it showed a religious bias. Model-2 depicted Prithvi Raj Chouhan, the last Hindu king before Islamic rule was established on Delhi by Mohammed Ghori. It was also rejected on grounds that it showed Prithvi Raj in Kesaria battle dress with a Kesaria flag which was presumed to be hurting Muslim sentiments. The message was clear that Hindus had to forget all past history that might cause annoyance to fundamentalist Muslims. Consequently, the pageant of Republic Day Parade of 1995 went without any tableaux from the capital state of Delhi.

The net result of the religious policy of the Congress and the Marxists is that the Indian Muslims have grown more fanatic than those of any other Islamic country.

The framers of the Indian Consitution, especially Dr. B.R. Ambedkar, were well aware of the evil effects of the Shariat law. They, therefore, wanted to rid India of it by introducing Article 44 which directs the Government to enact a common civil code for the whole country so as to do away with both the Shariat law of the Muslims and the Shastric law of the Hindus. It was essential for a country like India which made secularism its basic creed. Simultaneously, they provided in Aritcle 13(1) that all previous laws which were inconsistent with the provisions of the fundamental rights would, to the extent of their inconsistency, be null and void. But, while the Congress government hurried to replace the Hindu customary law based on Hindu Shastra, through a Hindu Code Bill, in 1954, it let the Shariat law prevail among the Muslims. To all pleas for a common civil code, Jawaharlal Nehru's reply was that time was not ripe for bringing the Muslims under a common civil law. The actual reason was and remains to be that the political interests of the Congress are, more or less, identical to those of the erstwhile British imperialists and it had had a vested interest in retaining the Muslims and Hindus in separate compartments. It, therefore, let the Shariat have full play in continuing the Muslims as a distinct political force to keep the Hindus at bay.

The Shariat law allows a Muslim to have more than one wife. Lured by this provision, an appreciable number of Hindus gets converted to Islam every year only to marry another woman of their choice while their former wives are living. According to an estimate, their annual number is one lakh. In addition, quite a large number of Hindu girls, uprooted from their Hindu ethos and ignorant of the rigours of the Shariat law, elope with Muslim boys. Recently (1995), in one case where a Hindu male became a Muslim only to marry another girl, while his own Hindu wife was living, the Superme Court declared the second marriage void and his conversion to Islam illegal. While delivering the judgment, the Supreme Court also directed the Government of India to bring out a common civil code in implementation of Article 44 of the Constitution to prevent such malpractices, causing lots of miseries to the existing Hindu wives and their childern. There is considerable resentment among the Muslim clergy over this judgment. The members of the Muslim Personal Law Board have met the Prime Minister who, as expected, has assured them that till the Muslims themselves ask for it their personal laws (Shariat) shall not be touched. Little wonder that the Indian Muslims, regimented behind the Shariat law and Urdu language written in Persian script, during the last 45 years of post-Partition period, have enjoyed a veto power in Indian politics.

Shri Vijay Kumar Malhotra, Lok Sabha member and former Executive Councillor of Delhi, states:

> "When I was Chief Executive Councillor of Delhi, the Managing Committee of Queen Mary School issued an advertisement for the post of Principal. It provided that the candidate must be Catholic Christian. Somebody complained that such an advertisement was against the educational code and the education department advised the managing committee of the school that they may appoint a principal according to their choice but should not include 'Catholic Christian' as an essential requirement.
>
> "The Management Committee did not agree to it and went to the Court of Law. The education department argued that all the students in the school were Hindus and as such how could this school be treated as a Christian school? The court pronounced the judgment that in accordance with the constitutional provisions religious minorities can run their own educational institutions and the Government cannot interfere in their management. Even if all the students, teachers and workers are Hindus in such an institution the institution shall

> be called a minority institution provided the managing committee belongs to religious minority."[19]

Education institutions run by Hindus, like the Arya Samaj, the Sanatan Dharma Sabha, etc., have no similar choice to appoint the principals or teachers of their religious faith alone.

Shri Malhotra further states that when Dr. V.K.R.V. Rao was the central minister of education, he enthusiastically declared that during his tenure he would like to see that the Vice Chancellor of Banaras Hindu University was a Muslim and that the Vice Chancellor of Aligarh Muslim University was a Hindu. A movement against this move was started from the Aligarh Muslim University. It was demanded that the AMU was only for the Muslims and for the protection of Islam and Islamic principles and it must, therefore, maintain its Muslim character. Dr. Rao argued before the deputation of the AMU that the University was being run with 100 per cent grant from the Central Government and that the Government money could not be utilised for promotion of one particular religion. The Supreme court endorsed the view point of Dr. Rao, but the Government passed a bill in Parliament to provide for completely religious character of the AMU.[20] There are at least five other such Muslim universities—Jamia of Delhi, Hyderabad, Jammu and two of Srinagar.

The University Grants Commission prepared a plan in July 1984 under the heading "Training Classes for Minorities for Competitive Examinations". The scheme aims at coaching of students from the minority communities so that they can take up examination for appointments to administrative posts. According to this scheme, 100 students from minority communities are admitted to every university which prepares them for Indian Administrative Service, Indian Foreign Service and other All India Services, 50 students for Provincial Civil Services and others, and 300 students for banking, LIC, etc., examination. Every college is admitting 50 students from minority communities. The position is that Muslims and Christians get free coaching whereas much poorer Hindus are left with no option but to receive this training after spending thousands of rupees.[21]

Shri Malhorta further states:

> "During 1969, communal riots broke out in different parts of the country. Smt. Indira Gandhi called the meeting of the

National Integration Council. I used to be then the Chief Exectutive Councillor of Delhi and also a member of the NIC. The then Home Minister, Shri Y.B. Chavan, obtained a report from the CBI and got it circulated. This report revealed that out of 32 riots noted, riots at 31 places were intiated by Muslims....When the meeting took up the agenda, the members started condemning the report with vigour. Many of the members even challenged the bonafide of the report and said that the report aims at defaming Muslims....They flatly refused to accept the report and asserted that Muslims could not initiate riots.

"Other members were of the opinion that even if this report was correct, it should not have been published or circulated. it can create tension...I submitted before the honourable members that the report was prepared by the Intelligence Department. They have made independent investigation without being prejudiced to the observations of local police. Therefore, rejection of the report will not be justified... The members from Muslim League and both the Communist parties forcefully reitcrated that communalism cannot be initiated by minorities. In fact communalism is of the majority community...

"What surprised us all was that not a single central minister of Congress or the Chief Ministers of the States came forward in defence of the said report. Even Shri Y.B. Chavan, Home Minister, spoke nothing to support the contention of the report."[22]

CONGRESS CULTURAL AND EDUCATIONAL POLICY

Since 1947 to 1957, the education and culture of India was placed in the hands of a renowned Muslim theologian, Maulana Abul Kalam Azad followed by men like Prof. Humayun Kabir and by Prof. Nurul Hasan. Even later on, when these vital departments were assigned to a non-Muslim, his pro-Muslim and pro-Urdu credentials were ensured. It was a well-thought-of plan to submerge Hindi and Hindu culture amidst Islamic thought and Urdu language. No wonder that, during the past 48 years, numerous institutions of Islamic studies and Urdu academies have sprung up and are getting handsome government grants. Maulana Azad always spoke and wrote his official notes in Urdu and desired that the noting on files put up for his orders should be in Urdu. Had the Prime Minister and his other Hindi knowing ministers spoken in Hindi and desired that the files submitted to them should be in Hindi, the *de-jure* official language of the Union, Hindi would have *de-facto* replaced English by now. But that was not to be because the Government was made up of English wielding modernist Hindus and Pan-Islamic Muslims.

As a result, almost the entire literary work done at the State expense or assistance was devoted towards finding fault in Hindu history, Hindu mythology, Hindu religion, Hindu society, and glorifying Islam, eulogising Muslim kings and emperors and in singing praises about their contributions to Indian art, culture, education, etc. Indian culture was given a new name "Composite Culture". Sanskrit, the mother of all Indian languages, was bracketted with Arabic and Persian. While Urdu has been Persianised, Hindi has been Urduised by replacing about forty per cent of its commonly used words by Persian or Arabic words. A close look at Hindi cinema and various Hindi serials on Indian TV would reveal that the language used in them—a mix of Urdu, Hindi and English-can be understood only by the educated hybrid population of the big cities and towns. Stoppage of the usage of the salutation "Ram-Ram" in the folk programmes on the TV and starting Urdu news bulletins, both in 1994, are other examples of the cultural policy. The education policy has benefitted only the English medium schools and colleges: English that networks and benefits just two per cent of the elite Indian population, is used as a weapon to browbeat and keep at bay the 98 per cent of the Indian population. So long as English remains the virtual visa for entry into every field and office of profit, all talk of democracy in India is false. If English is not replaced by Hindi and vernaculars, a bloody war in the near future between the disgruntled young men coming out of the poorly maintained government schools and those from the prestigious public schools cannot be ruled out. It is the former category of youth that is rallying behind political parties like the Bahujan Samaj Party and Samajwadi Party and is increasingly taking to crime.

An outcome of the Muslim domination in the fields of education, literature, art, culture, cinema, radio, and TV, has been that whenever a script requires introduction of a religious bigot, a cheat, a traitor, a womaniser, a tyrant, or a corrupt officer, it is always a Hindu, seldom a Christian, but never a Muslim. For all practical purposes, India has become an Islamic country where even freedom of speech and expression is subject to Shariat Law, interpreted by the Indian Ulemas. No newspaper or periodical can dare publish anything that may remotely touch Muslim sentiments, but there is every freedom to assail Hindu religion *ad nauseam*. Even the Parliament submits to the whims and fancies of the Muslim fanaticism.

On March 11, 1992, the Muslim members of the Lok Sabha, supported by Hindu MPs of the Janata Dal and the Congress, rose up to seek a ban on a book "Some Blunders in Indian Historical Research" by Shri P.N. Oak, which in their opinion, hurt the Muslim sentiments. The objectionable part was said to be where Shri Oak had stated that Prophet Mohammed was born in a Hindu family and that Kaaba was originally a Hindu temple. It was alleged that the book did not talk of history but was an attempt to outrage the Muslim sentiments. The Speaker immediately ordered withdrawal of the book from the Parliament Library. The Minister for Parliamentary Affairs, Shri P. Kumaramangalam, rose to assure the House that he would get the book examined with a view to banning it. In this connection, it ought to be remembered that there is no dispute that, before the birth of Mohammed, there were close trade and other links between India and Arabia, that there were three religions in Arabia—Judaism, Christianity and 'Polytheism'. The last one is not properly defined. Mohammed was born neither in a Jewish family nor in a Christian family. He was born in a family of 'Polytheist' (Pagan) tribe of Qurayish of Mecca who were also in control of the Kaaba temple. It is also not in dispute that the Kaaba housed 360 or so idols of different gods and goddesses all of which were broken by prophet Mohammed, except the Black Stone (Sang-e-Aswad). At that time, Shaivism, Buddhism and Jainism were the predominant religions of India. Traces of these religions have been found in excavations in West Asia, Central Asia and China in the North, Sri Lanka in the South and Japan in the East. Keeping in view the links and proximity of Arabia through the sea route, it is most likely that Shaivism, Buddhism and Jainism, parts of Hindu religion, did also exist in Arabia (along side Judaism and Christianity) and followers of these religions were given the name of polytheists. As Islam came to

Arabia only with Hazrat Mohammed, there is no denying the fact that his parents were not Muslims. They were also neither Christians nor Jews. Thus, the only possibility is that Hazrat Mohammed was born in a family which followed one of the religions of Indian origin and which now bear the common name of Hindu religion and that their temple of Kaaba was a Hindu temple. The presumption may be wrong, but that must be rebutted by arguments and evidence, not by banning the book or silencing the researchers. Such instances can be multiplied.[23]

Recently, a Muslim poet, Mohammad Alvi, of Ahmedabad, who had got the Gujarat Urdu Academy Award (1993) for his poetic work 'Chautha Aasman' was ex-communicated through a 'fatwa' issued by the chief of one Dar-ul-Uloom, who alleged that two of his couplets were blasphemous: one being critical of the omni-potence of Allah and the other implying a question mark on the finality of Mohammad's prophethood. The hapless poet was hiding underground in Bombay for some time but came out only to apologize for the couplets called in question by the Ulemas. During the past five years, many poets, scholars and open-minded Muslims have been penalised through similar fatwas. Not one of the Indian law enforcing agencies, the judiciary, the self appointed secularists, human right activists, the award giving academies, has ventured to come to the rescue of such Muslims. No one has raised a voice against the institution of this kind of extra-judicial 'fatwas'. The all powerful central Government is a silent spectator. Nay, to lend further support to the clergy of Islam, it has recently decided to make an annual grant of Rs. 300 crores to the State Wakf Boards to ensure minimum wages and perks to over three lakhs of Imams who lead congregational prayers in the mosques.[24] This is in addition to the subsidy granted for the Haj pilgrims and the grants-in-aid to Muslim educational institutions.

Keeping all this in view and the facts of the Shariat law earlier stated, only a fool or a knave would say that there is secularism and democracy in India. The process of *de-facto* Islamisation at the hands of Congress had been going on smoothly and continuously since 1920. Only its pace was accelerated after Congress got the political power in 1947. The process is being carried on under the attractive catchwords of 'socialism', 'secularism', 'composite culture' 'social justice', 'protection of minorities', 'unity and integrity of the nation', etc. The fact is that the Congress strived for none of these. For it, India was Congress and the Congress was India until it became "Indira (Smt. Indira Gandhi) is India and India is Indira". Since then onwards, the Congress has been converted into a private Limited Company of the Nehru dynasty. Even Sardar Patel was a victim of Congressism. Knowing fully well that Article 370 was ominous for India, he agreed to defend it before the Congress Legislature Party just to maintain "unity" in the party.

To quell any doubt about the Congress aim to convert India into a fundamentalist Islamic state one ought to refer to late Prime Minister, Rajiv Gandhi's speech made from the remparts of the Red Fort of Delhi on the Independence Day, August 15, 1988, in which he said, "Our endeavour should be to take the country to the heights to which it belonged about 250-300 years ago, before people from different corners of the world set out to discover India."[25] Students of history all know that it was exactly the period of Aurangzeb, who still haunts the Hindu mind as their worst persecutor but who is hailed by the fanatic Muslims as their ideal sovereign. When, due to the infamous Bofors scandal, Rajiv's Government was ousted and Janata Dal, a breakaway group of the Congress, took over, its Prime Minister, V.P. Singh, outshining Rajiv Gandhi, declared from the same Red Fort on the next Independence Day, that the birthday of Hazrat Mohammed would be observed as a public holiday throughout India. To catch up with the Janata Dal, the Congress coalition Government in Kerala decided that Friday, instead of Sunday, would be observed a public holiday in public schools. Further, succumbing to the pressure of the Islamic fundamentalists, the Indian Government cancelled its programme of commemorating 450th anniversary of Akbar's coronation, in 1992, for which Rs. one crore had been earmarked. It may be remembered that Akbar, the great grandfather of Aurangzeb, was a Sunni Muslim by faith but in course of time turned a Hindu by culture. When his mother died, he got himself tonsured like a Hindu. A noted historian (Dr. A.L. Srivastava) has remarked that, had a reformist like Swami Dayananda been in those days, Akbar would have been converted to Hindu faith. The fundamentalist Muslims of India (and Pakistan too) now denounce Akbar for having equated Islam with the Hindu religion.

In its latest move, the Congress Minorities Cell has demanded creation of a ministry for minority affairs with departments like the Haj pilgrimage, Waqf, Minorities Commission and Minorities financial Development Corporation.[26] It is often argued on behalf of the Muslims, "The Shariat (Muslim Personal Law) applies only to Muslims. Why should Hindus agitate over it and force them to adopt a common civil code?" It may sound plausible for a simpleton and please the modernist Hindus of the type earlier stated, but the Hindu masses have experienced its evil effects on them. Their concern is real and genuine. Firstly, The very fact of Hindus following one law and the Muslims another, stands like a rock in their coming together and socialising with each other. Secondly, the Shariat is greatly responsible for the backwardness of the Muslim masses, but the responsibility for their backwardness is thrown on Hindus. Thirdly, the Shariat allows a Muslim to take a Hindu girl but does not allow a Hindu to take a Muslim girl. If a Hindu wants to marry a Muslim girl, he has to first embrace Islam. All hue and cry on the recent film 'Bombay' arose because it showed a Muslim girl marrying a Hindu boy. Fourthly, Shariat allows a Muslim to have upto four wives at a time while a Hindu cannot have more than one. A recalcitrant but resourceful Hindu just gets converted to Islam and marries another girl even when his first wife is living. The Shariat gives him full protection. It is one of the causes, next only to the illegal migration of Bangladeshi Muslims to India, for the number of Hindus in India going down from 85 per cent in 1951 (including Jains and Boudhs) to 82 per cent in 1991 and the number of Muslims going up from 10 per cent to 13 per cent during the same period. The Muslim leaders gleefully say that there is more polygamy among Hindus than among Muslims. Even if it be true, the villain of the piece is Shariat.

Islamisation of India is thus continuing under the deceptive nomenclature of minority rights.

REFERENCES

1 VP Menon, Transfer of Power in India, p. 417.
2 Ibid, p. 419.
3 Organiser weekly, New Delhi, Nov. 12, 1995, Interview with Swami Ranganathananda, Vice President of R.K. Mission, who

was in Karachi from 9.8.1942 to Aug 9, 1948, CF Bhavan Journal, Aug. 15, 1995.

4 VP Menon, Transfer of Power, p. 419.

5 Durga Das, India from Curzon to Nehru, p. 279.

6 Hind Swarajya translated in Hindi by Amritlal Thakordas Nanavati and Published by Sarva Seva Sangha Prakashan, Rajghat Varanasi July 1994 p.6.

7 Ibid pp. 30-33.

8 Gandhi, Hind Swarajya, (Hindi), p. 49.

9 Maulana Azad, India Wins Freedom, p. 187.

10 Gandhi, Hind Swarajya (Hindi), p. 49.

11 Durga Das, India from Curzon to Nehru, p. 272.

12 Durga Das, India from Curzon to Nehru, p. 273.

13 Times of India, New Delhi, June 23, 1995, p. 13.

14 M.J. Akbar, 'Nehru: The Making of India' p. 580.

15 KP Karunakaran, Indian Political Thoughts, 1833-1921, pp. 56-57.

16 BN Mullick, My Years with Nehru-Kashmir, pp. 101-103.

17 Baljit Rai, 'Is India Going Islamic, p. 71, B.S. Publishers, Chandigarh, 1994, Distributors: Voice of India, 2/18 Ansari Rd., ND-2

18 Census figures of 1981

19 V.K. Malhotra, Is it a Sin to be Hindu in India, pp. 4-5, Published by Vishwa Hindu Parishad, Sankat Mochan Ashram, R.K. Puram Sec. VI, ND-27.

20 -do- pp.5-6

21 V.K. Malhotra, Is it a sin to be Hindu in India?, pp. 12-13.

22 Ibid pp. 20-21.

23 A book "Ahl-e-Arab Ka Kadim Mazhab", written by Pandit Gjyanendra Dev Sufi (formerly a Muslim, Haji Maulvi Abdul Rehman Sahib), published by Arya Tarkshalini Sabha,Chowdi Bazar, Delhi, in 1936, contains a number of verses from an ancient book "Sairulkool" by an Arab poet "Asmai", during the period of the famous Khalifa Harun Rashid, which is a collection of poems of many Arab poets who lived before Hazrat Mohammed. The author has quoted from other poets also. These verses show that the Arabs had great reverence for India, the Vedic religion, and Shri Krishna. The author has stated that he saw 'Sairulkool' in the ancient library of Jeruslam.

24 Indian Express New Delhi, 19th June 1995.

25 Rajiv Gandhi, Restore India's Glory with Unity and Strength, Govt. of India, DAVP, 1988.

26 Indian Express, daily, New Delhi, April 16, 1995.

Chapter XVI

IN RETROSPECT

The foregoing chapters have shown how both Congress and British patronage contributed to the growth of Islamic fundamentalism which later resulted in the complete Islamisation of one-third of Indian territory in 1947, a feat which even the most powerful and zealous Muslim emperor of India in the 17th century could not perform. And, during the past 48 years, Congress has assiduosly created conditions to turn even the truncated India into a virtual Islamic state, larger than even Pakistan.

In retrospect, the Partition of India in the words of noted writer Nirad C. Choudhuri took place because of "a combination of three factors—Hindu stupidity in the first instance and Hindu cowardice afterwards; British opportunism; and Muslim fanaticism."[1] Just as the Hindu stupidity and cowardice were personified in Gandhi, Muslim fanaticism got its expression in Jinnah. The British have gone, but the Hindu stupidity and cowardice on the one hand and Muslim fanaticism on the other have remained unabated in the truncated India. (India's role in J & K and IPKF's misfortune in Sri Lanka are the two living examples). The irony of fate is that the same set of people who had caused the gruesome Partition have remained at the helm of affairs.

Pakistan was a windfall for the Muslims and a great loss to the Hindus. But it does not mean that the Hindu loss resulted in Muslim gain, either in India or in Pakistan. The sole beneficiaries on both the sides were the unscrupulous politicians, the bureaucrats, the power brokers, the big businessmen, and the high profile criminals. If Pakistan subsists on American aid and the remittances made by Pakistani Non-Residents in Arab countries, India subsists on internal and foreign loans. The political condition in both the countries is pathetic. The ethnic fights among the

Punjabis, the Sindhis, the Pathans, and the Baluchis, in Pakistan, together with Shia-Sunni riots and the bloody war between the Muslim migrants from India (Muhajirs) and the locals have made Pakistan a virtual hell. Most of the Pakistanis now regret the day when they voted Pakistan.

The internal turmoil of Pakistan, however, is no consolation for the Hindu India. It is in the nature of Islamic politics that it keeps its adherents perpetually at war. So long as there is a non-Muslim entity, the Muslims would be engaged in eliminating or subjugating it. When that is done, an enemy is found within. It ought to be recalled that all the Muslims in Pakistan jointly first set out to kill, convert, or throw out all the Hindus and the Sikhs. As already stated, the Hindus and Sikhs of Pakistan who formed twenty-two per cent of its population in 1947 were reduced to less than two per cent by 1981. The funnier part is that the Indian Government never raised the point of this enormous genocide and persecution of Hindus either with Pakistan or in any international forum while it always showed serious concern for the (Muslim) Palestinians who were rendered refugees because of the creation of Israel. For a discerning eye it should be a proof enough that India is virtually an Islamic state inhabited by a Hindu majority population. Anyway, after Pakistan got rid of Hindus and Sikhs, it targetted Ahmediya Muslims and the Shias. And, now it is set against Muhajirs (Muslim migrants from India). But all these warring factions of Pakistan are one against the Hindu India. For the last one year, persecution of Muhajirs has been on the increase. Karachi, the port town of Pakistan, is burning and bleeding in the internecine war. The Pak Prime Minister, Begum Benazir Bhutto, has branded Muhajirs as traitors, agents of India, and even carrying bad blood, different from Pakistan blood. Even under this provocative situation the viewpoint of the Muhajir leader, Shri Altaf Hussain, towards India, remains the same as that of Pakistan Government or other Pakistanis. In an interview given to Shekhar Gupta (then Chief Editor, India Today) in London, the following questions and answers are a pointer to this fact:

Q. (S.G.)- Is a similar (as in Europe) South Asian confederation possible in the sub-continent?

A. (A.H.)- That is my wish also. All the countries of South Asia should talk and look at the West's example. It is possible as long as it does not affect the integrity of any nation. India should accept Pakistan's existence. The two should solve the Kashmir problem. The Indian Government must stop atrocities over the Kashimirs. They should be allowed to decide their fate, whether they want to live with India or Pakistan, or if they want to choose another option. Ask them to stop the atrocities.

Q. (S.G.)- What have the Muslims of the subcontinent lost and gained since Partition? How does the balance sheet read?

A. (A.H.)- If you look at it materialistically, we have lost everything. But if you look at it spiritually, we have built a country for the Muslims. So the spiritual success is there. That satisfaction is there. As far as material gains are concerned, bhai, we have gained nothing. Materially, it is a case of na Khuda hee mila, na visaal-e-sanam, na idhar ke rahe, na udhar ke rahe. (I got neither God nor a glance of my beloved; I ended up neither here, nor there).[2]

REFERENCE

1. Nirad C. Choudhuri, The Continent of circe, Jaico Publication House, Fort Bombay-1, Fifth edition, 1974, p. 292
2. India Today, fortnightly, July, 1995, pp. 44-47.

Chapter XVII

HINDU AILMENTS

For the last one thousand years, Hindus have been fighting against Islamic onslaught with marginal success now and then. In the meantime Christian Missionaries sponsored and funded by foreign countries have been an added dimension. They have carved out three Christian states in India's North-East frontiers—Nagaland, Mizoram and Meghalaya. Had they preached only Christian religion, there would be nothing wrong. But evil creeps in when the Missionaries introduce politics into their activities.

LOSS OF FIGHTING SPIRIT

Hindu philosophy is older and superior to either Islam or Christianity. Still, Hindus had to bow before both of them. Historians have assigned various reasons for it. What all of them have failed to take note of is the fact that while Islam is predominantly a political philosophy with a code of military conduct, Hinduism or Hindu religion, as practised for over 1500 years, had been bereft of any political thought or militancy. Lord Buddha had denounced nationalism. Politics and militancy were made the exclusive domains of Rajputras or Kshatriyas (princely or martial caste) and the Brahmins. It is difficult to say as to when this development took place. Vedic Mantras, the original source of Hindu religion, are full of community life, of eating together, sleeping together, praying together and fighting together. The Aryans collectively prayed to God to protect them and their belongings and to kill their enemies. But when we pass on to the epic age, all discourses are centred around the individual. The Rig Veda had proclaimed:

Samani va aakuti samaanaa hrdayaani vah;

Samaanamastu mano yathaa- vah; susahaasati. (Rig. 10/191/4)

(May you resolve with one voice; may your hearts and thoughts be united so that you may live together with unity and happiness)

In the later period, the stress was on "Uddareta aatma aatmanen", meaning, develop your own self through own effort. Even the Bouddha prayer was "Buddham sharanam gachhami; Sangham sharanam gachhami..", meaning, "I go to the shelter of Buddha, I go to the shelter of Sangha (the Buddhist school).." Thus collectivism of the Vedic period gave way to individualism.

There is, however, an episode in the Mahabharata in which the Kaurava prince, Duryodhana is captured and being taken away by Gandharvas. The Pandavas were then in exile in the forests as a result of Duryodhana's foul play in the dice game. Nevertheless, the eldest Pandu prince, Yuddhishthira, asks his brothers, Bhima and Arjuna to go and rescue Duryodhana. He tells them that though Duryodhana and his ninetynine brothers were enemies of the Pandavas, all of them made a single force of a hundred and five when faced with a foreign enemy. Bhima and Arjuna were convinced and rescued Duryodhana. This lesson of the Mahabharata was completely lost much before Islamic invasions. May be, the change came after Buddhism and Jainism rose to prominence in about the first century of the Christian era or when the Varna (caste) system became rigid. The subject needs a deeper probe.

It is no wonder that individually Hindus have had all wealth, wisdom, and chivalry, but as a community or nation they have been the weakest lot. Barring stray exceptions, Hindu community has, throughout the ages, known only the politics of compromise and self sacrifice. It is because of this trait that Mahatma Gandhi acquired such a great following. Islam, on the other hand, lays all stress on Islamic brotherhood (Umma) and aggression on non-Muslims. The very same Hindu who displays all cowardice and dreads even a mouse, turns into a wolf just by converting to the Islamic faith. There, he immediately becomes a mujahid (fighter for Islam). Thus, every Muslim is deemed a fighter while a Hindu is deemed a mere trader, farmer or craftsman. Adoption of Islam does not mean mere change of religion. It means change of one's entire personality, political thought, and perception of past events.

THE DOMINANT MINORITY

The resistance power of Hindus has further gone down during the past hundred years. It is because of the dominating tribe of the intellectual slaves among them. It was a small tribe in the medieval period who served the Muslim monarchs. Later, it expanded and served the British Raj. Now it is serving the anti-Hindu Congress regime. During the past 50 years, the tribe has expanded geometrically. It has become the dominant minority of India. It includes bureaucrats, prominent lawyers, contracters, ambitious industrialists, big businessmen, doctors, engineers, professionals, officers of the armed forces, police officers, mediamen, film makers, politicians of shifting loyalties, educationists, and lakhs of other beneficiaries of the Congress Raj. They form the bulk of the middle and upper classes of the Indian population and can be called the creamy layer of India. They are as far removed from their unprivileged Hindu brethren as were Britishers or the Mughal nobility. Their number is less than two per cent of the population but they are the actual moulders of India's destiny. Their sole religion is careerism, and material prosperity. Wealth is their deity and Charvaak (propounder of the theory, eat, drink and be merry) their Prophet. They formulate and implement the economic, educational, financial, and administrative policies in such a way that, while the public welfare measures of their political bosses seem to be set in motion, they and their bosses are the real beneficiaries. They are the people who devour 85 per cent of the Government funds earmarked for public welfare. Indeed, they are the real strength and carriers of the Congress culture and Congress ideologies in a measure greater than the Rajputs did for the Mughal empire. They and their progeny are completely detached from their religion, their culture, their vernacular, their age old sense of ethics and morality. They pride themselves in aping western lifestyle and mannerism. Thousands of them have got foreign assignments. They are educating their wards in prestigious English medium public schools, colleges and even in foreign countries. Through their clout, they would fix them in lucrative jobs in India in Government Departments, Public enterprizes or multinational companies. The worst part of the game is that almost everyone in the lower middle class is also racing on to join this very elite class. Thus, though the Hindu society is changing fast, it is changing for the worst.

This elite class of the modernist Hindus is in the forefront of ridiculing Hindu revivalist movement. It is this class which cries hoarse that India is a multinational (not multi-religious) country. This very class is wittingly or unwittingly supporting the Islamic fundamentalist movement. Muslims of India would have long ago joined the Hindu mainstream, but the Hindu mainstream itself is shrinking and drying up at the hands of the modernist Hindus and half-baked pundits. The elitist Hindus would go to a church on the Christmas day, to a mosque on the day of Id, and a temple on the day of Shivaratri or Janmashtmi, but are true to none. In this situation the fate of the weaker and the larger part of the Hindu society can better be imagined than described.

EROSIAN OF CULTURE

Earlier, the ruling Turks and the Mughals settled in India gave birth to a new language 'Rekhta' or 'Hindavi' by mixing Persian with Hindi, which later got the name of "Urdu". The official language remained Persian. Likewise, the dominant minority of India, the successor of the British Raj, has retained English as the official language and has simultaneously developed another language by mixing English with Hindi and Urdu. It is yet to get a name, but can be called Hinglish for convenience sake. During 1989-90 general elections, the late prime minister, Rajiv Gandhi, used the phrase "Chahe hum jeeten ya loozen, yani haren (whether we win or lose...)". Since then, Rajiv's linguistic progeny has come a long way. The news reader has come to say, "Aaj Bosnia mein peace process ko set back ho gaya hai (The peace process in Bosnia has suffered a set back today)" or "Bihar election mein violence hua aur ballot boxes snatch kiye gaye (The Bihar elections were marked by incidents of violence and ballot snatching)". A programmer of popular Hindi film songs says "Arright, iss hafte top of the charts par hai once again Madhuri Dixit singing Nazren milee tum se" (This week, Madhuri Dixit singing the note 'Nazren milee tum se' is once again on the top of popularity chart). This is the language which is now dominating the so called national programmes of the all permeating and most powerful network of the Indian television. For whom is it meant? what culture does it propagate? These are matters which ought to exercise the minds of the nation builders.

Language is an instrument that binds as well as divides people. It was the language, namely Urdu, which had united the Indian Muslims against the non-Muslims and created Pakistan. It was again Urdu which separated Bangladesh from Pakistan. It was the language that made the basis for reorganisation of states in India in the fifties. The latest breed of the language, say Hinglish, unites the privileged two per cent of the Indian population to the detriment of the remaining ninety-eight per cent. Yet, through all kinds of propaganda, the former has kept up the show of being the only Messiah of the latter. The propounders of Hindi and other vernaculars are well set against one another and are yet to realise the dangers of English monster and, through it, of the western culture because most of them are hirelings or proteges of the existing power bloc.

DEGENERATION OF BRAHMINS

The other stumbling bloc of Hindus are the half-baked Hindu intelligentsia, called Pandits or religious teachers. They are of two types, one who are semi literate but, born of Brahmin parents, know some of the Hindu religious rites and a bit of astrology (reading Hindu almanac). They deal with the ceremonial part and are mostly poor. Quite often they are objects of much ridicule. Very few of them are proficient enough in astrology, chanting of hymns, or making religious discourses in vernacular, to make a confortable living. This lot neither commands respect not credibility. They deserve pity and need proper education and training in Sanskrit and basics of Hindu religion. The other type consists of the English speaking swamis or godmen. They have a limited proficiency in some or the other Hindu philosophic thought, like the Geeta, the Upanishadas, or the Bhakti cult. English being the hall-mark of modernity, they have a good clientale among the middle and upper class Hindus and they make good capital out of their trade. But each one has his own interpretation of religion which creates more confusion than cohesion. Hindu Dharma, the philosophy of Hindu religion, covers all aspects of life in its four fold objectives, namely, *Dharma* (duty towards self and society) Artha (production and distribution), Kama (wants and their satisfaction), and Moksha (spirituality and deliverance). But the

Hindu Pandits and teachers supposed to be the store houses of knowledge and light houses of the society have all along concentrated on spirituality alone, neglecting all other aspects of the Hindu society which also form important parts of the holy Vedas, the Mahabharata, the Ramayana, the Manusmriti, and other holy books. It is the four fold objective of human life which gave birth to the concept of dividing the life-span into four parts, namely, Brahmacharya (education, training and discipline corresponding to Dharma), Grihasta (family life corresponding to Artha and Kama), Vanaprastha (spirituality and preparation to renunciation), and Sanyas (renunciation corresponding to Moksha, deliverance). The social and political aspects are never the subject of the teachers of Hindu religion. They are to be told to study more and widen their horizon.

There is yet another set of yogis, swamis and godmen patronised by high ranking politicians, rich businessmen and professionals. They run various kinds of ashramas, social, educational or charitable institutions, get handsome grants from Government, and private donations. Most of them serve as chests for depositing ill-gotten money of their patrons and for running clandestine business in connivance with the rich and high. This high profile lot of godmen is doing great harm to the Hindu society. They need chastisement and even severe punishment in many cases. Only a few institutions and individuals of missionary zeal are genuinely engaged in the cause of Hindu religion and Hindu society. Thus, Hindus suffer from an acute shortage of genuine intellectuals, scholars, teachers, and trustworthy priests.

FAILURE OF HINDU REVIVAL

Towards the later part of the nineteenth century, Swami Dayananda, Swami Vivekananda, Lokamanya Tilak, Smt. Annie Besant, and many others, devoted their lives to remove the prevailing confusion, defeatism, and superstition, among Hindus and infuse self reliance, a feeling of brotherhood on the one hand and to prepare them for freedom from the British Raj, on the other. The ground prepared by them was used by Gandhi for his political struggle against the British. His relentless campaign for a Hindu-Muslim unity, more than against the British Raj, eclipsed the process of Hindu revival. The Arya Samaj and other Hindu organisations rallied behind the Congress. Rashtriya Swayamsevak

Sangh (RSS) established in 1925, took up the work of Hindu revivalism, but its plank was Hindu nationalism, not Hindu religion. It could not, however, make much headway upto 1945. The relevance of the RSS was realised only when the Muslim League adopted a threatening posture for partitioning India and the Congress appeared helpless and in a way paving the way for the League. Gandhi's assassination in January 1948 gave a severe jolt to RSS. It was banned. Even when the ban was lifted, it was subjected to all kinds of wild tirade. Through scores of its branch organisations in the fields of education, religion, social service, industrial workers, tribal areas, slums, etc, the RSS has done a lot[1], but the net result is not very encouraging because the forces pitted against it have been at work with greater force and expediency. Moreover, the RSS has always borne a defensive posture, restricting itself to pleadings, petitioining and protests.

If today we find a militant tone among the Hindu masses, it is less a making of the RSS or its sister organisations, the Vishva Hindu Parishad (VHP), the Bhartiya Janta Party (BJP), and the Bajrang Dal, all together called the Sangha Parivar. It is more a reaction to Congress's unabashed apeasement policy towards Muslim fundamentalists, its shoddy secularism, self destructive economic policies, and rampant corruption. Although the truncated India, say, Hindu India has been proceeding on an Islamic path since 1947 itself, there was no perceptible reaction to it upto 1985. Hindus got alarmed only after the Supreme Court judgment in the Shah Bano case was annulled under pressure from the Islamic fundamentalists. It was followed by the incident of the wholesale killing and expulsion of Kashmiri Hindu population from the Kashmir valley. The bomb blasts by the Islamic terrorists in Bombay, Calcutta, Madras, Jammu and other places since 1993 have panicked the Hindu masses. So far, there has been no counter action against these bomb blasts from the Hindu revivalists.

The work being done by the RSS, the mother body of the BJP, VHP and the Bajrang Dal is grossly inadequate. According to an estimate, RSS's annual budget is not more than Rs.25 crore which is a very meagure amount compared to funds invested in anti-Hindu operations and propaganda by the Islamic institutions, the Christian Missionaries, and their supportive political parties. This writer is told that a single multi-national company operating in India spends about Rs. one thousand crore annually on advertisements alone of its products. The reason for the slow progress of the Hindu revival is its lack of resources, both in finance and manpower and antagonism of the mass media which is largely dependent on the huge finances and patronage coming from anti-Hindu establishments. The Sangha Parivar does not have a single daily newspaper. Consequently, its image in the public eye remains of 'the lunatic fringe of the Hindus', a term very much used by the English scribes. The Sangha Parivar is known more through its enemies than its adherents or its literature. In order to retrieve the situation, it must have its daily newspapers, at least in the capital and metropolis cities of India, so as to convey its message to the masses on day to day basis. A look at the RSS's own publications would reveal that it is not against the Muslims nor against the Dalits nor the Christians. It is only against the politics being played in the name of Christianity, Islam, Shariat and Urdu which created Pakistan. All allegations of militancy against the RSS are false. It has been a non-violent, armless, spectator to the killings of its own volunteers in Panjab at the hands of Sikh terrorists and in Madras at the hands of Islamic fundamentalists. Even after so much, its weaponry continues to be the bamboo stick and dummy sword.

A critical study would reveal that all movements of Hindu resurgence, during the past one hundred years, came to a dead end after a period of time. It is because each movement started and proceeded in isolation. When the Arya Samaj took up the Shuddhi (conversion of Hindu converts to Islam back to Hindu fold) and removal of untouchability, other Hindu organisations either opposed it or kept silent. Arya Samajists also did not bother to have a dialogue with the heads of other Hindu sects, convince them of the need of the hour and read to them relevant Vedic injunctions in support of their movement. Savarkar was a great patriot, a great orator, a great freedom fighter, but he was an atheist and, therefore, could not make much impact on the masses. The RSS might have gone to oblivion had it not floated the Vishwa Hindu Parishad (VHP) to bring all religious sects on one platform. The success of the Ramajanmabhoomi movement of the VHP was only due to the support of all Hindu religious heads. There is, however, a greater need for revitalising and re-organising the Hindu masses, streamlining Hindu rituals, correctly interpreting Hindu philosophic thoughts, eliminating false dogmas, superstitions and adulteration in Hindu religious texts. All this work needs thousands of whole time workers, dedicated scholars, professionals, and huge finances, say Rs 500 to 1000 crores annually. The Islamic institutions and the Christian Missionaries are spending greater amounts of money in propagating their religion and related activities. Mere blaming or finding fault with them makes little sense. The finance should not pose a great problem for the Hindu community which, according to this writer, squanders away Rs. 10,000 to 20,000 crores annually on avoidable festivities and bursting crackers on the Deepavali and Dushehra days even while their enemies are collecting AK rifles and RDX explosives.

The worth of the VHP will be known only if it can bring together and motivate the Dharmacharyas to re-write the Manusmriti, to prepare a minimum common code for the Hindus (with suitable dos and don'ts), to streamline and redefine the degenerated caste system, the social and family rights and duties of a Hindu, the penance and punishment for social and religious misconduct, and the like. The Dharmacharyas should choose a common language of Indian origin for their inter-state dialogue because use of English for their own religious matters would, besides being incongruous, be sinful and funny. It would be belying their claim that theirs is the oldest and richest philosophy or culture. For over 2,000 years, Sanskrit was the link language of Hindu religious heads, but now let them adopt Tamil, Bengali, Hindi or any one else. Further, there is an urgent need for an all-India Dharma Sabha, like the Akaal Takht of the Sikhs, to guide and decide day to day matters of religious disputes, inter-caste or inter religious marriage, entry to temples, performance of rites. This Sabha should have powers to ex-communicate or punish the recalcitrants. In the absence of such an institution, the number of Hindus who go on just castigating Hindu religion and Hindu society for the sake of money, name and fame among Hindu baiters, is fast increasing.

In the absence of a strong all India Hindu Dharma Sabha, Hindu religion has degenerated into numerous religious segments with dubious religious heads called 'godmen'. This has led to an anarchy in the ancient Hindu religious thoughts. The concepts of God, soul, truth, varnaashrama Dharma, have become totally confused. The distinction between a believer and a non-believer has become extinct. Atheism has become a part of Hindu religion. Silence of Buddhism and Jainism on the existence of God is being interpreted as a negation of God and a revolt against Hindu religion.

Such a Dharma Sabha was there at Varanasi till about a hundred years back after which it declined and is now non-existent. It needs to be revived and reorganised with branches at suitable places. It is also necessary to oversee and prevent disintegration, caricaturing, perversion, of Hindu religion and misuse of Hindu mythological figures, signs or symbols. A time has come when Hindus must set their system of assimilation and elimination in proper working order. Mere focussing attention on assimilation to the utter neglect of elimination of bad blood will do no good.

REFERENCES

1. H.V. Seshadri's RSS- A Vision in Action', Jagarana Prakasan, Bangalore, Reprint Dec. 1988 (Distributors, Rashtrothana Sahitya, Kempegowda Nagar, Bangalore, 560019.

Chapter XVIII

HINDU-MUSLIM QUESTION

The most nagging question, for over a century, has been one of Hindu-Muslim unity. During all these hundred years frantic efforts were made for the unity, but every effort resulted in widening the gulf between the two, leading to the partition of India. Instead of solving the problem, the partition has made the matter worse. The reason is that every move for unity was made by the Hindus, none by the Muslims.

For Hindus, led by Gandhiji, Hindu-Muslim unity was an article of faith and they made enough sacrifice for it. For the Muslims, it always remained a political game, a bait to advance their demands and political aims. In the attempt to accommodate the Muslim sentiments, Hindus have secularised themselves to the extent of becoming irreligious. The Muslims have, however, responded in greater bigotry and Pan-Islamism. In Kashmir, where they are in a majority, they sought India's help to save them from the invading Tribals of Pakistan. Later, they themselves joined hands with Pakistan and either gunned down the Hindu population or drove them out from the Kashmir valley.

Unless, therefore, the Muslims too feel the need for Hindu cooperation they will not care for Hindu sensibilities nor can there be a meeting ground between the two. In their homes and temples, Hindu secularists have been verily chanting "Ishwar Allah tere naam, sab ko sanmati de Bhagwan", but a corressponding note of the type has not yet come from a mosque or a Muslim home. On the death of a Hindu secularist, a pundit is called to recite from the Geeta, a priest to recite from the Bible, a granthi to recite from Guru Granth Sahib and a mullah to recite from the Quran, but on the death of a 'secular' Muslim, there is no pundit, no priest, or granthi; only the mullah prevails.

Many historians, scholars, and political analysts, including late Congresss leader Lala Lajpat Rai and the renowned Dalit leader Dr. B.R. Ambedkar had opined that Hindu-Muslim unity was an impossibility because of the exclusive nature of Islam. Once, one Shri Nazir Ali, a Muslim Sufi saint from Kashmir, met the previous RSS Chief, late Dr. M.S. Golwalkar (popularly known as Guruji) to seek latter's cooperation in fighting against the menace of communism and materialism. Guruji agreed but said that the greatest difficulty was that various segments of the people had partitioned God in so many parts, each segment fighting for his part. How to bring them together? The Sufi said, "Why don't you all accept Islam?"[1] The fact is that Islam does not believe in coexistence of religions. Secularism has never been its grain, except as a temporary measure by way of political expediency. There are numerous verses in the Quran and directions in the Hadis to kill, torture and persecute the 'non-believers', a term used for those who do not put their faith solely in Prophet Muhammed and his teaching in the Quran. This aspect of Islam is already explained in earlier chapters, especially chapter VII—Aftermath of Khilafat—and subsequent chapter XXI—Global Threat of Islam. There are, however, verses in the Quran which allow co-existence of different religious faiths. Here are verses 104 to 107 of Surah VI, as translated from Arabic by Maulana Abul Kalam Azad, an authority on Islam and Arabic language:

> 104. Now are things clearly disclosed to you to reflect on. Should any one take note of them, that will be to his own advantage; (on the other hand) should one choose to remain blind to them, that will be to his own disadvantage. (Remember) I am not a keeper over you (to force you to reflect over).
>
> 105. So clear have We made our revelations (in diverse ways) that they exclaim: "Thou indeed hath been well instructed (and have not minced anything in the expression of truth)", and We do this in order that you may make clear their significance to a people who may be disposed to understand.
>
> 106. Follow thou that which hath been revealed to thee from thy Lord (other than whom) there is no god but He: and hold aloof from the polytheists.

> 107. Had God pleased they would not have taken others for God; (not that God hath not the power to do so; but that is not His way). He leaves every one to be responsible for his thought and action. (The task of the prophet was but to point out the truth and exercise no compulsion). And we have not appointed thee a keeper over them nor art thou(of thy own choice) a guardian over them.

The Quran also says that Prophets like Mohammed were sent on various parts of earth at different times. Surah IV/ 163-165 read:

> 163. Verily We have inspired in thee Our 'word', as We had inspired in Noah, and in the prophets after him and also as We had inspired in Abraham and Ishmael and Isaac and Jacob and their progeny and in Jesus and Job and Jonah and Aaron and Solomon and (in like manner) did we give the Psalms to David.
>
> 164. Of some apostles have We already given thee account, and of some, We have not given thee any account. (In like manner) did God converse with Moses.
>
> 165. All these were apostles, bearers of glad tidings and warners, raised in order that men may have no plea against God after they had come. And God is Mighty, Wise.

Surah XXIX/46 reads:

> 46. Do not argue with the followers of earlier revelations otherwise than a kindly manner—unless it be such of them as are set on evil doing—and say, "We believe in that which has been bestowed upon us, as well as that which has been bestowed upon you: for our God and your God is one and the same, and it is unto Him that we all surrender ourselves."

The Quran also says in Surah IV/152

> 152. But those who believe in Allah and His messengers and make no distinction between any of them, unto them Allah will give their wages; and Allah was ever Forgiving, Merciful.[2]

Thus, the Quran emphatically speaks of one God but many prophets or apostles and enjoins upon the Muslims to follow not just only one prophet but other prophets as well who obviously appeared in places other than Arabia, like Christ in Jerusalam, Lord Krishna and Lord Rama in India. Prophet Muhammed was sent to Arabia for the Arabs as stated in Surah XLII/7:

> 7. And thus we have inspired in thee a Lecture (Quran) in Arabic, that thou mayest warn the mother-town (Mecca) and those around it, and mayest warn of a day of assembling where of there is no doubt...[3]

Surah CIX, relating to A1-Kafirun, or infidels of Mecca says:

> 1. Say: O disbelievers!
> 2. I worship not that which ye worship;
> 3. Nor worship ye that which I worship;
> 4. And I shall not worship that which ye worship;
> 5. Nor will ye worship that which I worship.
> 6. Unto you your religion, and unto me my religion.[4]

The above verses read together would convey that the Muslims must respect and honour the customs and traditions of the country to which they belong and should not try to turn every land into an Arabian desert. Hence, former Chief Justice, M. Hidayatullah, was perfectly right when he said that the Quran was the Geeta of Arabia and the Geeta was the Quran of India.

Five hundred years ago, Abdur-Rahim Khankhana of emperor Akbar's court had expressed the same sentiments about Tulsidas' Ramayana. He said, "Ramacharit-manas vimal, Santan jeevan pran; Hinduvan ko Ved sam, Yavanahi pragat Quran". (This sacred Ramcharit-manas is the life stream of the saints; it is like they holy Vedas for the Hindus and a book of Revelation for the Muslims and the Christians). However, the cosmopolitan part of the Quran has been overshadowed by the earlier stated conservative one, for it suits the imperial and expansionist designs of the Ulemas. It is because of this that at times the Ulemas give more credence to the Hadis than the Quran, although Prophet Mohammed gave only the Quran. The Hadis is a man-made book, about two hundred years after Mohammed.

Akbar the Great was a product of the liberal and secular teachings of Islam whereas his great grandson, Aurangzeb, was a product of the exclusive and uncompromising part thereof. Aurangzeb's own blood brother Darashikoh, who followed Akbar's line of thought and action, was branded a 'Kafir' and executed at the behest of Aurangzeb. Later, when the political supremacy of the Muslims declined in the eighteenth century, liberal and secular face of Islam reappeared. It continued upto the last quarter of the nineteenth century when, having got the British patronage, the ideology of Aurangzeb started gaining ground once again. Presently, the Indian Muslims are following this very line of thought. In brief, Islam has two faces. The face that suits a particular situation is conveniently brought forward. But, apparent contradictions appear in almost every Scripture. Our Indian Constitution is no exception. The rule in such situations is that the text should be read in the context of the situation in which it is stated. In this way, we will find harmony even where we are faced with an apparent contradiction.

A dispassionate reading of the Quran and the life of Hazrat Mohammed would reveal that the Islam was more of an Arab national movement than a religion. Mohammed's greatest contribution was to bring together different warring Arab tribes and to make them, at one time, the most powerful nation on earth. He declared that the Arabs were the chosen people of God. Initially, the Muslims offered their prayer facing Jerusalam, the homeland of Jews. Mohammed asked them to turn their faces to Mecca in prayer. Earlier, the Arabs were only traders or farmers. Mohammed made them formidable fighters. However, drunk deep with the new found religio-political creed of Islam, the Arabs expanded their empire far and wide. In whatever country they conquered, they introduced their Arabic language and Arab culture. But when the Turks, and the Persians regained their self consciousness, they revived their culture, overthrew the Arab rule, and replaced Arabic language by their own, Turkish or Persian. Holding this very view, an India born Muslim scholar settled in UK, Anwar Shaikh, states in his well researched book, "Islam–The Arab National Movement", that the Arab nationalism has done more damage to the national dignity and honour of non-Arab Muslims than any other calamity that may have affected them. He also rightly says that Islam has become the biggest business for the Mullah and an effective source of power for the politicians.[5] An example of brain washing effect of the Quranic teaching of Madrasa style is provided by an incident quoted by the noted author Nirad C.Choudhari in his "The Continent of Circe". Nirad once asked a Moulvi of his native place (East Bengal), "Which fruit do you like the most?". Prompt came the answer from the Moulvi, "Palm dates of Iraq".

It ought to be remembered that the Hindu-Muslim unity in medieval period dawned only when Hindus developed a kill instinct under Shivaji and Guru Gobind Singh and when the Muslim rulers lost their political supremacy. It was the maximum when the actual political power passed to Hindu hands, namely the Marathas, the Sikhs and the Jats. The atrocities committed by Nadir Shah of Iran and Ahmad Shah Abdali of Afghanistan on Hindus and Muslims alike, also turned the Muslims further to their Hindu neighbours. During the popular upsurge against the British in 1857 when Delhi was under occupation of the rebel army, the Britishers were pinning their hopes on the day of Id (on Aug 1, 1857) when they were sure of serious Hindu-Muslim riots due to cow killing by the Muslims. Historian Surendra Nath Sen states:

> "The Muslim festival of Id was approaching and Hodson confidently expected Muslim fanatics to fight the Hindus over the customary killing of cow in the Jami Masjid. His spies had reported of dissensions going on. 'Some of the Mahomedan fanatics, we are told, 'have declared their fixed intention of killing a cow as customary on the day at the Jumma Musjid. It is hoped that they will religiously adhere to their determination, and there is then sure to be a row between the Mahomedans and Hindoos.'.......there was a large number of Hindus in the rebel army, and responsible Muslim opinion was disinclined to alienate them in any way....Hakim Ahsanullah hesitated to forbid a time-honoured practice and would fain be guided by the Maulavis. But the King (Bahadur Shah Zafar) took courage in both hands and informed the General and officers of the army that no cows were to be killed within the city during the festival of the Id, and if any Mohommedan should do so he would be blown away from a gun; and whoever, on the part of a Musalman helped to kill a cow, would also be killed. The King himself set an example to his subjects by sacrificing a sheep at the Idgah. So on the first of August, the day of the Id, there was no internecine war of factious fight at Delhi".[6]

But, the Hindus had lost their initiative to the British simply because, saddled with power, every Hindu principality adopted a narrow sectarian and regional outlook. The Marathas, who had risen on the note of Hindu padpaadshahi (rule according to Hindu ideals) soon got engaged in establishing a Maratha Raj. Later, they themselves got divided into four mutually warring dynasties. The Khalsa Panth that was set up to protect Hindus and promote Hinduism got confined to a Sikh Raj in the Punjab. The Jats similarly worked for a Jat kingdom. This very internecine Hindu conflicts were exploited by the British and are now being exploited by the contemporary politicians.

Hindu-Muslim unity is, therefore, not impossible. It is possible and desirable too. But it cannot be bought nor begged. It will automatically come if only Hindus could stand as Hindus and show that they can also fight with a kill instinct while Muslims need to get out of the captivity of the Ulemas. As a matter of fact, Hindus need Hinduising themselves more than attempting to Hinduise Muslims or Christians.

REFERENCES

1 Dr. Saifuddin Geelani, Guruji Ke Muslim Samasya Par Vichar, p. 11, Suruchi Prakashan, Jhandevala (opp. Naz Cinema), New Delhi-55.

2 Meanings of the Glorious Quran, English translation by Muhammed Marmaduke Pickthall, Kitab Bhavan, New Delhi-2.

3 -do-

4 -do-

5 M.M. Shankdher's 'Political Question, a review of Anwar Sheikh's book "Islam the Arab Nationalism", Indian Express, Magazine Section, p.4, July 23, 1995.

6 Surendra Nath Sen, Eighteen Fifty-Seven (Forewarded by Maulana Abul Kalam Azad), Publication Division, May 1957 (Reprint Feb 1958) pp. 92-93.

Chapter XIX

MYTH OF MUSLIM GRIEVANCE AND DALIT POLITICS

Following the pro-Muslim policies of Congress, it has become a lucrative business to invent and magnify Muslim grievances. Popular English dailies and periodicals (apart from the Urdu media) give them wide publicity. Here is a specimen from a famous national daily, authored by Nirmal Goswamy, under the caption "Banality of Evil":

> "The Muslims of India have been systematically dispossessed by a vengeful majority. Their homes and properties have been robbed under the infamous Evacuee Property Law. Their share in civil administration, the armed forces and the corporate sector is abysmally low compared to their numerical presence in the nation. Their cherished language, Urdu struggles for survival. Suspicion, ridicule, obsessive hatred and murderous hostility of the Hindus have condemned them to a life of dark fear. They are the prime targets of the infamous TADA. Massive, cyclic programmes culminating in the evil at Ayodhya on December 6, 1992, have irretrievably damaged their psyche. No sane Hindu could even begin to deny these absurdities."[1]

Referring to a novel 'Lajja' by a Bangladeshi authoress, Tasleema Nasreen, which depicts the plight of the persecuted Hindus of Bangladesh, Goswamy laments, "Will an Indian (Hindu) author write the same way about the Muslims of India?" These very grievances have been ventilated by Dr. Rafiq Zakaria in his recently published book 'The Widening Divide'. He has posed the question, "Whether the sins of the forefathers of Muslims should be visited on the present generation?". The falsehood and absurdity of all these allegations and assertions would be evident from the facts stated hereafter.

After Partition, Hindu majority of India did not take a wholesale vengeful action against the Muslims on a national level as the Muslims did against the Hindus in Pakistan and Bangladesh. The truth is that whenever the Muslims were attacked in any part of the globe, the Muslims of India have been targetting Hindus and Hindu temples. Even when the Americans bombarded Iraq during the Gulf war of 1990, Muslims rose against the Hindus. In J & K, the Kashmiri Muslims armed with the guns and bombs received from Pakistan, have killed or driven out the entire Hindu population from the Kashmir valley. Yet, there is no retaliatory action from Hindus in any other part of India where they are in an overwhelming majority. It is an ominous sign that the propounders of Muslim grievances have failed to take note of this positive phenomenon. On the contrary, some Urdu papers off and on brand Hindus as cowards.

Demolition of the Babri structure in Ayodhya is an isolated and exceptional case. Hardly anyone lamenting over it had seen it. Except the domes, there was nothing like a mosque in it. The structure built with the material of an ancient Hindu temple on the birth site of the Hindu god, Lord Rama, an incarnation of lord Vishnu, had been a matter of dispute for centuries. Even so, the Muslims demolished hundreds of undisputed Hindu temples in retaliation, caused communal riots throughout the country, and a gruesome serial bomb blasts in Bombay which took a toll of about 300 lives and loss of property worth crores of rupees. The Evacuee Property Law was a natural consequence of the Partition but its implementation in Pakistan and Bangladesh was far more rigorous than in India. Thousands of Muslims who had gone to Pakistan returned in 1950 and the Indian government gave them their properties back. Not a single incident of a Hindu returning to Pakistan(or Bangladesh) took place. From the very beginning, the Muslims have held high political, administrative, and military positions in India. There have been two Muslim presidents of India, a sizeable number of them has been cabinet ministers in the Central Government. At least one Muslim, Air Marshal Latif, was the Chief of Air Staff. Two Chief Justices of India (Justice Hidayatullah and Justice H.M. Beg) were Muslims. The present Chief Justice of India (Justice Ahmadi) is again a Muslim.

The Muslim share in Parliament and state legislatures has recently declined as a result of Muslims themselves taking to Islamic fundamentalism and terrorism during the past few years and certain acts of the Congress and some other political parties which have hurt the sensibilities of Hindus. Earlier, many Muslim candidates were getting elected from Hindu majority areas. Muslim representation in civil services, the armed forces, etc., is definitely low, but it is again a making of the Muslims themselves. In pre-Partition days, the Muslim share in the armed forces and the police was over sixty per cent. In civil services also their number was over fifty per cent, far in excess of their population, that was about 24 per cent. Of the six army Regiments of the Panjabis, five Regiment strength consisted of Muslims while Hindus comprised only one Regiment strength. After Partition, all the Muslim Regiments of the Indian army, ninety per cent or even more of the Muslim police personnel and the civil servants went to Pakistan in the hope of better promotion prospects and bright future. This fact has been conceded even by Shri Sita Ram Kesari, the most vociferous central minister in advocating job reservations for the Muslims.[2] For the first twenty years, these very Muslim government officers and other ranks migrated from India (Now called Muhajirs) dominated the Pakistani services and other fields, leaving very little room for the natives of Pakistan. It was very much resented by the locals of Pakistan—Panjabis, Sindhis, Baluchis and Pathans. After the first generation of Indian Muslims in Pakistan passed away, the resentment snowballed into a fierce anti-Muhajir movement in Pakistan, especially in the port city of Karachi. The Muslims who remained in India were mostly craftsmen, farmers, weavers, and other lower class men who had no tradition of Governmemt service, nor education. Admittedly, they did not take to modern education because their leaders kept them tied up with Urdu language and Madrasa education. One should not, therefore, grudge their low share in public services. Those alleging discrimination against the Muslims in public services and lamenting over their low percentage should first look into the reasons for their abysmally low numbers in the competitive examinations held for the services and the numbers who qualify in the written examination. The alleged discrimination, if any, is possible only where selection is made after a personal interview. Fortunately, no Muslim candidate (to the knowledge of the present writer has ever complained against it. Here is a letter from a Muslim lady, Naseem Bano, of Delhi, published in the widely circulated national daily, Indian Express, New Delhi, Aug 16 1995:

> "About 40 years ago, I had applied for the post of a principal in a girls college in Lucknow. I was the only Muslim candidate and there was no Muslim member on the selection committee. But it was I who was selected for the job. I served my college for 35 years and received a lot of affection from my colleagues and students.
>
> "Never did I feel like a second class citizen. I am proud to be an Indian and I am equally proud that others treat me that way. So, why do leaders of all political parties cry wolf whenever issues concerning Muslims come up in public forums? The truth is that the community can advance only if it takes care of its educational status. What it needs is modern education and not crutches."

Interestingly, most of the Muslims who were engaged in radio, films, literature, education, TV, music, other creative arts, and journalism, remained in India and they continue to dominate in these fields. It is because of them that Hindi has been Persianised to a great extent. It can now be called Urdu in Devanagari script.

The talk of their "cherished language Urdu" is ridiculous. Urdu is an artificial language that cropped up, like the "butler English", as a means of communication between the invading Turks and Iranis on one side and natives of India on the other. The tragedy is that while the Iranis and the Turks settled in India got engaged in Indianising themselves and their language, their descendants in the twentieth century are engaged in reversing the gear. To say that Urdu is the language of all Indian Muslims is utterly false and perfidious. It first divided India in 1947 and later, in 1971, divided Pakistan when East Bengal became Bangladesh because the Bengalis refused to accept Urdu as their language. In the truncated Pakistan today, the Sindhis, the Panjabis, the Baluchis and the Pathans are all set against Urdu's domination. Muslims in India, like their neighbours, speak and write the local language of the areas where they reside; in Panjab, Panjabi: in UP, Hindi; in Andhra Pradesh, Telugu; in Kerala, Malayalam; in

Bengal, Bengali; and so on. It is the Mullahs and Moulvis, supported by anti-Hindu politicians, who have thrust Urdu on the Indian Muslims by giving it a religious colour. Seeing the sad situation in Pakistan, it is strange that the Muslims in far flung areas of West Bengal, Kerala, and Assam, would really want Urdu. The demand is from the political fringe of the Muslims and is artificially inflated and sustained with the help of Anglicised Indians and power hungry politicions.

It is noteworthy that Muslim backwardness is more pronounced in the Hindi speaking states of U.P., Bihar, Rajasthan, Madhya Pradesh, where the Muslim population is being increasingly provoked against the regional language Hindi—which according to the Constitution, is also the official language of the Union of India. In other states,like Andhra Pradesh, Karnataka, Kerala, Tamilnadu, Gujarat, etc., where the Muslims have adopted the regional languages, they are much better off.

For the past ten years or so, Muslims in India are no doubt seen as suspects for the reasons already stated. The allegation of obsessive hatred and murderous hostility towards them or assertions like "they are prime targets of the infamous TADA" are baseless. The TADA was enacted in 1985 when Punjab was in the grip of Sikh terrorists armed with Pakistani weapons. Naturally, the persons then targetted were predominantly Sikhs. During the past five years, Islamic terrorists and Pakistan agents have extended their activities in J & K, Maharashtra, Gujarat and other parts of India. They are also dominating in smuggling activities of narcotics, prohibited arms and ammunition across the country. Naturally, the persons targetted during this period were predominantly Muslims in the said areas. Still, on an all India basis, the numbers of non-Muslim detainees under the TADA were more than of the Muslims.

We now come to the question, "Why should the Muslims of today suffer for the sins of their forefathers?" It is just natural. Are we all, Hindus and Muslims, not suffering from the pangs of Partition, a sin committed by our forefathers, be they Jinnahs or Gandhis? Are we all not paying for the sins of our forefathers committed against the SC/ST centuries ago, by way of making reservations for them in Government jobs? However, the funny part is that the sins of persecuting Hindus and demolishing Hindu temples were committed by the invading Turks, Afghans, Gaznis, or Mughals, whose descendants, by and large, are still well placed.

The suffering lot of Muslims consists of poor Hindu converts to Islam.

Lastly, the lamentation as to why an Indian or Hindu author does not write a novel like 'Lajja' on Muslims in India, is another perfidy. The alleged suffering of Muslims in India is mostly imaginary, a concoction. This should be evident from two glaring facts. Firstly, in 1951, in Bangladesh the Hindus formed thirty per cent of the population. Due to acute persecution, they have been reduced to ten per cent according to 1981 census. By now, their percentage must have further gone down. Secondly, while Bangladeshi Hindus fled to save their life and honour, Bangladeshi Muslims, numbering about 20 million, have crossed over to India for a better living. There is no incidence of Indian Muslims migrating to Bangladesh or Pakistan during the past twenty years. The truth is that the Muslims in India enjoy greater safety and security, greater than what is available to Hindus themselves. The fact remains that all the Muslim suffering in India are attributable to their Mullahs and their political masters, aided and abetted by the forces which want to make India an Islamic state and those who want to introduce western culture and western system of governance in India.

Unfortunately the propagators of Hindutva and Hindi, by and large, have been unable to see the harm in conceding Urdu as the common language of Indian Muslims. The political fall out of Urdu before India's Partition has been brought out in the early chapters of this book. After the Partition, a Muslim poetess of Gujarat, Rehana Tayyabji, wrote to Gandhiji in Nov 1947 in the context of Hindu-Muslim unity. Her foresight on the continued use of Urdu is revealing. She wrote:

> "Bapu! If you want the Muslims to be truly loyal Hindustanis (Indians) don't differenciate between them and the other Hindustanis. If they want to live in India, they should live like other Indians, learn Hindi and Devanagari script...
>
> "Bapu! It is an injustice on the Muslims that you don't let them have an opportunity to shed their rigidity.....
>
> "You will please excuse my impertinence, Bapu! you have lived so much away from the Muslims that you do not know

their psychology. That is why Pakistan came into being. And I believe that if, in addition to Hindi, you make Urdu an official language you will create another Pakistan well within India.

"Now, as an Indian Muslim I pray, for God's sake, don't encourage the Muslims to live like foreigners in their own country. By themselves, they definitely want that you continue to play the game of Britain and Pakistan and let the Muslims go on getting more and more. Bapu! I am greatly scared because I am well acquainted with the Muslim society. I know their aspirations which you may or may not appreciate. For God's sake, give a careful thought to what I have stated....."[3]

It is often said that the Muslims belong to this country as much as Hindus. The question is, in what way? Is it for de-Hinduisation of Hindustan, that is India? Is it not a fact that for their Urdu, their Shariat, their separatist political aspirations, slaughter of cows, *et al.*, the Muslims have already been given thirty per cent of the Indian territory in the form of Pakistan (partly converted into Bangladesh)? This is what a rustic semi-literate farmer of Uttar Pradesh told this author sometime back. "We had a joint family of four coparceners in an ancestral house having sixteen rooms. One of the coparceners, 'B', wanted separation. He got away with his proportionate share of four rooms, but left behind two of his children with the remaining coparceners in 12 rooms. Can these two children, when grown up, claim equal or proportional share in the remaining property? The answer is 'No'". On this analogy, the Muslims who did not go to Pakistan are legally and morally bound to speak the same language, follow the same traditions, be subject to the same laws, adopt the same culture, as the Hindus do with whom they chose to cast their lot in 1947 and of whose family they now form a part. Otherwise, their proper place is in Pakistan. But the Muslims in India, pampered by the power hungry politicians of the Congress, its offshoots, and the anti-Hindu Marxists and communists, are now insisting on having Urdu in Persian script, separate Shariat laws, reservation in Government jobs, freedom to slaughter cows in utter and absolute disregard, and contempt, to Hindu sensibilities, and separate Shariaat courts to be manned by Mullahs and Qazis. If, in this situation, Hindus suspect the Muslims, what is wrong in it? Indeed these very points were advanced to seek Partition of India, which the Muslims have already got.

RELIGIOUS FUNDAMENTALISM

For some time, a new proposition has been advanced that Islamic fundamentalism and Hindu fundamentalism are both dangerous and need to be curbed with an iron hand. It is making a lot of impact on those who neither know Islam nor Hinduism. Islamic fundamentalism, whose specimen is available in J & K, in our neighbourhood Pakistan, Bangladesh, and Afghanistan, aims at converting India into an Islamic state. Hindu fundamentalism, on the other hand, aims at establishing a secular polity in the background of Indian culture where there is no discrimination on grounds of religion, sex or caste. It is sometimes given the name of Hindutva after the name of this country Hindustan. We have 'India' only so long as English remains the official language of Hindustan.

Presently, there are separate personal laws for men and women based on religion which means different treatment to different religious denominations. Hindu fundamentalists want to remove this distinction while Muslim fundamentalists want to countinue with it. The propaganda that Hindu fundamentalists want to impose their *Shastric* laws or the *Manusmiriti* on non-Hindus and the Dalits is utterly false. Even during the medieval period, there were large areas governed by Hindu kings but nowhere religious persecution took place as in the areas governed by Islamic zealots.

Islamic fundamentalists want to ban the national song "Vande Mataram", perpetrate cow-slaughter, rule by the Shariat, promote Urdu as the official language, and treat Hindus as 'Kafirs'. Hindu fundamentalists want respect for 'Vande Mataram' as India's mark of nationalism, ban on cow-slaughter, rule by secular laws (neither Shastric nor Shariat), Hindi as the official language of the Union and inter-state communication, treatment of all citizens alike, no 'Kafirs', no untouchables.

Islamic fundamentalism and Hindu fundamentalism are thus diametrically opposed to each other. Islam as a religion (save its political aspect) can honourably live with Hindu fundamentalism, but Hindu religion, Christianity or any other religion cannot have equality with Islam under Islamic fundamentalism. Within India itself, J & K is a living example of the intolerance of Islam. For the true meaning of Hindutva, see chapter XX, 'Quibbling over Hindutva'.

JOB RESERVATIONS

As a consequence of the Muslim disenchantment due to demolition of the 'Babri Mosque' in Ayodhya on Dec 6, 1992, the Prime Minister and some other leaders, notably Sitaram Kesari, have been making various offers to the Muslim community to win them over. Shri Kesari, a prominent central minister, has been more vocal in pleading for job reservations for the Muslims. Interestingly, though the Muslim leaders here and there had been demanding reservations of seats in Parliament and State Legislatures, they never sought reservations in government jobs, because to do so they would have to plead their own backwardness, something which they thought would be beyond their dignity. The thinking, however, took a change in the past decade when the Muslim leaders felt the need for making a united front with the Dalits and the OBCs. In 1990, the then Prime Minister V.P. Singh, leader of the Janata Dal Government, made 27 per cent reservations in Government jobs for the OBCs, pursuant to the Mandal Commission's Report. A year or so later, the Janata Dal leaders started making out a case for similar reservation for the Muslims. The Muslim leaders readily adopted it in their charter of demands. Now, Congress leaders have also come to support it. Here is an instance of history repeating itself.

Before the Muslim League was born in Dec 1906, a petition for the Muslim delegation to the then Viceroy, Lord Minto, was drafted by an Englishman, Sir Archbold, which included the demands for reservations of posts in all the services and separate electorate for the Muslims. These demands received a pat from the Viceroy. On its formation, the Muslim League adopted them and, as time passed, made further additions. All prominent historians agree that the edifice of Pakistan was gradually built on the foundation of the separate Muslim electorate and reservations in the Council and other public bodies. Many conscientious intellectuals who know the history have pointed out that job reservation for the Muslims and similar offers were bound to exacerbate communal sentiments to the detriment of the Muslims. Reservations for the SC/ST and the OBCs have been made on the premise that they had been badly treated for ages by the upper caste Hindus. Admittedly, they have suffered societal discrimination for centuries due to the birth based caste prejudice in the Hindu society which in turn resulted in their economic backwardness. Surely, that is not the case with the Muslims. Indeed, they got a preferential treatment during the Muslim rule and they were also the pampered lot of the British Raj, before Partition. The Muslim backwardness is solely due to their self imposed isolation and hawkish nature. Making reservations for them would mean putting a premium on their separatist thought and bullish behaviour.

The question of reservations on the basis of religion, with special reference to the Muslims, was thoroughly discussed in the Constituent Assembly in 1949. Both Jawaharlal Nehru and Sardar Patel vehemently opposed it in the interest of the nation and also in the interest of the minority communities. In his forceful speech, a Muslim League Member from Bihar, Tajamul Husain said:

> "Reservation is the offspring of separate electorates. Do not bring in reservation in the place of separate electorates....I ask the members of the majority community who are present here today. Will you allow us to stand on our own legs? Will you allow us to be a part and parcel of the nation? Will you allow us to be an equal partner with you? Will you allow us to share your sorrows, grief and joy? If you do, then for God's sake keep your hands off reservation for the Muslim community...." (Proceedings of the Constituent Assembly quoted in Organiser weekly, New Delhi, Aug 20, 1995, P.2)

The national leaders should think of ways and means which would provide employment and honourable livelihood to all, irrespective of caste and religion. Most of the forty per cent Indians under the poverty line are Hindus. The Muslims constitute only about 13 per cent of the total population, according to the latest 1991 census report.

SILVER LINING

For a long time, the Muslim community has been a captive of Mullahdom or Mullahshahi. It is the tyrannical overlordship in the name of Islam which provokes its adherents to attack and destroy non-believers. The Indian Ulemas have chosen to categorise Hindus as non-believers, i.e. Kafirs or infidels. A few years back, when a prominent Muslim, the Director of Khuda Baksh Library of Patna, said that it was wrong to use the word 'Kafir' (non-believer) for Hindus, the Ulemas castigated him and issued 'fatwa' against him. The Ulemas of this kind are not interested in the basic tenets of religion but they insist on some dogmas that suit their overlordship. They are interested in their own pelf and power.

After the demolition of the Babri structure in Ayodhya on Dec 6, 1992, a small but significant section of the Muslim intelligentsia, has gathered courage, even at the risk of their lives from the Ulemas, to denounce the Muslim leadership for having kept the whole Muslim community isolated and tied to superficial issues of Urdu, Shariat, Babri Mosque, Madrasa education, and so on, resulting in alround backwardness of the community. This section needs all protection and encouragement. Unfortunately, Hindu organisations, because of their own weaknesses, have done nothing so far for these Muslims. A classic example is that of Ms Taslima Nasreen of Bangladesh who carries a fatwa on her head from the Bangladesh Ulemas. Presently, she is passing her days in Germany. She wanted to come to India, but the Indian Government did not allow her the visa. The propounders of Hindutva have exploited her name upto the hilt, but have offered no help. Naturally, she is equally critical about the Sangha Parivar.

Another silver lining came about in 1995 from the Uttar Pradesh, the most populous state of India where the Bahujan Samaj Party (BSP), a party of the Muslims and the Hindu Dalits, and the Samajwadi Party (SP), headed by a powerful group of Yadavas, surresptitiously categorised backwards, had formed a coalition Government even though the Bharatiya Janata Party (BJP) was the largest single party in the legislature. Sick of the treacherous behaviour of the SP, the BSP withdrew which brought about the fall of the coalition government. However, with the unconditional support of the BJP, the BSP formed the Government which gave India, its first ever Dalit woman Chief Minister, Km. Mayawati. This coming together of two utterly antagonistic political parties was very much resented by the perpetrators of class-wars, caste wars, and communal wars who, over a long period of time, had painstakingly created a wide wedge between the two by projecting the BJP as a party committed to 'Brahminical' order of society that was allegedly determined to eliminate the Muslims, and enslave the Dalits. The BSP, on the other hand, was projected as a party of crusaders against the so called 'Brahminism'.

There is an ancient Sanskrit play in which a prince, betrayed by his ministers, escapes in disguise to another kingdom where he earns his livelihood by giving tutions in music. On hearing the high reputation of this new music teacher, the princess of the kingdom requests the king, her father, to engage him as her music teacher. The king finds that the musician is extremely handsome. He is afraid that the princess might fall in love with the musician. So, he tells the musician, "The princess is very dark skinned and has a very ugly face. You have to teach her from behind a curtain to avoid the ugly sight. "The musician agrees. Now, the king tells the princess, "Look my child! The musician is excellent in music, but is a swarthy hunchback. He has an abominable face. You have to take your lessons from him from behind a curtain." The music class starts. A heavy silk curtain is put up betweem the princess and the music teacher. One evening, the princess is unable to pick up the new musical note (Raga). In disgust, the musician says, "Not only is your face ugly, your head too is brainless". The princess, a paragon of beauty, gets enraged and retorts, "You swarthy hunchback! How dare you call me ugly?". A verbal duel ensues. In a fit of rage, the prince turned music teacher, draws the curtain. Face to face with the princess, the prince is stunned to see her beauty. The princess is equally ecstatic to see the majesty of the musician. The trickery of the king is out. The inevitable happens. The prince and the princess fall in love with each other.

The UP provided a God-sent opportunity for the Sangha Parivar as well as the BSP to get a first hand knowledge of each other. The former could show that it is really concerned with the ill fated Dalits and would do every thing to raise their social and educational status in the Hindu society and to improve their economic lot, ensuring them at the same time, security of life and property against all kinds of exploitation and oppression. Till recently, the Sangha work was centred around big cities and towns among the educated middle or lower middle class citizenry. The Sangha Parivar availed of the opportunity to come close to the villages and rural life and started working even among the Dalit and backward Muslims and those terrorised or victimised by the Mullahs and Moulvis. They have, however, touched only a fringe of such Muslims whose number is very large and who need urgent help for liberation from the clutches of the Ulema and unscrupulous politicians. Only by doing this, the Sangha Parivar would be giving proper answer to their detractors.

Incidentally, the Dalit Hindus and the oppressed and muzzled Muslims can be the most fertile ground for recruiting dedicated workers and crusaders for the national cause. Without their active participation in large numbers, the cries of Hindutva will not go far enough. It ought to be remembered that the brave armies of Shivaji and Guru Gobind Singh largely consisted of Backward and Dalit Hindus and the victimised Muslims, especially the Pathans. Upper caste Hindus were few and far between. This historical fact was very well known to the Muslim politicians and the British rulers. Hence, from the very beginnning of the current century, both of them took extra pains to alienate the Dalit Hindus from the main Hindu body. More about it in the next heading–The Dalit Politics.

On its part, the BSP needs to shun its fascist stance against upper caste Hindus, namely, their oft repeated slogan, "Tilak-Tarazzu-aur-Talwar, inko maaro joote chaar", meaning give shoebeating to the Brahmin, the Trader and the Kshatriya caste men.

As expected, the enemies of Hindu revival and detractors of the Sangha Pariwar used every trick to break the BSP and the BJP alliance. In a few months time, the BJP was forced to withdraw its support to the BSP government. Consequently, the BSP Government fell. There is a President rule in U.P. However, in the recent Lok Sabha elections held in April 1996, the BJP candidates won more seats reserved for the Scheduled Castes/ Scheduled Tribes in U.P. than the BSP candidates. A greater test of the Sangha work done among the Dalits would be provided by the U.P. Assembly elections scheduled to be held in October 1996.

THE DALIT POLITICS

The power hungry Pan-Islamists of India, like the Christian missionaries, have been well aware of the importance of the so called "Backward" and "Dalit" Hindus since the medieval period and, therefore, have always been trying to segregate them from the Hindu body. In his 'Thoughts on Pakistan' written in 1941 (reprinted in 1946 as 'Pakistan or Partition of India'), Dr. B.R. Ambedkàr stated:

> "The Muslims have always been looking at the Depressed Classes with a sense of longing and much of the jealousy between Hindus and Muslims arises out of the fear of the latter that the former might become stronger by assimilating the Depressed Classes. In 1909 the Muslims took the bold step of suggesting that Depressed Classes should not be enrolled in the Census as Hindus. In 1923 Mr. Mohammed Ali in his address as the President of the Congress went much beyond the position taken by the Muslims in 1909.
>
> "The quarrels about ALAMS and PIPAL trees and musical processions are truly childish; but there is one question which can easily furnish a ground for complaint of unfriendly action if communal activities are not amicably adjusted. It is the question of conversion of the Suppressed Classes, if Hindu society does not speedily absorb them...It has been suggested to me by an influential and wealthy gentleman who is able to organise a Missionary Society on a large scale for the conversion of the Suppressed Classes, that it should be possible to reach a settlement with leading Hindu gentlemen and divide the country into separate areas where Hindu and Muslim Missionaries could respectively work (Hindus for assimilation and Muslims for conversion), each community preparing for each year, or longer unit of time if necessary, an estimate of the numbers it is prepared to absorb or convert."[4]

Mohammed Ali's clear signal was that either Hindus absorb the Depressed Classes in a given time or allow the Muslims to convert them to Islam. But does conversion to Islam change the fate of the Dalits? No. The Hindu Dalits, who had embraced Islam earlier, remained Dalits even after becoming Muslims. Indeed, they form the bulk of the Muslim population in India, backward-both socially and economically. Only for the past 4-5 years, the Muslim leadership is agitating for a reservation for them in government jobs. The Dalits by alienating themselves from the Hindu fold, would thus be exposing themselves to Islamic fundamentalism, nothing more.

Indeed, the Dalit question in Indian politics was introduced by the British for their own imperial designs. They first planted it in the South in 1920s through E.V. Ramasamy Naicker in the name of Dravidianism. Following British historians, Naicker said that there was an ethnic and racial divide between the Aryans called Brahmins, having migrated from the North, and the native Backward Classes, that the backwardness and all other ills, like poverty, of the nativeTamilians were due to these alien Brahmins. Dravidianism was , therefore, to free the Tamil land (Tamilnadu) from all 'alien' influences of the allegedly immigrant Aryans, purify Tamil language and culture, eliminate 'Sanskrit', denounce all gods and goddesses originating from Northern India, remove the caste system of the Hindu Dharmashastras, and oppose introduction of Hindi. Naicker was an atheist and wanted to replace religion by logic. But his followers, rooted deep in idol and hero worship, deified his own self. This Anti-Brahmin and Anti-North movement greatly influenced the politics of Tamilnadu. Its torchbearer, the Dravid Munetra Kazgam party ruled over Tamilnadu for a long time. But soon the truth came to the fore. Hindu religious practices, the worship of gods and goddesses, remained unchanged. It was realised that the Tamil music, of which the Tamilians, are so proud was given by the early Tamil Brahmins. Also, the Bhakti cult of India, the greatest contribution of Tamilnadu to the Indian subcontinent, originated from the Tamil Brahmins. Besides all this, the new Dalit leaders who replaced the erstwhile Brahmins from the seat of power did not prove any better. The DMK got split up. The stronger group AIDMK, chose Ms. Jayalalita a Brahmin, as its leader.

But, the devisive forces of India have carried the anti-Brahmin movement of Tamilnadu to other parts giving it some more teeth. It is now being propagated that the actual conflict was between the Brahminical social order comprising Brahmins and those forming part of the Hindu Chaturvarna (caste structure) namely, the Kshatriyas and the Vaishyas which include Thakurs, Banias, Kayasthas, Mudaliars, Reddis. It was highlighted that the Dravidian movement in Tamilnadu failed only because it did not address itself to the Muslims and the Christians. The above theme has generated the slogans, 'Dalit-Muslim Bhai-Bhai; Hindu Kaum Kahan se Aai' (Dalits and Muslims are brothers; wherefrom comes the Hindu community) and "Tilak, Tarazu aur Talwar; inko maro jute char' (Give severe shoe beating to the Brahmin, represented by Tilak, Bania, represented by balance, and the Kshatriya, represented by sword.) In fact, the Dalit politics is being played, financed and directed mainly by the overzealous Christian missionaries and fundamentalist Islamic institutions and organisations. Their sole aim is to alienate the SC/ST and OBCs from the Hindu body and make them fight against their own source and sustenance. It would be clear from the news report in the Indian Express, New Delhi (Oct.11,1995) which says, "The Dalit issue has now entered the agenda of the World Council of Churches (WCC) which intends to play the role of a facilitator in the Dalit Solidarity Programme for members from all religious affiliations. It will serve as a link to foster solidarity 'within the Dalit community', announced Dr Konrad Raiser, General Secretary of the Geneva-based organisation. The main initiative is expected to come from within India itself as it did in South Africa". There is a warning that "The WCC would also initiate interventions to internationalise human rights violations in this regard through the UN Human Rights Commission (UNHRC) . Mr Ipe Joseph, General Secretary, National Council of Churches in India (NCCI) revealed that almost 60 to 70 per cent of the Christians in India are Dalits".[5] The report also states that "The whole initiative for Dalit solidarity took shape three years ago at the NCCI headquarters where a national conference of Dalit leaders of all faiths was held. That was the starting point for an affirmation of what the Indian church community could do for Dalits irrespective of their religious affiliations, he said."[6]

The recently formed 'National Front' government at the centre (after the general elections of 1996), has declared its intention to pass a law to extend the job reservations to the Scheduled Caste Hindus converted to Christianity.

Truly speaking, all Hindus are Dalits and all Dalits are Hindus. Various castes and sub-castes are the limbs of the same Hindu body of which some have overgrown and some suffer malignancy. It is impossible that all people in the society be Brahmins or Kshatriyas; some have to be Vaishyas and Shudras. What is possible and needed is human dignity to each and all. In every society, there is a ruling class, a class of academicians or specialists, a trading class, and a class of servants. This four-fold division (Chaturvarna system of the Hindu Dharmashastras) is universal.

It is also true that, time changing, sovereigns become servants and servants become sovereigns. What needs to be fought against is exploitation of one class or individual by another. No Shastric law allows exploitation. The overriding principle is "Yadyapi shuddham lokaviruddham, ma karniyam ma karniyam", meaning, even if some act is permitted by the scriptures but is against the common conscience, it must not be done. It is so because the society is always in the process of evolution. A principle or law fair today, may become obsolete or unfair after a period of time. The reprehensible birth based caste distinction is un-Shastric. It had started losing ground a hundred years ago with the reformist movement launched by the Arya Samaj of Swami Dayananda and preachings of Swami Vivekananda, etc., in the North and Narayana Guru, Mahatma Phule in the South. It has stayed back because of the later day pervert politicians. Maharishi Veda Vyasa, the author of the Mahabharata and the Bhagvatgeeta, was not a Brahmin by birth; he was born of an unwed low caste boatsman's daughter. Krishna himself was from a farmer (Gopal) family. Maharishi Valmiki, the author of the Ramayana and the first poet of Sanskrit, was from a Dalit class. Brahmins have been just parroting the Ramayana, the Mahabharata and the Bhagvatgeeta. Kabir, a half-Hindu and a Half-Muslim weaver is held in greater reverence in the Hindu society than any of the present day Shankaracharyas. All the reservations for the SC/ST after Independence, have not yet produced a single Kabir or Dr. B.R Ambedkar. As already stated the Dalits who embraced Islam, Christianity or Neo-Buddhism continue to be Dalits. Thus, escapism is not the way. Remedy lies in self emancipation, self-assertion from within, and giving out true meaning to 'Hindutva'. Shivaji and most of his men were from backward classes but attained Kshatriyahood by their own merit. Interestingly, the Brahmins of Maharashtra had refused to coronate Shivaji alleging him of low birth. Then, the Brahmins from Banaras (Varanasi) were invited to coronate Shivaji. Conducting themselves well, the Dalits can confront the hypocrite Brahmins, "Aachar-heenan na punanti Vedah" meaning, the characterless do not get sanctified by the Vedas. (Bhavishya Purana.)

A lot has been said and written against Manu, the first Hindu law giver, and his Manusmriti which is alleged to be responsible for all the ills of the Dalits. The fact is that Manu and his

Manavadharma Shastra, popularly known as Manusmriti, are very much misunderstood and misrepresented. But much of its share goes to Hindu dharmacharyas. Comparable to Noah in the Biblical mythology, Manu, accordingly to Hindu mythology, was the first king and law giver on earth. His name and his work find frequent references in the holy Vedas. The Mahabharata and the Ramayana contain some of the shlokas of the Manusmriti. The present text of the Manusmriti was compiled in the name of Maharishi Bhrigu, over a long period of time. Thus, it is difficult to know how much of it is from the original Manu. There is, however, a key to it. It is repeatedly said in the Manusmriti that whatever be against the Vedic scriptures should not be followed. All agree that birth based caste prejudice was absent in Vedic times. The Manusmriti has 12 chapters on various subjects, from evolution of the universe to kingship, taxation, crime and punishment, individual conduct, marriage, property, duties of each Varna, penance and outcome of various acts of omissions and commissions. There are contradictions as well. No doubt the Manusmriti gives a very respectable position to the Brahmin, but it also prescribes an onerous code of conduct for him. In the matter of crime and punishment, he is punishable eight to sixteen times more than a Shudra (Dalit). Even Western scholars have acclaimed the Manusmriti as the greatest work of its time. But, it is necessary that the Hindu dharmacharyas get together to rewrite or streamline it by omitting the spurious portions and explaining the controversial ones.

REFERENCES

1 Indian Express, New Delhi, Sunday Magazine, p.4, July 16, 1995.

2 T.V. Interview "Aaj Tak", conducted by Surendra Pratap Singh, July 19, 1995, 2130 p.m.

3 Itihas Ke Jharokhe se, part II, by Vachnesh Tripati, p. 103, (Hinduvani Hwai Rahoongi Main), Suruchi Prakashan, Deshbandhu. Gupta Road, New Delhi-55, 1995.

4 S.K. Aggarwal Dr. Ambedkar on Muslim Fundamentalism, 1993, Suruchi Prakashan, Jhandawala New Delhi-55.

5 Indian Express, New Delhi, october 11, 1995

6 -do-

Chapter XX

QUIBBLING OVER HINDUTVA

Of late, some prophets of doom have been creating a false scare of Hindu resurgence by implanting imaginary motifs. These prophets of evil are quite well to do and occupy vantage positions. Undoubtedly, the answer to present maladies facing the Indian sub-continent and those of the world at large, is Hindutva or Hinduism. There is, however, a lot of confusion about the terms — Hindutva, Hindu religion, and Hinduism. All the three terms are used indiscriminately. Briefly speaking, Hindutva is a clarion call for Hindu revival. It is a geo-cultural concept which,in the present circumstances, has acquired a political bias. It is rooted in Hindu culture, distinct from Hindu religion, and is poised against the present hybrid of Marxism or socialism and the capitalist philosophy of the West. Hindutva alone can be the true guide to national policy on defence, economy, foreign affairs and even the political structure — unitary or a federal set up. The word 'Hindutva' should not and need not raise an alarm in any quarters as falsely made out in the English media and reflected in vernacular press. It is only because English remains India's official language that this country is called 'India'. It makes us all 'Indians' and our feeling of being Indian may be called 'Indianness'. Had we changed over to Hindi by 1965, as envisaged by the Constitution makers, India would have become 'Bharat' or 'Hindusthan'. Our nationality would then have been 'Bharatiya'/'Bharati' or 'Hindi/'Hindu'. The term 'Hindutva', meaning Hinduness, would not have then caused a stir. So much for the language!

Hindutva based on Hindu culture must be catholic and must aim at peaceful co-existence with all sections of mankind and with nature too. In other words, it has to be eco- friendly, respectful to all great souls, irrespective of their origin or religious faith, who devoted their lives for the upliftment of man or contributed in the fields of science, art, or literature. The Hindu culture has been enriched not only by those born in Hindu religion but also by scores of others, like Amir Khusro, Abdur-Rahim Khankhana, Malik Mohammed Jayasi, Ras Khan, etc. who followed Islam, but bore Hindu nationality. A political philosophy based on such a rich, powerful and multi-dimensional culture, will by its very nature proceed towards decentralisation of power, maximum freedom to the individual, minimal government, preservation of ecology, respect to ethical and moral values. Just because ethics, morality and spirituality ceased to form essential parts of our new found political and educational system since Independence, the country is moving fast into a world of chaotic materialism, narrow mindedness, and criminality. Hence the relevance of Hindutva.

Many a well meaning ex-civil servants and ex-military officers has lamented over the emerging war clouds and the nemesis that faces India today. The future Indo-Pak conflict would be a confrontation between the forces of true secularism and democracy on one side and the forces of fundamentalism (supported by the US and a host of Islamic countries) on the other. In concrete terms, it is going to be a war between the forces of Hindutva and the forces of Islamic fundamentalism. Today's India is neither a democracy nor a secular country. Rule of law, the first requisite of a democracy, enshrined in Articles 14 and 16, is so fettered that it has become a rule of hypocrisy and minorityism. Secularism as propounded by the Congress, the communists, and some others, taking shelter under Articles 29 and 30, make Hinduism subservient to Islam and Christianity. Of late, Hindu businessmen have started opening educational institutions with Christian names so as to get the benefits of the minority institutions.

Today, the Muslim masses suffer from religious fanaticism. Hindus, on the other hand, suffer from irreligiosity or false dogmas. Their predicament can be gauged from the fact that every other day, they invent a new god or goddess. Even the idols of actors and actresses are being installed as temple deities (in the South). Muslims suffer from a false superiority complex or imaginary fears, while Hindus suffer from diffidence. While Muslims are displaying all aggressiveness, reflected in day-to-day gun-shots and bomb blasts, far and near, Hindus only show signs of helplessness. By and large, Muslims suffer from poverty and are an easy prey to the call of 'jehad' on dubious promises of 'jannat' (heaven) from Pak-funded Mullahs, Moulvis, and other anti-India agencies at work in India and abroad. Hindu elite, as stated earlier, is deep seated in abundance of wealth which is flaunted anywhere and everywhere with its 5 star living, — ostentatious marriages and birthday parties — huge financial rackets, unaccounted wealth that is revealed in every day police raids, bank frauds, the huge amounts of money passing in horse trading, etc. This dominant minority of India is oblivious to the dangers looming large on the Indian horizon. The Hindu poor is in bewil derment, resigned to his fate. Hindutva, therefore, has to address itself to the economic plight of the poor without religious or communal bias and to relieve the rich of their extra fat, through persuasion as a rule, but through coercion where needed. It needs to generate confidence among the law abiding citizens and infuse terror among the criminals, the exploiters, the anti-nationals and anti-socials. The truth that has been the worst casualty after independence from the British Raj has to be revived to its pristine glory. Thus, Hindutva, instead of being a mere political slogan, needs to touch every field of Indian life- education, economy, social reform, ethics,morality, health, unemployment, law and order. Human life needs adequate material support for an honourable living and freedom of faith for spiritual bliss. One at the cost of the other is harmful. In this sense, Hindutva cannot be the monopoly of any one political party or a religious community, or organisation. It has to be nourished and nurtured by all nationalist forces engaged in various facets of life.

Hindutva bereft of Hindu culture is dangerous and even suicidal. Basically, culture emerges out of the family and educational institutions. Government can do very little in this matter. Hindu social, educational, and religious institutions have the onerous responsibility of imparting the right type of education to the masses to save families and put the educational institutions on the right track. Hindu religious institutions who receive donations worth crores of rupees should utilize greater part of their income on education, training, rebuilding of the Indian nation and public welfare activities of secular nature that should attract and emancipate even the so called minorities. The right way to finish minoritysm is that the votaries of Hindutva themselves take care of the needs and legitimate aspirations of the minority communities. The examples thus set by Hindu institutions would, in due course, be emulated by the minorities also.

The theme of Hindutva emerged mainly as a reaction to the British Raj, Islamic aggression, economic and cultural invasion of the West. But, reaction alone is a negative approach. Hindutva, to make a dent in the civilized world, needs to have positive programmes. It is necessary that the political power comes to the forces of Hindutva, but that should not be the end of it.

Understandably, the talk of Hindutva on a public platform was a crime during the Turkish Raj. Likewise it was a crime during the British Raj. But irony of fate is that it has continued to be a crime during the past 48 years of the Congress Raj. On that very ground the election of many MLA's had been declared void by one or the other High Court, from time to time. In a land mark judgment on Dec 11, 1995, the Supreme Court of India ruled that the use of the expressions "Hinduism" or "Hindutva" in election speeches does not automatically amount to seeking votes on religious ground. Accordingly, the Hon'ble Supreme Court quashed the order of the Bombay High Court which had held the election of Maharashtra Chief Minister, Manohar Joshi, and some others to the state Assembly as void because they had made references to Hindutva or Hindu Rashtra in their election speeches.[1]

As expected, a number of anti Hindu politicians and their high flier supporters have sharply reacted to this judgment and have demanded amendments to the Constitution and the Representationof the People Act (RPA) to let the old order continue. It is argued that "the concept of Hindutva, whatever be its intellectual meaning, had acquired a very insidious electoral meaning". A senior lawyer of the Supreme Court (PP Rao) remarked "It is difficult to appreciate the court's view that Maharashtra Chief Minister Manohar Joshi's statement that he would establish the first Hindu state in the country did not amount to appealing to the electorate in the name of religion... tomorrow someone else can say he would establish a Muslim state".[2] Indeed, they are the specimen of the Hindu elite who refuse to understand the difference between a Hindu Rashtra ruled by secular laws, like the USA and UK, and a Muslim state ruled by the Shariat, exemplified by Pakistan and Bangladesh in our own neighbourhood.

Interestingly, Arif Mohammed Khan, former Union Minister of the Congress who had resigned from the Rajiv Gandhi's government on the famous Shah Bano case, has said that the judgment "does not apear to have condoned communalism". Shri Tariq Anwar, Chairman of the AICC minority cell has concurred with Shri Arif Mohammed Khan. Hailing the judgment, Shri L.K. Advani, president of the Bharatiya Janata Party (BJP) has hopefully said that his party has never endorsed bigotry or fanaticism of any kind, whether religious, linguistic or casteist. He asserted, "For us, nationalism is not just a geographical concept; it is essentially a cultural concept. Whether you call it Hindutva or Bharatiyata or Indianness, the nomenclature does not matter; the content is the same".[3]

REFERENCES

1. Indian Express, New Delhi, Dec. 12, 1995 (Front page)
2. Ibid Dec. 13, 1995 (p.9)
3. Indian Express, New Delhi, Dec. 13, 1995 (p.9).

Chapter XXI

GLOBAL THREAT OF ISLAMIC FUNDAMENTALISM

In recent times, Islamic fundamentalism has taken an alarming global proportion because of the changes in world politics. Earlier, it centred round the Arab-Israeli conflict and the Soviet occupation of Afghanistan. Now, the Islamic States of the Middle-East have come to terms with Israel. Soviet forces are no more in Afghanistan. Various Islamic fundamentalist forces (numbering about 70), with their arms and ammunition, are now targetting the democratic world and secular polity in the name of pure Islam. Even the Muslim countries which do not strictly follow the Shariat law are under threat. Egypt, Algeria, Turkey, are some of the Muslim countries where Islamic fundamentalists are fighting against the established secular and democratic regimes.

On August 7, 1994, in London, about eight thousand radical Muslim academicians and religious leaders, including headscarfed women, representing Islamic fundamentalists the world over, gathered at an 'International Khilafah Conference'. It was organised by the Muslim Unity Organisation led by Hizb-ut-Tahrir, a fundamentalist outfit, banned in the Middle East for its extremist activities. Its spokesman, Farid Kassim, said:

> "All negotiations between (Arab) regimes and Israel are illegal. There will be no peace with the state of Islam until the state of Israel is demolished. All international organisations such as United Nationals International Monetary Fund and Arab League are in the hands of the imperialist superpowers. They are unacceptable to Muslims and Islam."

As the speeches, like the above, were being made, the audience raised cries of "Allah-o-Akbar", the war cry of Muslims.

There were speakers from West Asia, Pakistan and the United States also. Islamic fundamentalism has, therefore, become a universal threat. India, which has already been reeling under it for centuries, faces the greatest danger. In any plan or scheme to ward off this threat, one must take into account the global view of Islamic fundamentalism. And, before an effective counter action is taken, it is necessary to know the *raison d' etre* of this fundamentalism, the reasons why it has found so much of acceptability throughout the globe and why thousands of men and women have come forward to sacrifice their lives and property, crossing their territorial boundaries?

THE BACKGROUND

After Christianity, Islam has the largest following in the world. Since its very birth, 1400 years ago, Islam has been aggressive. To start with, its founder, Hazrat Mohammed, laid claim over the ancient temple of Mecca (Kaaba). Had Mohammed built a new shrine for his new found religion, there was no need for him to migrate to Medina (Hijerat), collect a formidable army, and, after eight years, raid Mecca to occupy the Kaaba temple, destroying all the 360 idols in it and slaying everyone who did not follow his commandment. Following this example, the creed of co-existence, except for a temporary period, became anathema to pure Islam.

Islam says that there is one and only one God, Mohammed is His prophet, and the Quran is a Book of Revelation. Good enough! The politics of Islam, the reign of coersion and oppression of the people of other faiths, emanates from its insistence that (a) Mohammed is the last prophet on earth who superceded all previous ones, (b) that there can't be any other prophet in future till eternity, (c) that everything contrary to the Quranic injunctions is falsehood, fit for destruction, and (d) that the best service to God (Allah) is to bring a non-Muslim to Islamic fold or kill one who might speak ill of Islam, its prophet or the Quran. The life of Mohammed and his various acts detailed in the Hadis and pronouncements in the Sunna allow Muslims to enter into a temporary truce or alliance alone with any non-Muslims and that too for furthering the cause of Islam. (Some of the verses of the Quran which stand in the way of peaceful co-existence of the Muslims and non-Muslims are given at the end of this chapter)

It is this religio-political thought of the Arabs who, over a thousand years ago, established their vast empires in the West and Central Asia, parts of North Africa, and Sindh in India. But, when the Arabs came into contact with the ancient civilizations of the Greeks, the Persians, the Romans, and the Indians, they borrowed a lot from them. The Arabs not only conquered territories, they converted the local populations of Jews, Christians, Zoroastrians, Buddhists, Hindus, or others into Islam and imposed their Arabic language on them. Even in the Sindh province of India, they introduced Arabic. Later, as and when the Persians, the Turks, and other non-Arab people regained their national consciousness, they overthrew the Arab rule even while retaining the Islamic faith. They set up their own kingdoms in Persia, Egypt, Syria, Turkey and elsewhere. The Turks and the Persians even removed the Arabic language and revived their own Turkish or Persian. There were contant wars among various Muslim principalities and ethnic tribes, or factions, right since the death of Hazrat Mohammed (632 AD), succeeded by Abu Bakr, the first Khalifa. Abu Bakr was succeeded by Omar (634 AD), assassinated in 644 AD. His successor, Usman was murdered in 656 AD. Usman's successor Ali was murdered in 660AD. As a result of these internal fights, the seat of the Khalifa shifted from Medina to Damascus, to Baghdad, to Cairo and finally to Istambol (Turkey). Of these warring factions, some Turko-Persians and Afghanis marched towards India through the North-West Frontiers and settled there.

From the 15th century, the Europeans (Portuguese being the first) set out on eastward journey to protect their commercial interests which had been seriously jeopardised by the Egyptian rulers of the Mamluk empire. These Muslim rulers (since 1425) had taken control of the main commercial ports and banned circulation of the European gold coins. Both these steps were intended to increase the revenues of the Mamluk empire and ruin European traders.[1] The rich spice trade between the East and the West was being carried through an exclusively Egyption route.

With their superior sea power, the Europeans wrested greater part of the trade and commerce between East and West. It considerably ruined the economy of the Muslim countries. The industrial revolution in Europe aggravated the situation further. By the end of the 19th century, the Ottoman empire and Persia at one end of Asia, and China and Japan at the other were the only areas out of European subjugation. Then started the political and economic pressures on the Ottoman empire from the Tsarist regime of Russia and European powers. They helped Christian majority provinces of the Ottoman empire to get independence from the Turkish rule. Greece, Rumania, Serbia, Bulgaria, Cyprus and Egypt were occupied by Britain, while Tunisia was occupied by France. Germany had emerged as another great European power but it did not get any share out of the disintegrating Ottoman empire. Being a rival of Britain and France, Germany helped Turkey, internally and externally. With the help of the Russian government, the Balkan states became independent from the Turkish rule. All these developments aroused Muslim ire against the British and other colonial powers. It was in this background that Turkey joined Germany against Britain and France during the first world war (1914).

Muslim resistance to the growing European powers got expression in two ways. One was from the educated elite, influenced by the Western thoughts and culture. Jamal al-Din-Afghani (1839-97) was the most influential intellectual Pan Islamist ideologue of the 19th century in Persia and Egypt. His thought is well summed up by Bernard Lewis:[2]

> "For Jamal al-Din, Islam was a civilization, potentially a world power, and only incidentally a faith; its basic demand was for loyalty rather than for piety. The Muslims were to be united as the Germans and Italians were united, and Jamal al-Din passed his life in the search for a Muslim monarch to whom he could be a Bismarck or a Cavour. The enemy from which Islam needed to be saved was Europe, and especially Great Britain, the imperial power in India and Egypt."

Since its earliest times, Islam blended religion and matters of state, ethics, law and politics into its fold, but Al-Afghani's emphasis on the political aspects of Islam had a novel Eurpoean influence. Though antagonistic to Western encroachments, Afghani favoured adaptation of Western concepts. He had also come to India where he met Muslim leaders in Bombay, Calcutta, and other places to prepare them for a global confederation of Muslim states. He was the first man to give a scheme of Pakistan to the Indian Muslims. (Sir Sikandar Hyat Khan referred to him in his speech in the Punjab Assembly on 11-3-1941, in connection with the concept of Pakistan).

The other type of resistance came from the Orthodox Mullahs and Moulvis who thought in terms of superiority of Islam, stressed on Pan-Islamism (unity of the Umma) irrespective of territorial boundaries, and all out jehad against political and cultural domination of Europe. The European powers made alliances with the elite groups in each Muslim country and helped them in getting political power after the former were forced to abdicate in favour of the locals.

After world war II, all Islamic and non-Islamic countries got independence. All of them got engaged in making rapid progress in every field so as to catch up with the European countries. But, all of them, saving a few small countries like Singapore, failed because the new power groups thrived on populist slogans and heavy borrowing. During the cold war period, the USA, the UK, and the USSR made all out efforts to win over these power groups by promising financial, technological and other aids. This way almost every Muslim country got a god-father. Billions of dollars of grants and loans passed from the Soviet Union to Afghanistan, Egypt, Syria and Iraq, while equal or greater amount of aid passed from the USA to Pakistan, Iran, Turkey and Egypt. Pakistan has been the shrewdest or the luckiest to have got all types of assistance from the West as well as the East. The oil producing countries of the Gulf received large amounts of Western private and public capital to develop their resources which yielded billions of dollars in profits to the investors and royalties to the Gulf countries.

In retaliation to the shameful defeat at the hands of the US supported Israel in 1971, the Arab nations (dominating the OPEC-Organisation of the Petroleum Exporting Countries), effected a steep rise in their petroleum prices. A large part of the huge profits made thereby has been used in promoting Pan-Islamism the world over. It has found expression in three ways — Politicising Islam (raising political upsurge in the Muslim world), Petrolising Islam (using wealth earned through petroleum for the upliftment of Muslim brotherhood), and Nuclearing Islam (acquiring nuclear capability for Islam in any subsequent conflict involving the Muslim countries).

RISE OF PAN ISLAMISM AND TERRORISM

In the above given situation, Pan-Islamism and Islamic terrorism have taken a serious turn. They are now challenging even those Islamic countries which have adopted secularism and democracy, like Algeria, Lebanon, Turkey, Indonesia, Malaysia and so on. The fundamentalists have already forced Pakistan and Bangladesh to shed their secular character and pass blasphemy laws, which make the lives of non-Muslims, and even open-minded Muslims, miserable. In all secular countries where Muslims are in sizeable numbers, Islamic fundamentalism combined with terrorism is growing fast. In the Muslim world, it is the Mullah or Ulema controlling the mosque who has a direct audience with the common man. He is considered the true and authentic interpreter of the Quran and the Shariat. No Muslim government can, therefore, afford to ignore the call of the Ulema claiming to represent the umma (Muslim community). It is never difficult for a Mullah to find fault with any Muslim officer or minister to condemn him as an apostate, infidel or for violating this or that part of the Shariat.

Presently, Muslim countries with democratic set up are under severe threat of Islamic terrorism from within and without. Countries which are strictly under the rule of Shariat, like Saudi Arabia, Iran, and Pakistan, are also engaged in mutual rivalries for supremacy in the Muslim world. Having a population and military force larger than any other Islamic country and also the atom bomb, Pakistan is trying hard to emerge as the custodian and protector of Muslim interests on a global basis. It is getting all material support from the USA and China, and financial support including mercenaries from a number of Muslim countries to fight its undeclared war against India, in Kashmir, Punjab and even in the North-East.

It is ironical that while almost every Muslim country is entangled in internal turmoils, like the Shia-Sunni disputes, ethnical or racial prejudices, fights between locals and immigrants, they would make a common cause against a non-Muslim country, like India, where a sizeable number of Muslims reside but Islam is not the ruling religion. Everywhere the Ulema tells his Muslim audience that they are born to rule, not to be ruled; that their forefathers were the masters of the globe; that they have fallen to bad days only because their leaders had deviated from the Quranic injunctions, in that, instead of simple life-style of the Prophet, they had adopted a luxurious life style imitating Europeans; that they have to revert back to the Quran and the Islamic traditions and resort to jehad against one and all whosoever comes in their way. This sort of preaching and propaganda from the mosques the world over goes deep into the brains and hearts of the gullible, illiterate or semi literate masses of the Muslims. The Ulemas have the backing of a number of Muslim countries and international militant organisations, like the Ikhwan-ul-Musalmeen, the Jamat-e-Islami, and the Harkat-ul-Ansar. The last one is headquartered in Islamabad (Pakistan) whose branch Hizbul Mujahideen is operating in Jammu & Kashmir (India).

A DISTURBING FACTOR

A much disturbing factor is that the USA and the European nations have not yet taken due note of the dangers of the fast growing Islamic fundamentalism, backed with well equipped and dedicated Mujahids in hundreds of thousands. Their complacency emanates firstly from the fact that the areas of operation of these fanatics, at present, are far from Europe and America and, secondly, from an over confidence on their arsenal of superior weaponry. The United States has been well aware of Pakistan's clandestine imports since the mid-seventies for its nuclear weapon programme, but the US administration kept on certifying Pakistan's nuclear innocence. It was motivated by the American interest in equipping Pakistan to counter Russian interventian in Afghanistan. For the same reason, the US desisted from declaring Pakistan a state supporting terrorism even when it knew fairly well that Pakistan was providing all material and diplomatic support to subversive activities in Punjab, J & K, and even in Afghanistan after Soviet withdrawal.

According to India's former Foreign Secretary, Shri J.N. Dixit,

> "Pakistan remains an important factor in US strategic and security schemes in relation to the subcontinent, in relation to the Gulf and in relation to Central Asia. Through the negative prism, the US would want to sustain its close relations with Pakistan to prevent it from becoming even

more close to China or becoming a part of the Pan-Islamic fundamentalist movement. Similarly, US economic interests in China are of a scale which would make the US think twice before taking any drastic action against China".[3]

This humble author thinks that the American policy towards Pakistan is erroneous and suicidal. Pakistan itself is a product of Islamic fundamentalism. It has not only subsisted on religious bigotry, but is now the greatest breeder and exporter of Islamic fundamentalism and terrorism. Islamic fundamentalism has three pronged strategy-one for the Muslim countries themselves to bring them round to strict Shariat laws, the other for those Asian and African countries where Muslims are not in a majority but are in sizeable numbers, and the third for the Christian world of Europe and America. Islamic institutions funded by the oil rich Arabs and mafia dons, like Dawood Ibrahim, are already engaged in prosylitising activities in Western countries and carving out large or small Muslim pockets to be the jumping grounds for their future terrorist and subversive activities and guerilla war-fare. It is going on a much larger scale than the erstwhile Communist movement. In this sort of warfare, long range missiles, fighter/bomber aircraft, and atom bombs are useless. The Islamic fundamentalists have shown enough samples of what they are capable of doing through various bomb blasts in various parts of the globe, including the one in New York (USA)'s World Trade Centre on 26 Feb 1993 and another of blasting a seven storey Jewish centre at Buenos Aires in Argentine, killing 26 persons and injuring over 120. It is not possible to correctly list out the bomb blasts and other acts of mass killings, loot and arson, committed by Islamic fanatics in India during the past few years.

Here are some of the areas where the anti-West Islamic fundamentalist groups, seeking to establish 'pure' Islamic states, are at work:

(a) Palestine—Sunni Hamas and Islamic Jihad;
(b) Palestine—Shiite Iranian-backed Hezbollah, or party of God, with offshoots like Islamic Jihad and Organisation of the Oppressed on Earth; Iranian Revolutionary Guards contingent.
(c) Jordan— Muslim Brotherhood; Hamas and Jesh Mohammed (Army of Mohammed).

(d) Algeria—Sunni Islamic Salvation Front, driven underground in 1991 while fighting the leftist regime.
(e) Egypt—Sunni Muslim Brotherhood; Islamic Jihad (Sheik Abdel-Rehman's group); Al-Gamaa al-Islamiya, or Islamic Group which is an offshoot of the Islamic Jihad.
(f) Sudan—Sunni fundamentalist regime linked to Iran; Iranian Revolutionaly Guard Corps contingent. (Accused of harbouring fundamentalist militants active in Egypt, Algeria and Tunisia.)
(g) Somalia—Sunni Islamic Union of Somalia (Opposed to US presence).
(h) Iran—Shiite fundamentalist regime which has long been linked to Shiite and Sunni fundamentalist factions in the region: Revolutionary Guards Corps.[3a]

Since Islamic fundamentalists do not believe in co-existence or secularism, they are always at war with some one or the other. In West Asia, their main target still remains Israel. In Sudan, Cyprus and Lebanon, they are fighting with Christians. In the Indian subcontinent they are fighting with Hindus, Christians, Buddhists, and all non-Sunni Muslim sects—like Ahmediyas, Shias, and Muhajirs. The position, more or less, is the same everywhere-China, Russia, Central and South East Asia, Sri Lanka. In Afghanistan, after having got rid of the Soviet troops, they are fighting among themselves. In U.K., they have launched a Muslim Parliament to fight the British government with the slogan, "Dictatorship of the majority dressed in democracy is unacceptable".

PROMOTERS & CONTRIBUTORS OF ISLAMIC FUNDAMENTALISM

The greatest contributing factor of Islamic fundamentalism is the wide spread illiteracy, coupled with the phenomenal growth rate of Muslim population throughout the world. This illiteracy, together with the enforced aloofness from and even hatred towards the non-Muslim people, their institutions, philosophy or literature, and a blind faith on the dog headed Mullahs make a queer cocktail to baptise the young Muslim boys and girls into the false cry of Islam in danger and to render them incapable of pursuing a life of peace and tranquility. They make easy prey to the lustful Arab

Sheikhs, resourceful Syeds or Ulemas, smugglers, dealers in narcotics, adding to their harems, becoming their touts or fodder for their Islamic guns.

In order to retain their age-old hold on the Muslim body and mind, the Muslim clergy repeatedly exhort their followers to distance themselves from the mainstream of their respective countries. This aloofness naturally causes them economic backwardness and deprivation resulting in discontentment. The discontentment is exploited by the clergy by alleging that all their ills have emanated from the discriminaton and oppression of the non-Muslim government or the community of non-Muslims. Thus starts the demand for a separate homeland or autonomy for the Muslims. This tragic story has repeated itself uniformly in every non-Islamic country from Cyprus in Europe to Philippines in South East Asia and from India to the (erstwhile) USSR.

After dissolution of the USSR, the fundamentalist Muslim countries, like Saudi Arabia, Iran, Pakistan, etc., made a beeline to woo the newly independent six Central Asian Muslim republics (Azerbayjan, Kazakistan, Tajkistan, Turkmenistan, and Uzbekistan) with offers of social, religious, financial, commercial and political assistance, but their real aim was to Islamise the secular character of these republics.

These republics have huge arsenal of all kinds of deadly weapons, including nuclear weapons and missiles which they are ready to sell to tide over their financial difficulties. Unless nations of the world professing secularism and humanism, especially India, provide adequate financial aid and moral support, these republics alongwith their arsenal are sure to fall to Islamic fundamentalist forces. Through its Afghan links, Pakistan is already providing men, material, and guidance to local fundamentalist elements in the said republics to wrest power from the present secular set up. Russia is well aware of the dangers ahead and spoke to Pakistan's foreign minister during the latter's visit to Russia in 1994.

THE WESTERN ATTITUDE

The oil reserves of the Middle East are not only the source of fabulous wealth of the Muslim countries of the region, viz Saudi Arabia, Kuwait, Iraq, UAE, etc, but these reserves are equally important sources of income to the western oil companies and their parent nations, including the USA. Their economic interests are interwoven with their political aims in the Middle East. They have, therefore, been striving hard to win over the Arab regimes where possible and to eliminate or subdue their enemies. Saudi-Arabia, the UEA and some other Arab kingdoms have alligned themselves with the USA who has also brought about a peace agreement between the PLO and Israel. Still, there are some countries, like Iran, Iraq, etc. and various fundamentalist outfits in other countries, like Egypt, Sudan, etc., who bear the age old animosity towards Americans and European nations.

In the Gulf war, of 1990-91 though the USA came victorious, its economy was greatly strained which even caused the defeat of its president, John Bush, in the subsequent presidential election. The event brought home the need to prevent any large scale war in the Middle-East. Hence, while making frantic efforts to bring about peace between the Arabs and the Israelis, the USA tried to shift the area of tension. The J & K provided the softest ground. By alleging human rights violation by the Indian security forces in Kashmir and supporting Pakistan version on J & K, the USA and pro-West Arab regimes have shrewdly diverted all the Islamic fundamentalist forces towards India and Afghanistan. In spite of all available evidence that Pakistan was arming, training and sending the terrorists to the Indian side of J & K, etc., for subversive acts of arson, loot, kidnapping, murder, and creating disaffection, the USA did not declare Pakistan a terrorist state. The US administration has been touting Pakistan as a moderate and liberal Islamic state and a bulwark against fundamentalism. In 1991, uncontroversial evidence came to surface that Pakistan had either made the atom bomb or was very much near it. In this situation, the USA, following its own policy on nuclear armament, had to ban military aid to Pakistan. In 1995, a decision was taken to lift this ban temporarily to enable the US Government to supply military hard-ware to Pakistan worth $ 368 million. (The amount is under-valued. The actual cost of arms to be supplied would come to over a billion dollars).[4]

According to a Washington based report in the daily Indian Express, March 8, 1996 (p.11), the US annual human rights report for 1996 has severely criticised Pakistan for its utterly discriminatory and inhuman treatment of religious minorities, like Hindus, Christians, Ahmadiyas (declared un-Islamic by Pakstan Government). The report seeks repealing of Pakistan's blasphemy laws.

The Assistant Secretary of State, Robin Raphel, said there had been more than 50 cases in Pakistan of blasphemy charges since 1986, mostly against members of the Ahmadiya community and Christians. According to her, as long as Pakistan's blasphemy laws remain on the books they are likely to encourage intolerance of minority religions whether Christian, Ahmadiya or Hindu. She said, "We will continue to urge Pakistan's leadership to find a way to phase out these discriminatory and inflammatory laws". Another annual report of the State Department for 1996, released on March 6, states that "during 1995, India made significant progress in resolving human rights problems". For the first time since the start of the insurgency in J & K, a mention of the plight of the Pandits of the Kashmir Valley who have been rendered refugees in hundreds of thousands, has been made in the said report.[5] These instances would prime facie show a shift in the US policy towards India and Pakistan from a policy of favouritism towards Pakistan to a policy of even handedness towards the two countries. But we have to be cautious and must not be led by such one time small gestures which might have been taken by US administration to appease the Christian clergy who have, for long, been agitating against Pakistan's blasphemy laws.

TRAINING AND EQUIPPING ISLAMIC FANATICS

The cold war period offered a great opportunity to the zealots of Islam to get military training and hardware from the Western bloc for use against the Soviet sponsored communism and from the Soviet bloc for use against capitalism of the West. The doctrinal training was provided by numerous ancient and modern Islamic institutions, madrasas and universities in Egypt, Iran, Iraq, Saudi Arabia, Pakistan, and India. After the end of the cold war, the Western and the Soviet sources are nearly dried up, but the deficiency has been amply made good by Pakistan. For more than a decade, Pakistan has been running a number of training centres for the secessionist elements of Punjab and J & K. The whole job is being carried out by Pakistan's Inter Services Intelligence (ISI) wing. The major source of financing this stupendous task is the clandestine narcotics trade which Pakistan has allowed to grow unbriddled and which sometimes worries even its best friend and benefactor, the USA. In a Washington based news item published in the daily Hindustan Times, Sept 13, 1994, the former Pakistan

Prime Minister, Nawaz Sharif, is reported to have said that in 1991 Pakistan's Army Chief, General Aslam Beg, and its Intelligence Chief, General Asad Durrani, had sought his approval for a detailed "blueprint" to sell heroin to pay for the country's covert military operations. A Western diplomat who was based in Islamabad at the time and who had occasional dealings with the two generals is reported to have said, "it is not inconceivable that they would come up with a plan like this...There were constant rumours that ISI was involved in rogue drug operations with the Afghans...." The same report also states that about 70 tons of heroin was being produced in Pakistan annually of which a third was smuggled abroad mostly to the West according to the State Department's 1994 report on international drug trafficking. Incidentally, one kg. of heroin costs Rs. one crore in the international market.

Earlier, Pakistan had been training Arab and other nationals, sponsored by various Muslim governments or NGOs under a 'Kafil' system* to fight jehad in Afghanistan against the Soviet forces. Huge quantities of arms, ammunition, and finances were provided to Pakistan for the purpose by the USA. After the end of the Soviet-Afghan war and withdrawal of the Soviet forces in 1989, a part of the jehad force and its weapons found their way to India, in J & K, Punjab, and North-East.

According to intelligence reports, foreign money amounting to Rs. eighty crores has been clandestinely pumped into the Kashmir valley, mostly through Pakistan, during the past five years to sustain fundamentalism and terrorism.[6] This information, gathered by Indian intelligence agencies, forms the basis for the Central government for issuing notices under public pressure to

---

* Kafil system is a method of recruitment for jehad. Every Friday, the Mullah or Khatib in the mosque would urge the rich gentry to finance those who are willing to go for jehad. A kafil is the person who finds a potential fighter, pays for his passage to the place of jehad and undertakes to support his family in the absence of the jehadist. Between 1983-86, over 5,000 Arabs, financed under this system, entered Pakistan. An equal number or even more, came at their own from as far as Senegal, Sudan, Somalia, Turkey, Upper Volga, Algeria, Morocco, Egypt, Indonesia, Malaysia, Turkey, Burma, Nepal, Bangladesh, even Britain, and the United States. After the Soviet pull out from Afghanistan in 1989, many of the jehadists moved to J & K (India)- Indian Express, New Delhi, Aug 30. 1993, based on a report published in Pakistan monthly, Herald, (Aug 1993), reproduced in POT (Public Opinion Trends, Vol. XXI No.195) dt. Aug 24, 1993, published from New Delhi.

21 fundamentalist associations and 42 individual leaders of the valley, under the Foreign Contribution (Regulation) Act, 1976. The last date for receiving replies to these notices was March 12, 1996. Intelligence agencies have identified Pakistan as the major supplier of the money, along with a Gulf country. Pakistan has repeatedly pledged "diplomatic and material" support to the "liberation" movement in the Valley.[7]

Thus, Pakistan has become the largest breeding ground and exporter of Islamic fundamentalists and saboteurs, catering to the needs of the entire Muslim world. It has set up a full-fledged university, Markaze Dawat-ul-Arshad (MDA) for promotion of international terrorism in the name of jehad for Islam. Its main centres are at Lahore and Peshawar, but its offices are scattered at many places. This university is getting funds from Pakistan government and many other Muslim countries. Youths from Sudan, Egypt, Lebanon and other countries are getting training in jehad in the camps run by the MDA. A special report called "The Kashmir Connection", prepared by the "Task Force on Terrorism and Unconventional Warfare" of the Republican Party of America, that was placed on record of the US Congress on June 22, 1994 by Congressman Nill McCollum of Florida, warned that the fighting in Kashmir was likely to be escalated and expanded to other parts of India by highly trained and armed specialised terrorist forces led by Pakistan and supported by other Islamic fundamentalist forces.[8] According to this report, Iran, Afghanistan, Saudi Arabia and other Gulf countries, besides Ikhwan in Sudan, Algeria and Egypt, see the fighting in Kashmir as jehad. It also stated that there were already extensive stockpiles of weapons as well as large sums of money to sustain and support the extended conflict on all India basis. Pakistan government, the report stated, saw three distinct advantages of keeping Kashmir tension at a high level. First, it "created a diversion from frustrations at home". Second, "Kashmir cause allowed Islamabad to rally the support of Pakistan's Islamic parties and their loyalists in the military and the Inter Services Intelligence". And, third, "it served the regime as an important access point to the markets of Central Asia". This American report also confirms that Islamic terrorists are trained at the Markaze Dawar centre set up by the ISI in Pak-occupied Kashmir and that the training is imparted primarily by instructors from the Armed Islamic Movement and then by Ikhwan-ul-

Musalmeen from Algeria, Sudan and Egypt. The trainees, who include Sikh militants, have now been provided long range chemical missiles, called Saqr missiles. These were developed by Pakistan in the 1980s with the help of US for use in Afghanistan by the Mujahideen.

Shifting of Afghan Majahideens to camps in the POK, the said American report says, began in 1992[9] and that "Many Islamic groups believe that wresting of Kashmir from India would be a great prize at minimum cost, and would inspire their followers". It adds that "Iran considers that escalation of the jehad in Kashmir a key to the assertion of its own strategic prominence, particularly under the auspices of the Islamic Bloc. The Afghan Deputy Prime Minister, Maulana Arasalan Rahmani, is reported to have said that Afghanistan had played a major role in a recent development among the Islamic organisations fighting in Kashmir, namely, the merger of Harkat-ul-jehad Islami and Harkat ul Mejahideen into 'the potent Harkat ul Ansar group' as a part of the active support to the Islamist fighters in Kashmir, Tajikistan and Bosnia. Their number was stated to be 8,000.

A new brand of mercenaries of Lashkar-e-Toiba has started its operation in the south Kashmir Valley, Arizal (Badgam). These mercenaries, mostly Pakistani nationals, are trained in speaking chaste Haryanvi and Punjabi and they wear Indian army uniforms and pass off as Indian security men. The group was originally raised as a private army by an emir of Sudan. It later turned into a mercenary group with a global network. In Kashmir, it is working under the ISA direction.[10]

Incidentally, the Arabs in Saudi Arabia and the Gulf countries considered Pakistanis as second rate Muslims. But, by making the 'Islamic' atom bomb, internationalising the Kashmir question,opening terrorist training centres for the whole of the Islamic world, and with the active support of the great power that is the US, Pakistan has secured a respectable place in the Muslim world. The US sees Pakistan as its advance guard in the West, Central, South and South-East Asia regions. The Taliban, the Islamic fundamentalist army of young students who have marched from the Pakistan border to Kabul and is out to dislodge the present government led by president Rabbani, has been funded and armed by Pakistan. Taliban members are young Afghan refugees who were enrolled in religious schools in northern Pakistan. Many are ethnic Pashtoons.

Young Pakistanis have also joined the Afghans in Taliban. President Rabbani is making desparate requests to the US and others to stop Pakistan from interfering in Afghan affairs through the Taliban, but all in vain. Incidentally, if Afghanistan falls to the Talibans it will seriously affect India's economic and strategic interests.

Now that India has been pushed on to the fore-front to face the rising tide of a fully armed Islamic fundamentalism, it is naturally saddled with the greatest responsibility. Being the largest democracy on earth and being the hardest hit target of the fundamentalists, India has not only to defend itself, but also contribute and guide the entire civilised world to tackle the problem. Truly speaking, almost every country in Asia and Africa is sick of the fast growing menace of Islamic terrorism. But, either for fear of a global Islamic reaction or for immediate political expediency, every one has opted to compromise with it. The Indian government is a classic example of this fear psychosis. For the last 48 years, it has been acceding to every separatist demand of the Islamic fundamentalists and chastising the Hindu majority as if vivisection of India to accommodate the Shariat-bound Muslim in the Islamic state of Pakistan was not enough. During the past five years, thousands of lives have been lost and property worth hundreds of crore of rupees destroyed by the Islamic terrorists, throughout the length and breadth of India, but not a single person has yet been convicted. As against this Indian complacency, ten Islamic terrorists responsible for the bombing of the World Trade Centre in New York on 26 Feb 1993 have been convicted with tough sentences. Their leader, a blind Egyptian cleric Omer Abdel Rahman and another one have been given life imprisonment while others have been given imprisonment of 25 to 57 years. In his pre sentence address, Abdel Rahman called the US as the "fiercest enemy" of Islam.[11]

The Indian government has to come out of its dichotomy and inertia[12] and ensure that while all people follow their respective religions without let or hindrance, no one is allowed to tamper with the secular character of the country or a part thereof. It means that though every religious denomination has the liberty to worship its own god or deity in its own way subject to public order, health and morality, no one can be allowed to put obstacles in the power of the state to regulate the social behaviour, financial or property transactions, and to maintain the unity and integrity of the nation.

It will be a foolhardiness to believe that India, or say Hindus, can by themselves defeat the nefarious designs of the world wide heavily armed Islamic fundamentalism. India has to enlist moral and material support of all secular governments and the people, like those in Egypt, China, the newly independent Central Asian republics, Turkey and European countries. In 1994, Egypt declared Pakistan and Sudan as the terrorist states and snapped telephonic links with them. India, by not taking similar action against Pakistan even while lamenting that Pakistan was waging a 'proxy war' against it, only weakens its case and also the cause of countries like Egypt. (No wonder that in the ongoing anti terrorism meet at Cairo (Egypt) in consequence of four successive bomb blasts by the Hamas in Israel, India has not been invited).

Islamic fundamentalism and terrorism needs to be fought on the battlefield and also on the ideological plane. It must be admitted that the consumerist culture of the West, fed on exploitation of the poor and backward countries of the East, and eroding moral standards in the name of liberty (an outcome of affluence), are some of the real irritants which, among others, provide strong base for the Islamic fundamentalism to grow. While remedying these evils, the masses need to be educated that humanism, not fundamentalism, is the right answer, that militancy and terrorism on the part of one section leads to the same on the part of the other. Fortunately, some Muslim intellectuals, even at the risk of their precious life, have come up to speak against Islamic fundamentalism. The cases of Salman Rushdie of Britain and Taslima Nasreen of Bangladesh are well known. A Muslim Nobel Laureate, Neguib Mahfouz, who also carried death sentence from Islami zealots, says through one of his lady characters, Samia (in 'The Journey of Ibn Fatouma'), "The difference between our Islam and yours is that ours has not closed the door of independent judgment; and Islam without independent judgment means Islam without reason".[13] About a year ago, Turkey's head of the Department of Religious Affairs, Mr. Mehmut Nuri Yilmiz, gave a call for a new interpretation of the Quran to bring it in line with the modern society.[14] A Muslim scholar, Hazrat Allama Anwar Shaikh, born in India (1928), but settled in England since 1956 has taken the courage of tracing his roots in Sanatana Dharma without formally changing his religion. There, he edits a quarterly journal 'Liberty'. He concludes that "India and Islam cannot live together. If the Hindus do not realise this danger, they must surrender to another 1,000 years of humiliation".[15] But, such free thinking men and women belonging to the upper strata of society have little impact on the largely poor and illiterate multitudes. For them, the voice of sanity should come from the ones who live among them and speak their vernacular. It is heartening that such people are also now coming up, though smaller in number. Maulana Wahiduddin Khan, head of the Islamic Centre, Nizamuddin West, New Delhi-13, and Maulana Allahma Hazek Tahfuri of Nagpur (a 105 year old linguist) are doing commendable work. Maulana Tahfuri[16] took the courage of questioning the supremacy of Mohammed's prophethood among hundreds of prophets preceding Mohammed. He opined that unless and until Quran's chronology was set right, Muslims would continue to suffer from various problems.[17] The clerics declared the Maulana a 'Kafir' or gone berserk. An unpurturbed Tehfuri said, "I may be poisoned, hanged or gunned down. I am least bothered about the fatwa. What I am saying is a reality whether one accepts it or not". In Pakistan, Ms. Asma Jahangir, winner of 1995 Ramon Magsaysay award, has been fighting for the women rights against the rigours of the Shariat laws.[18]

In Nov 1995, Municipal elections were held in UP towns. The prestigious Muslim religious institute, Darul-ul-Uloom Deoband, issued a 'fatwa' that Muslim women should not offer themselves as election candidates for that would expose them to public gaze. Defying the 'fatwa', an appreciable number of Muslim women came into the open, contested, and won the elections. Darul-ul-Uloom had to withdraw the fatwa. Smt. Zeenat Naaz, a 32 year old Muslim woman and a mother of four children, got elected as the Municipal Board chief of the Deoband town itself. She had publicly took off her veil at a Republic Day ceremony in 1989.

It is necessary that all forces, government or non-government, who subscribe to the idea of an open door policy in the matter of religion, and believe in the co-existence of different religions, join together to take a concerted action against the gun and bomb wielding fundamentalists/terrorists who are spread in every nook and corner of the globe. At the same time all help, protection, and encouragement should be provided to the free thinking Muslim scholars, ulemas, men and women.

THE INDIAN SCENE

The fundamentalist Islamic world sees India as the safest and the softest target. It is because, in spite of its vast territory, huge population and world's fourth largest armed forces, India is surrounded by an inimical Islamic state of Pakistan in the West, an equally irritant Bangladesh in the East, a hawkish neighbour in China in the North, and above all, it is being run by men of straw. In the past 49 years, Indian armed forces defeated Pakistan thrice on the battlefield (1947,1965 and 1971), but each time the political masters of India lost everything on the negotiating table. The Indian weakness is reflected in the following.

a. After dissolution of the USSR, India has become friendless in the international political arena.
b. Although about 130 million Muslims of India constitute only about 13 per cent of the total population, they make the largest organised political lot whose support has always been sought by the ruling party, the Congress, or its splinter groups, e.g., the Janata Party, or the Janata Dal. Virtually, the Muslims have enjoyed a veto power in the power game of India. It is no exaggeration to call India a semi-Islamic state.
c. Islamic fundamentalism has already taken over one of the largest Indian states, J & K, and has created strong bases in the border areas of Maharashtra, Gujarat, Kerala, West Bengal, Tamilnadu, and the hilll states of the North East.
d. India is the only country against whom the entire Muslim world is expected to stand united.
e. Strategically, if India is overpowered by the forces of Islam, there will be nothing to stop them from overpowering the world.

Thus, for their own survival, the rational Muslims, the Christians and in fact all non-Muslim communities of India, have to get united and act swiftly to eradicate the monster of Islamic terrorism. It has got to be done at the district level, provincial level, national level, and international level. The present government of India has proved incapable of doing anything in this direction.

Almost from the beginning of the century, India has been in the whirlwind of a triangular contest of socialism, democracy, and Islamic fundamentalism. Socialism has gone, democracy has turned into a farce, the Islamic fundamentalism is rising high. By now, it is well known that the Islamic fundamentalists have collected huge quantities of arms and ammunition in almost every big city. Only a fool will believe that all this happened without the knowledge of the Indian government. A special report in 'India Today,' New Delhi, (Feb. 15, 1986) under the heading 'A lethal invasion' states:

> "If you thought the Purulia[19] arms drop was a serious threat to national security, then consider these facts. The total arms recovered in that incident are less than what flows into the country every fortnight through the maze of 'conventional' routes. In Jammu and Kashmir alone, ever since full-scale insurgency began in the '90s' the army and paramilitary forces have seized more than 15,000 AK-type rifles, 2.4 million rounds of ammunition and close to 10,000 kg of explosives—enough perhaps to reduce the entire state to rubbles. Punjab and Haryana police in the past month have seized 250kg of RDX following a series of raids. To get an idea of what that quantity of RDX means, here is an example: the human bomb that had felled chief minister Beant Singh wrapped himself with only eight kg of RDX. Still, intelligence sources in these states say that the amount seized is only a third of what is actually in circulation.
>
> "India is in fact ranked by international arms experts as among the worst-hit countries by the illegal proliferation of what is known in defence parlance as Non-Major Weapons Systems. The terminology is misleading: short of tanks and heavy artillery it encompasses a vast range of lethal weapons including machine guns, rocket launchers, anti-aircraft guns, grenades and explosives. In short, enough for any militant group to wage a sustained war of attrition against the state."[20]

The ominous trends are that the Kashmir and Punjab militants are now importing RDX by the quintals, instead of AK-47 rifles, to cause maximum damage with minimum loss to themselves. Fundamentalist groups in Tamil Nadu, Kerala and Uttar Pradesh are also acquiring RDX as well as AK-47s. There is a nexus between arms smugglers and drug peddlers.

In 1983, 10,000 tons of weaponry was supplied to Afghan fighters through Pakistan channels.The supply rose to 65,000 tons by 1987. An estimated $ nine billion were spent by the US National Security Council and the CIA to arm the Mujahideen. These arms were bought by the CIA conduits from different sources: Romania, Czehoslovakia, Egypt, China, Israel, and East Germany. The arms were routed mainly through the Inter-Services Intelligence (ISI) to Afghanistan. There were about 3 million Kalashnikovs two years ago. After the Soviet pull out from Afghanistan Mujahideen Commanders and ISI intermediaries have made a profitable business of this deadly stock.[21]

Though late, the lethargic Hindu intelligentia and the nationalist Muslims, Christians, and members of the other so-called minority communities have started realising the duplicity and deception of the leaders who have been at the helm of affairs since the British left India, but it will be imprudent to pin all hopes on any one person or organisation, be it the RSS, BJP, or any one else. It must also be remembered that no foreign power will come to fight for us. As explained earlier, the multi-dimensional Islamic fundamentalism is desparately bent upon making India an Arabian desert. Greater damage is being done by the Anglicised Hindus, masquerading as secularists who should actually be termed as Ansars (helpers) of Islamic fundamentalist terrorists. It is unfortunate that the propounders of Hindutva have, during the past years, mostly concentrated on construction of a grand temple on the Ramajanmabhoomi in Ayodhya or deliverance of Gyanvapi Shiva temple in Varanasi and Shri Krishna temple of Mathura. They have done nothing concrete to meet the imminent danger of Islamic fundamentalism. If a right atmosphere is created the Muslims will themselves offer to vacate these ancient temples for the Hindus. The nationalist forces of India need to improve their public relations. For it, they must cultivate a few daily news papers in English and vernaculars.

TACKLING TERRORISM

According to a press statement of the Governor of J & K, Gen. (Retd) K.V. Krishna Rao, there were about 30,000 Pak sponsored armed Islamic fighters (including 8,000 foreign mercenaries) in J & K by the middle of 1994. The number of those spread in other parts of India, especially in Punjab, North East,

West Bengal, Bihar, U.P., Maharashtra, Gujarat, Kerala, Tamilnadu, and Delhi, is a matter of guess. The first and the foremost task is to identify and isolate these secessionists, terrorists, or subversives, and their harbingers. To combat this large force of unprincipled but highly motivated young men, the country needs at least 50,000 trained and well equipped non-governmental young volunteer force, besides the regular military and paramilitary forces. The project requires huge financial outlay, meticulous planning, and man power. While there is no dearth of planners and the requisite man power, one would wonder as to how to get the money in this poverty ridden country that is India. The fact, however, is that in this very country, people, especially Hindus, incur a wasteful expenditure of no less than Rs. 1,000 crores annually on fire works on various festivals and over Rs, 10,000 crores on extravagnt pomp and show of marriages and birth day parties. Just ten to twenty per cent of this wasteful expenditure would be adequate to take care of the financial aspect of the counter measures against the said fundamentalism and terrorism. The common Indian is intelligent and also partriotic. He only needs to be told about the magnitude of the danger to the national security, the actual national requirement, and convinced about the sincerity of purpose.

During the past two years, some of the Kashmiri militants, like Kukka Parrey, having got disillusioned with their mentor Pakistan, have turned against pro Pakistan terrorists and secessionists. Their efforts have paid high dividends. They need all help and encouragement to expand their area of operation and influence. Indeed, desparate maladies need equally and even more desparate remedies.

In short, the threat of Islamic fundamentalism and terrorism in India is real and hard hitting. It is spreading fast through propaganda and through the gun-powder. It is getting huge financial aid, men, and material support from within the country and from abroad. Moderate and secular Islamic countries are themselves under siege and are fighting against the fundamentalist forces. Almost the entire English and Urdu media of India are playing upon, or engaged on finding political justification and alibis to these forces. While Egypt has killed about one thousand of these terrorists, Algeria and Turkey are also hitting them in a big way, India remains a haven for them. Pakistan is their greatest nursery. Their number and their areas of operation, in spite of all claims to the contrary, have been increasing for the past five years. Islamic terrorists of all hues are active here. The present Government is incapable of taking hard decisions and effective action against them because of its own commitments to the fundamentalist Muslims. Even if all this does not motivate Hindus, the nationalist Muslims, and the Indian Christians, to unite and take a concerted counter action to ward off the evil their doom is sure and certain. However, Hindus being in the majority and also holding key positions, both in administration and financial institutions, it is primarily their duty and responsibility to first rise above their selfish ends and to devote their time and energy to thwart the fast approaching calamity.

In his well written book, "Is India Going Islamic?", Shri Baljit Rai, an ex Director General of Police, has stated:

"The Hindu can make his choice. In fact, he has no choice. It is either a Hindu Rashtra or a Dar-ul-Islam in India. Time available, only 20 years",

Shri Rai's view is based on disproportionately increasing Muslim population in India. But, if other factors are also taken into account, the tragedy may come about earlier. Let no one live in the false illusion, as many would like us to believe, that there is no danger either to Hindu religion or Hindu civilization because it has already survived all the vicissitudes of a 5,000 years old history.

• • • •

Some of the verses in the Quran which stand in the way of peaceful co-existence of the Muslims with people of other faiths. (Text from Meanings of the Glorious Quran, translated by Muhammad Marmaduke Pickthall).

SURAH IV (WOMAN)

Verse 14- And whoso disobeyeth Allah and His messenger and transgresseth His limits, He will make him enter Fire, where such will dwell for ever; his will be a shameful doom.

144- O ye who believe! Choose not disbelievers for (your) friends in place of believers. Would ye give Allah a clear warrant against you?

150- 51. Lo! Those who disbelieve in Allah and His messengers, and seek to make distinction between Allah and His messengers, and say: We believe in some and disbelieve in others, and seek to choose a way in between;

Such are disbelievers in truth and for disbelievers We prepare a shameful doom.

SURAH VIII- (SPOILS OF WAR)

Verse 12- When thy Lord inspired the angels, (saying:) I am with you. So make those who believe stand firm. I will throw fear into the hearts of those who disbelieve. Then smite the necks and smite of them each finger.

13- That is because they opposed Allah and His messenger. Whoso opposeth Allah and His messenger, (for him) lo! Allah is severe in punishment.

14- That (is the award), so taste it, and (know) that for disbelievers is the torment of the Fire.

SURAH IX (REPENTANCE)

Freedom from obligation of treaty with idolators.

Verse-1. Freedom from obligation (is proclaimed) from Allah and his messenger toward those of the idolaters with whom ye made a treaty:

2. Travel freely in the land four months, and know that ye cannot escape Allah and that Allah will confound the disbelievers.

3 And a proclamation from Allah and His messenger to all men on the day of the Greater Pilgrimage that Allah is free from obligation to the idolaters, and (so is) His messenger. So if ye repent, it will be better for you; but if ye are averse, then know that ye cannot escape Allah. Give tidings (O Muhammad) of a painful doom to those who disbelieve.

5. Then, when the sacred months have passed, slay the idolators wherever ye find them, and take them (captive), and besiege them, worship and pay the poor-due, then leave their way free. Lo! Allah is Forgiving Merciful.

123. O ye who believe! Fight those of the disbelievers who are near to you, and let them find harshness in you, and know that Allah is with those who keep their duty (unto Him).

SURAH XL VIII (VICTORY)

Verse 29- Muhammed is the messenger of Allah. And those with him are hard against the disbelievers and merciful among themselves...

REFERENCES

1 Cambridge History of Islam, vol. I, pp. 225-226.
2 Cambridge History of Islam, vol. I pp. 689-90.
3 J.N. Dixit's article in Indian Express, New Delhi, March 5, 1996, "Pakistan's nuclear policy-US TURNING A BLIND EYE".
3a Indian Express, daily, New Delhi; July 5, 1993, p.7
4 M.V. Kamath, "American blackmail of India," Organiser weekly New Delhi, Jan. 7, 1996.
5 Indian Express, New Delhi, March 7, 1996, News item "US has new praise for India's rights record."
6 Indian Express, New delhi, March 7, 1996, news item "Foreign funds used to foment terrorism".
7 Ibid
8 Indian Express, New Delhi, June 29, 1994, report "ISI backed militancy to spread in India, warns US report" and another news item "Islamic nations jump on J-K bandwagon for jehad's sake".
9 In fact, presence of foreign mercenaries in Kashmir, including the Afghans, had come to light in 1991. Since then, their numbers have swelled. Upto June 1994, 88 Afghans and 51 Pakistani Mujahideens were killed by the Indian security forces (Hindustan Times, New Delhi, July 3, 1994).
10 News item "Haryanvi speaking mercenaries take the edge off Army", Indian Express, New Delhi, July 24, 1995.
11 Indian Express, New Delhi, Jan 19, 1996, news item "Cleric gets life term for bombing".
12 Some of the compromises made by Indian government with the Islamic fundamentalism are: Carving out Muslim majority districts, declaring Urdu as the second state language even where Muslim population is less then 15 per cent, allowing the Muslim majority state of J & K to have its separate constitution, allowing mosques to make political and even secessionist speeches, even while swearing by secularism, allowing the Muslims to wage political wars in the name of Shariat and the Quran, banning any book or literary piece of work at the slightest hint from any Mufti or Maulana, non-implementation of the Constitutional provison for a uniform civil code for the whole country.
13 Ashok Chopra's "Myopia by Choice", Hindustan Times, New Delhi 6 July 1994.
14 Editorial, "New look at holy book", Ibid, 22nd June 1994.
15 Dr. Shreerang Godbole, "From Islam to Sanathanadharma-The journy home", Organiser weekly, Jan 15, 1995.

16 Indian Express, New Delhi, July 21, 1994, report "105 years old religious scholar declared gumrah".

17 The Quran available today was compiled about 30 years after the death of Mohammed, during the days of Khalifa Usman. The arrangement of the verses is not in chronological order. Even verses revealed in Medina are clubbed with those revealed in Mecca, and quite often, put in one Surah.

18 Times of India, New Delhi, Magazine Section, Aug 20, 1995.

19 Purulia is a town in West Bengal where, on the night of Dec 17, 1995, an AN—26 aircraft, having taken off from Karachi (Pakistan) dropped through parachutes a huge cache of arms and ammunition and made way to Yangon (Mayanmar). On its return journey next day, it was spotted and made to forceland at Bombay by IAF fighter aircraft.

20 INDIA TODAY, New Delhi, Feb 15, 1996, pp. 136.

21 Pankaj Pachauri, in India Today, Ibid, p. 140.

Chapter XXII

GANDHI'S RELEVANCE TODAY

Many eminent academicians, politicians, sociologists, and even scientists, have started showing greater interest in Gandhi and his thought. In the Indian context, one must take into consideration Gandhiji's own personality, his perception and his actual deeds. As a person, Gandhi had a feeble body but he was gifted with an extraordinary strong will and a missionary zeal to serve the cause of humanity. In his public life, Gandhi set high standards of simplicity, truthfulness, selfless service and financial integrity. Once, somebody gave his wife, Kasturba Gandhi, some money and a gold ring. Presuming that these items were meant for her personal use, she kept them with her. When Gandhi came to know of it, he publicly admonished her for this impropriety which he termed as nothing but theft.[1] These traits of Gandhi have greater relevance in today's world of rampant corruption and misappropration of public money.

Gandhi belonged to an upper class Vaishnavaite Bania (Vaish) family. Thus, non-violence and vegetarianism ran in his veins and blood since birth. His weapon of Satyagraha (coercive method of self-suffering to press a demand) was picked up from the Indian woman who, though dependent on man physically and economically, exercised great influence on him through her moral strength and Satyagraha. However, Satyagraha can be used only against one who has some common interest with you and has a sense of justice. Gandhi used it against the British and the Depressed Class leader, B.R. Ambedkar, as both claimed to serve the same lot. Gandhi could never think of using it against the Muslim League or Jinnah because they had nothing in common with Gandhi nor had they the sense of justice.

The basics of Gandhiji's philosophy of life, education, government, and independence (Swarajya) are contained in a small book, "Hind Swarajya", which he wrote in 1909, while he was still in South Africa, about ten years before he actively joined Indian politics. Gandhiji wrote that Swarajya did not mean just transfer of political power from the British to the Indian hands. It meant replacement of the British systems of government, the legislature and the judiciary by indigenous ones, rooted in Hindu culture and Hindu civilization which lay greater stress on development of mind and spirit rather than accumulation of wealth and ostentatious living. He advocated replacement of English by Hindi and other Indian vernaculars; forsaking western culture based on materialism; upliftment of villages; going back to nature instead of promoting rabid industrialisation and urbanisation. Gandhi favoured only those simple machines (like the sewing machine) which brought happiness to all. He abhored all those machines which were aimed at making profits or exploitation beyond one's actual needs. Gandhi laid great stress on simple living and high thinking. He set his own example for it. All these ideas have greater relevance today than ever before.

At the Gujarat Educational Conference held at Broach on October 20, 1917, Gandhi spoke as under on the evils of English education to Indians:

> "The greatest service we can render to society is to free ourselves and it from the superstitious regard we have learnt to pay to the learning of the English language. It is the medium of instruction in our schools and colleges. It is becoming the *lingua franca* of the country...This belief in the necessity of English training has enslaved us. It has unfitted us for true national service. Were it not for force of habit, we could not fail to see that by reason of English being the medium of instruction, our intellect has been segregated, we have been isolated from the masses, the best mind of the nation has become gagged and the masses have not received the benefit of the new ideas we have received. We have been engaged these past sixty years in memorizing strange words and their pronunciation instead of assimilating facts. In the place of building upon the foundation, training received from our parents, we have almost unlearnt it. There

is no parallel to this in history. It is a national tragedy. The first and greatest social service we can render is to revert to our vernaculars, to restore Hindi to its natural place as the national language and begin carrying on all our provincial proceedings in our respective vernaculars and national proceedings in Hindi. We ought not to rest till our schools and colleges give us instruction through the vernaculars..."[2]

Incidentally, Gandhi had only an inkling of the above thoughts which became firm after he read certain European philosophers and authors, like Tolstoy, Sherard, Carpenter, Thoreau, Ruskin, etc. In the preface to 'Hind Swarajya', Gandhi wrote:

> "The thoughts given here are mine and also not mine. These are mine because I hope to work on them and they are embedded in my soul. These are not mine because they did not originate in me alone. They were formed after going through some books. What I used to feel within my heart got confirmation from these books".[3]

Among the twenty reference books cited in the Appendix to the 'Hind Swarajya', only two are from Indian authors, i.e., 'Poverty and Un-British Rule in India' by Dadabhoi Nauroji and 'Economic History of India', by R.C. Dutt. Gandhiji's greatness lay in putting into practice the ideals which had remained as talking points in the countries of their origin. These ideals found ready acceptance among the Indian masses because they had been a part and parcel of the Indian way of life, especially in the villages for thousands of years of India's glorious past. These ideals, Gandhi's own conduct, and his bare body in a loin cloth (for which the British nick-named him half-naked fakir) made him an avatar, a prophet, among the gullible, simple, folks of India. During his extensive tour of the country in 1921, when Gandhiji and his party were stranded in rain, in a Bihar village, an old woman came to see him. She said:

> "Sire, I am now one hundred and four and my sight has grown dim. I have visited various holy places. In my own home I have dedicated two temples. Just as we had Rama and Krishna as avatars, so also Mahatma Gandhi has appeared as an avatar, I hear. Until I have seen him, death would not appear".[4]

Gandhi's fault lay in stretching the principle of 'Ahimsa' to a ridiculous extent and that too only for the Hindus while to the Muslims he said that they could use violence according to their Quran. After 1920, Gandhi's only obsession was Hindu-Muslim unity and thereby getting rid of the British Raj. Towards this end, Gandhi started compromising with each and every one of his ideals upto the Partition of India. He took extra pains to make Jawaharlal Nehru the Prime Minister of India, a man who was opposed to every aspect of the Gandhian philosophy, except the policy of appeasing the fundamentalist Muslims. As a matter of fact, there is a great difference between the Gandhi before 1920 when he was a loyalist of the British crown and authored the 'Hind Swarajya' and the one thereafter who turned against the British and ran after Mullahs. The latter aspect has already been discussed in the earlier chapters. The fact that Gandhi made several political blunders in the later part of his life, should not detract us from the great work done and the principles enunciated by him in his earlier part.

Now, in the midst of the failure of the socialist ideology, fast eroding moral values, increasing violence, terrorism and spate of other crimes, environmental pollution, ecological imbalance due to rabid industrialisation, spread of deadly diseases, like AIDS, due to permissiveness, drug addiction, mental depravity, machination for material prosperity and economic exploitation, arms race among nations, world attention has been drawn to the Gandhi thought and the philosophy of life propounded by the Vedic Rishis, which says—

Ishavaasyam idam sarvam yadkinchit jagatyamjagat, Ten tyaktenbhunjithah ma gridhah kasyaswiddhanam. (Ishavasyopnishad)

(All that we see in this world is permeated by God. Therefore, take only that much which is essential for you as a gift of God-not your own-and don't long for the one which belongs to others.)

The real happiness lies in renunciation, not accumulation; abstinence, not indulgence; and in poverty, not riches. But unless these virtues are adopted and displayed in life by those who are at the helm of affairs, the common man will not be attracted towards them. After all, people at the lower rung follow the example set by their superiors.

REFERENCES

1. D.G. Tendulkar, Mahatma, vol. II.
2. M.K. Gandhi, Evil Wrought By the English Medium, edited by R.K. Prabhu, p. 8, Navajivan Publishing House, Ahmedabad, Sept. 1958.
3. Gandhi, Hind Swarajya, Hindi translation by Amritlal Thakurdas Nanavati, p.3, Sarva Seva Sangha Prakashan, Rajghat Varanasi, 4th edition, July 1994.
4. Tendulkar, DG, Mahatma, Vol. II, p. 78.

APPENDIX A

A SUMMARY OF

RECOMMENDATIONS OF THE COMMISSION OF INQUIRY ON KANPUR RIOTS OF MARCH 1931, SET UP BY CONGRESS

SUGGESTION TO GOVERNMENT

The District Magistrate and the Superintendent of Police of the District where a communal riot occurs should be suspended and then allowed to submit explanations.

CLASSIFICATION OF REMEDIES

These are grouped under three heads: (1) Religio-educational, (2) Politico-economic, and (3) Social

I. RELIGIO-EDUCATIONAL

(1) The Congress should bring out a series of graded books in which essential truths common to all religions are presented in an impartial and attractive manner, illustrated, where possible, by parallel passages from the scriptures.

(2) The denominational institutions for the education of the youth should be nationalised:

- (a) In future no new school or college should be opened bearing the name of Hindu, Muslim, Christian, or any other community.
- (b) The names of existing denominational institutions should be altered.
- (c) Members of other communities should gradually be taken on the governing bodies of these institutions.
- (d) The courses of study and lectures should cover a broad cultural and national outlook.
- (e) All existing preferences in favour of students of any particular community should be abolished.

(f) In the interim period, students of Muslim institutions should be invited by Hindu institutions, on important festivals, etc. to live together for a week or ten days.

(3) New books on history should be written in such a way that while stating the truth, they may help in promoting national outlook and regard for the heroes of history and mythology as the common heroes.

(4) (a) Both Hindi and Urdu, written in Nagri and Persian scripts should be compulsorily taught to all students in Hindustani-speaking areas.

(b) All Congressmen in Hindustani speaking provinces should know Hindi and Urdu both. Those in non-Hindustani areas should learn Hindustani through the medium of either the Nagri or the Persian script

(c) Notices and circulars issued by the AICC should be in both the scripts.

(d) Hindi and Urdu authors, speakers, and news-paper editors should help in the evolution of a common Hindustani language, eschewing, as far as possible, difficult Arabic, Persian, and Sanskrit words.

(e) The Persian script should be somewhat simplified.

(f) Congress should undertake to issue a large weekly in Hindustani.

(g) Some Hindu youths should be induced to study Islam through original Arabic sources and some Muslim youths should be required to study Hinduism on the same lines. Comparative study of religions and cultures should be promoted.

(6) Speakers, writers, and editors of newspapers should refrain from speaking, writing or publishing things that may incite communalism.

(7) Persons changing their religion should not change their names. In the Indian Christian community, persons preserve their old names. Minors under eighteen years of age should not be converted unless it be along with their parents and guardians.

II. POLITICO-ECONOMIC

(1) Adopt the recommendations of the Fundamental Rights Committee. Congress should place before the people the outlines of a more complete scheme of Swaraj mentioning the fundamental rights and duties of individuals, economic

policy and methods for securing an upright and honest legislature. It should allay the fears of the minority communities and sections.

(2) Qualifications should be prescribed for persons proposed to be elected as office-bearers or members of an executive body:

(a) They must be at least 25 years of age for Provincial & subordinate Committees, and 30 for the All India Committee.

(b) They must have been members of the Congress for at least five years.

(c) They must not be members of any communal organisation which works for safeguarding the political rights of the Hindu, Muslim, or Sikh community as such.

(d) They should have faith in the doctrine of non-violence.

(3) The policy and methods of communalistic leaders should be exposed by members of their own communities.

(4) The system of separate electorates on the basis of religion should be abolished and the Congress should on no account agree to its continuance. Out of 26 Muslim witnesses whom we questioned 19 condemned the system of separate electorates and ascribed to it most of the present communal bitterness. Reservations of seats on a religious basis is also bad, but in view of the suspicions and fears entertained by a large number of persons among some minority communites, it should be permitted for a fixed period.

(5) The Congress should cease to deal with separate communal organisations for the settlement of communal rights.

(6) Organising Hindus and Muslims separately, such as the Sangathanas and the Tanzeem, for defending one community from the attacks of the other, shouid be stopped.

(7) All communal volunteer corps, like Mahabir Dals and Ali Ghols, should be abolished and Joint volunteer corps consisting of both Hindus and Muslims should be organized.

(8) Every Congress volunteer should take a vow of maintaining neutrality and bring peace to both the communities and help Hindus and Muslims alike and will not retaliate even if attacked personally.

(9) Every attempt at the economic boycott of one section of a community by members of other community should be put down.

(10) Economic co-operation between members of the two communities should be encouraged. Banking, Insurance, Trade, and Industry should be organized by joint efforts.

(11) Special efforts should be made to carry on Congress propaganda among the poor—the peasants, the labourers and unemployed.

(12) Joint Hindu-Muslim Panchayats, should be formed as widely as possible.

(13) In all Congress meetings and processions, cries with "Hai, hai and cries of "Jai! or "Zindabad!" should be stopped.

(14) Hartal, like picketing, should be absolutely peaceful. No coercion of any kind should be employed.

III. SOCIAL

(1) Every Hindu and every Muslim should try to be on familiar terms with at least one friend belonging to the other community.

(2) Hindus and Muslims should join more and more in each other's festivals.

(3) Joint clubs for recreation and sports, and joint reading rooms and societies should be established.

(4) All inhabitants of our country should call themselves Hindis or Hindustanis and differences in dress and appearance which tend to make obtrusive the distinction should be abolished or at least minimised.

(5) Efforts should be made for the abolition of Purdah. Chairman,Bhagwan Das adds: If Muslim women come out and mix freely with Hindu women, antagonisms and conflicts are sure to abate...the main reason why Hindus object to the presence of Muslims at, e.g. bathing ghats, and typically Hindu melas, etc., is that, while Hindu women go there, Muslim women do not, but only Muslim men—whence annoyance to Hindus. If Muslim women also went, all cases of annoyance would vanish at once.

(6) Untouchability should be abolished

(7) Partiality based on communal consideration should stop.

(8) All slaughter of quadrupeds, even for religious sacrifice,

should be governed by the general laws of the land, based on grounds of hygiene, sanitation, and public decency. Cow sacrifices should not be interfered with by any one, any more than the sacrifices of goats, sheep, buffalows etc. This does not apply where any arrangement has been arrived at through mutual consent.

(9) Playing of music in the vicinity of mosque should not be interfered with. Any arrangement arrived at mutually should be maintained.

(10) The Hindus should abolish the present hereditary caste system and shift the system of four main castes (Varnas) from the basis of rigid heredity to that of vocational temperament and class namely, (1) the learned professions for men of knowledge (2) the executive professions for men of action: (3) the wealth-producing and wealth-managing professions for men of desire; and (4) the labouring professions for men who are not intellectually evolved and educated as the other three and who can only assist them in minor capacities.

IN A SUPPLEMENTARY NOTE, THE COMMISSION MADE FURTHER SUGGESTIONS;

UNDER THE HEAD "II. POLITICO ECONOMIC"

(10) (a) Congress should appoint a special committee of Congress Muslims to go into the question of whether the Muslim community is poorer and less educated than the Hindu community and whether this is due to, as alleged, the manoeuvers of the latter and ascertain whether the allegation is correct and, if so, what are the remedies.

UNDER THE HEAD "III. SOCIAL" Re. Cow-sacrifice. The suggestion made is reiterated. So long as Hindus continue to offer sacrifices of any animals themselves, and sell cattle to butchers, as they do, they cannot justly claim injunction against any other in respect of cow-sacrifices or cattle-slaughter.

IN HIS DISSENTING NOTE, PURUSHOTTAM DAS TANDON STATED ABOUT COW-SLAUGHTER:

There are two ways of approaching this question. One is to ask the Hindus to give up their sentiment in favour of the cow and to reconcile themselves to the view that the cow can be sacrificed in the same manner as other animals. The other method is that which is traditional in this country, viz., that the inhabitants including Muslims, refrain from killing the cow. Several Muslim leaders have from time to time advised the Muslims to stop cow-sacrifice in India in the interest of brotherly relations between the two communities and have adduced religious and historical reasons in support of their argument. I do not feel competent to give that advice to the Muslim community, but at the same time, I am a dreamer of an absolute Hindu-Muslim fusion. I want Hindus and Muslims to live in the same Mohallas, in adjoining houses, and to have the most cordial relations. And I want Hindu and Muslim women to have social relations as much as men. This dream is not likely of fulfilment if cow may be sacrificed in private houses of Muslims situated side by side with Hindu homes. The Hindus may be persuaded to keep quiet when such sacrifices occur, but there would be no joy and happiness in living in a neighbourhood where such slaughter may take place....

DISSENTING NOTE OF ZAFARUL-MULK (OCT. 24, 1931)

As for the Musalmans, there can be very little doubt that the idea of keeping their general features distinctively separate from those of other nations and communities is as old as Islam itself, for the holy prophet (peace be on Him) has expressly commanded the Muslims to avoid all such fusion, by saying-

He who imitates a people is one of them.

Numerous examples can be cited from reliable historians that even long before the English became a powerful nation and English literature spread among the Musalmans, leaders of Islamic thought, theologians, Sufis, philosophers and poets, had been laying great stress on keeping as a model before them, the lives of the Prophet (peace be on him) the Khulafai Rashideen (Abu Bakr, Omar, Osman and Ali), and other companions of the Prophet (Sabha) and following their modes of life to their utmost capacity.

Akbar, who is so highly admired by English and Hindu writers and even Muslim graduates of modern Universities, however, much we may appreciate his superior political talents or his incomparable administration, has always been treated contemptuously by religious authorities of his own times, and the very fact, that Aurangzeb is generally regarded to be not only one of the greatest Muslim Kings, but almost a saint, clearly shows, which way the wind has been blowing in the Muslim mind.

.....I cannot acquiesce in the following recommendations of the Committee:

I. Under sub-clause (2) of the Social group it has been suggested that-

Holi, Diwali, Idulfiter, and Shab-i-barat should be regarded as common festivals of both communities, and new common national festival should be created."

Innovation in religious matters having been forbidden, it is absolutely impossible to accept the first portion of the recommendation, but the latter portion may be acceptable if this procedure in any established festivals is so regulated as to make it a purely social function and nothing is done that may not be acceptable to the Muslims from their religious point of view, as the manner in which Hindu festivals are generally observed cannot be followed by Musalmans.

II. Sub-clause (5) of the Social group recommends the abolition of Purdah. I know that the purdah system, as in vogue here, requires some changes, and I should be willing to accept any modifications that do not go beyond what is allowed by our religion, but the abolition of Purdah will mean an interference in religion which cannot and should not be tolerated by Musalmans.

III. .....I must clearly state that interference with the right of slaughtering of quadrupeds in one's house, either through legislation or executive orders, will always be a source of legitimate grievance to the Musalmans and other classes of people, and I hope that the phraseology of this section, specially the phrase "should be governed by the general laws of the land" will not be a pretext for enacting laws to infringe one's right to freely practising one's religion or the freedom of citizenship. A Musalman, while performing his religious obligation freely and without hitch or hindrance should take every care to see that he does not give any occasion for provocation to his neighbours.

IV. The recommendations classed under Religio-Educational group are generally agreed upon, but I should like to say a few words on the following points:-

(a)......

(b) The recommendation under Sub-clause (7) which prohibits the conversion of minors under 18, is against the Islamic law and cannot therefore be accepted by Musalmans. According to Muslim theologians, even those minors have the right of conversion whose powers of understanding are sufficiently developed and the age of minority does not go beyond 15 years, although many especially women, reach their age of puberty even at an earlier age.

V. Under sub-clause (4) of the Politico-Economic group, I do not see my way to agree to the suggestion that separate electorate on religious basis be abolished. Whatever my friends of the Muslim Nationalists Party may think, I am convinced that taking all the various circumstances in view, abolition of separate electorates is bound to affect the minorities adversely...mixed electorates should not be forced upon the minorities...

My own suggestion, therefore would be that the community in majority within a certain province be made to elect her representatives by mixed electorates, so that the rights of minorites may not be altogether neglected while the community which is in minority be permitted to elect her representatives, either by separate electorate or if it chooses by mixed electorates.

I have never been able to appreciate the view that separate electorate is or has been a source of Hindu-Muslim dissensions...Why should then separate electorate be singled out for such wholesale denunciation?...

VI. Under sub-clause (10) it has been suggested that banking and insurance, etc, should be organised by joint efforts of the two communities. Interest on money in every form or shape being prohibited by Islam, I cannot ask any co-religionists to join the banking or insurance business. On the contrary, I feel it my duty to advise them to refrain from all such immoral undertakings. I would go one step further and request my Hindu brethren also to desist from this sort of business which not only retards their moral and spiritual progress but tends to nourish capitalism, which is the source of incalculable mischief to humanity.

The experience gained during the centuries of Muslim rule in India, goes to show clearly that natural causes led to some sort of fusion between the two communities without making any fuss about it or adopting any artificial means to force its pace.

In order, however, to achieve a real and permanent unity and keep Hindus and Muslims on brotherly terms....manners suggested below:-

(1) The Hindus who form the majority community and are far ahead of the Muslims in wealth, modern education, organisation, and propaganda, should try to win the hearts of the Muslim minority by unhesitatingly giving the guarantees and facilities required by her for securing a proper place in the constitution of the country.

(2) If we really care to be truthful and honest and long to live in peace and harmony we should give up all cravings for Western ideals and habits and turn back to the old days of Vedas and Quran.

(3) The idea of the one supreme God is the central point of belief, not only of the Musalmans but among some of the Hindu sects also, as mentioned on p.353 (chapter on remedies). If constant and earnest efforts are made to propagate and inculcate this belief in all the Hindu sects, a certain degree of unity in religious thought can be achieved which will in its turn dispel feelings of contempt and hatred from the minds of the monist and the pagan both.

(4) When the weak has nothing to fear from the strong, lust has been generally subdued, and people have learnt to become God-fearing and live a purer life, Hindus and Muslims will easily become friends and learn to love each other like sons of the same parents.

APPENDIX B

CHARTER OF FOURTEEN DEMANDS PUT UP BY JINNAH IN 1931.

1. The proposed constitution of India should be federal in character and the residuary powers should vest in the states.
2. All provinces should enjoy equal self-rule powers.
3. All legislatures and local self-government bodies should be so reconstituted as to provide reasonable and effective representation to the minorities. While doing so, the majority in any state should not become minority.
4. The Muslim representation in the Central Legislature should not be less than one-third.
5. Separate electorates should continue. If any community decides to have joint electorates instead of separate electorates for itself, it should have the freedom to do so.
6. If, at any time, it is decided to reorganise the provinces, such reorganisation should not adversely affect the Muslim majority in Punjab, North West Frontier province and Bengal.
7. All communities should enjoy religious freedom.
8. If three-fourth of the repersentatives of any community in any legislature or self-government body opposes any piece of legislation as being against the interests of the said community, such a law should not be enacted.
9. Sindh should be separated from Bombay province.
10. All reforms should be extended to North-West Frontier Province and Baluchistan along with other provinces.
11. Provision should be made to ensure adequate representation for the Muslims in government jobs in all the provinces. While doing so, due consideration should be given to competence also.
12. Protection should be afforded to Muslim religion, culture and personal law.

13. At least one-third of the number of central and provincial council of ministers should consist of Muslims.
14. The Central Legislature should not make any alterations or amendments in the constitution without the consent of the provincial governments.

BIBLIOGRAPHY

1. Aggarwal, S.K., Dr. Ambedkar on Muslim Fundamentalism, 1993, Suruchi Prakashan, Jhandewala, New Delhi-55.

1-A. Akbar, M.J., Nehru—The making of India, 1988, Viking, published by Panguin group, 27 wrights LANE, London.

2. Anwar Shaikh, Islam—The Arab National Movement, 1994, Principality Publishers, Cardiff Great Britain.

3. Ayasha Jalal, The Sole Spokesman, Jinnah, the Muslim League and the demand for Pakistan, 1985, Cambridge University Press, London (South Asian Studies).

4. Azad, Maulana Abul Kalam, India Wins Freedom, 1960, Orient Longman, 17 Chittaranjan Avenue, Calcutta.

5. Azad, Maulana Abul Kalam, Tarjuman al-Quran, English translation 1967, By Dr. Syed Abdul Latif, Asia Publishing House, Bombay.

5-A. Baljit Rai, Is India Going Islamic, 1994, B.S. Publishers Chandigarh, Distributors—Voice of India, 2/18 Ansari Road, New Delhi.

6. Barrier, N. Gerald, Roots of Communal Politics, South Asia Books, Columbia, Missori.

7. Cambridge History of Islam, Vol. I, 1970 Cambridge University Press, London.

8. Choudhari, Nirad C., The Continent of Circe, Jaico Publication House, Fort Bombay-I, Fifth edition, 1974.

9. Durga Das, India from Curzon to Nehru and After (4th Reprint) 1977, Rupa & CO., 15 Bankim Chatterjee Street Calcutta-700073.

10. Doughlas, Ian Henderson, Abul Kalam Azad An Intellectual and Religious Biography, 1988, Oxford University Press, Delhi, Bombay, Calcutta & Madras.

11. Edwarde, Michael, Last Years of British India, NEL Mentor Edition 1967, New English Library, Barnard Inn, Halborn, London, ECI.

12. Gandhi, M.K., Hind Swarajya (Hindi), 1994, Sarva Seva Sangha, Rajghat Varanasi, 221001.
13. Gandhi, M.K., Evil Wrought by the English Medium, edited by R.K. Prabhu, Sept 1956, Navajivan Publishing House Ahmedabad.
14. Gandhi, Rajiv, Restore India's Glory with Unity and Strength.
15. Dr. Saifuddin, Guruji Ke Muslim Samasya par Vichar (Hindi translation), 1979, Suruchi Sahitya Jhandewala, New Delhi-55.
16. Guillauma, A Life of Muhammed (A translation of Ishaq's Sirat Rasul Allah) Oxford University Press, Great Britain, 1955.
17. Hali, Altaf Husain, Hayat-i-Javed, translation by K.H. Qadiri and David Matthews, 1979, Idarah-i-Adabiyat-i-Delhi, 2009 Qasimjan Street Delhi-6.
18. Hodson, H.V., the Great Divide, 2nd print 1988, Oxford University Press Karachi.
19. Jog, B.N., Threat of Islam, Unnati Prakashan, 1994, 1, Purvanchal Navghar Marg, Mulund (E) Bombay-81.
20. Karunakaran, K.P., Indian Political Thought (1832-1921), Peacock Press & Publisher, 1976, New Delhi.
21. Lal Bahadur, The Muslim League (Its History, Activities and Achievements), Agra Book Stores, 1954, Agra.
22. Madhok, Bal Raj, Hindu Rajya (Hindi), Vikalpa Prakashan, 3rd edition, 1990, 3314 Bank Street, Karol Bagh, Delhi-5.
23. Majumdar, R.C., History of Freedom Movement in India, vol. 3, 1963, Firma, K.L. Mukhopadhyaya, Calcutta.
24. Majumdar, R.C., Advanced History of India, MacMillan and Co., Ltd. 1946. St. Martin Street, London.

24-A. Mallick, B.N., My years with Nehru-Kashmir, 1971 Allied Publishers, Asaf Ali Road, New Delhi.

25. Menon, V.P. Transfer of Power in India, Orient longmans, 1968, 3/5 Asaf Ali Road, New Delhi-2.
26. Nomani, Mohammed, Rise and Growth of All India Muslim League, 1942, Kitabistan, Allahabad.

27. Muslim Personal (Shariat) Application Act, 1937.
28. Pickthall, Muhammed Marmaduke, Meanings of the Glorious Quran, English translation of the Quran, 5th reprint 1993, Kitab Bhavan, 1784 Kalan Mahal, Daryaganj, New Delhi-2.
29. Puri, B.N., A study in Indian History, 1971, Bhartiya Vidya Bhavan.
30. Pyarelal, Mahatma Gandhi-Last Phase, Vol. I.
31. Prasad, Rajendra, India Divided, Hind Kitab, Bombay, 1946.
31-A. Raghavan, GNS, M. Asaf Ali's Memoirs, 1994, Ajanta Publications, P. Box 2192, Malka Ganj, Delhi-7.
32. Ram Swarup, Understanding Islam Through Hadis, 1985, Voice of India, 2/18, Ansari Raod, New Delhi-2.
33. Seshadri H.V., RSS: A Vision in Action, Dec. 1988, Jagaran Prakashan, Bangalore.
33-A. Shahid Hamid (Major General), Disastrous Twilight, 1986, Leo Cooper and Secker & Warburg, 54 Poland Street London.
34. Sharma, T.L., Hindu-Muslim Relations, (1913-1925), 1987, B.R. Publishing Corporation, 29/9 Shakti Nagar Nangloi Park, Delhi-7.
35. Shourie, Arun, Religion in Politics, Roli Books International, 1987, 5, Ansari Road, Daryaganj, New Delhi-2.
36. Singh, Nihar Nandan, Lokmanya Bal Gangadhar Tilak, Congress Centenary Celebrations (1985), Committee, AICC, New Delhi.
37. Sitaramayya, Pattabhi, History of the Indian National Congress, Vol. I, 1969, S. Chand & Co., Ram Nagar, New Delhi-55.
38. -do- Vol. II, 1947, Padma Publication Ltd., Bombay.
39. Srivastava, A.L. (Dr.), The Sultanate of Delhi (1206-1526 A.D.), Shiva Lal Aggarwal, Agra, 1972.
40. Tara Chand (Dr.), Influence of Islam on Indian Culture, 1936, India Press (Publication), Allahbad.
41. -do- History of freedom Movement in India, Vol. III, publication Division, Government of India, 1972.

42. Tendulkar, D.G. Mahatma, Vol. I, 1951, Vithalbhai K. Jhaveri, 64 Walkeshwar Road, Bombay-6.
43. -do- Mahatma, Vol. II, -do-
44. Tripathi, Vachnesh, Itihas ke Jharokhe Se, Part II (Hindi), 1995, Suruchi Prakashan, Deshbandhu Gupta Road, New Delhi-55.
45. Wali Khan, Facts Are Facts. The Untold Story of India's Partition, 1987, Vikas Publishing House 576, Masjid Road Jangpura, New Delhi.
46. Zakaria, Rafiq (Dr.), The Widening Divide, Viking, Penguin Books India (Pvt) Ltd., Nehru Place, New Delhi-19, 1995.
47. Malhotra, V.K. (MP), Is it a Sin to be Hindu in India?, Vishwa Hindu Parishad, Sankat Mochan Ashram, R.K. Puram, Sec. VI, New Delhi-27.

NEWS PAPERS/PERIODICALS

1. Indian Express, daily, Bahadur Shah Zafar Marg, New Delhi-2.
2. Times of India, daily, -Ibid.
3. India Today, fortnightly, New Delhi.
4. Hindustan Times, daily, Kasturba Gandhi Marg, New Delhi, 110001.
5. Organiser, weekly, Jhandewala, New Delhi, 110055.

INDEX